Solutions Manual

to accompany

Principles of
Corporate Finance

Ninth Edition

Richard A. Brealey
London Business School

Stewart C. Myers
Massachusetts Institute of Technology

Franklin Allen
University of Pennsylvania

Prepared by
Bruce Swensen
Adelphi University

McGraw-Hill
Irwin

Boston   Burr Ridge, IL   Dubuque, IA   Madison, WI   New York   San Francisco   St. Louis
Bangkok   Bogotá   Caracas   Kuala Lumpur   Lisbon   London   Madrid   Mexico City
Milan   Montreal   New Delhi   Santiago   Seoul   Singapore   Sydney   Taipei   Toronto

Solutions Manual for use with
PRINCIPLES OF CORPORATE FINANCE
Richard A. Brealey, Stewart C. Myers, and Franklin Allen

Published by McGraw-Hill/Irwin, an imprint of The McGraw-Hill Companies, Inc., 1221 Avenue of the Americas, New York, NY 10020. Copyright © 2008, 2006, 2003, 2000, 1996, 1991, 1988 ,1984, 1981 by The McGraw-Hill Companies, Inc. All rights reserved.

1 2 3 4 5 6 7 8 9 0 QPD/QPD 0 9 8 7

ISBN: 978-0-07-328699-0
MHID: 0-07-328699-0

www.mhhe.com

TABLE OF CONTENTS

Chapter 2   Present Values, the Objectives of the Firm, and Corporate Governance 2-1

Chapter 3   How to Calculate Present Values 3-1

Chapter 4   Valuing Bonds 4-1

Chapter 5   The Value of Common Stocks 5-1

Chapter 6   Why Net Present Value Leads to Better Investment Decisions than Other Criteria 6-1

Chapter 7   Making Investment Decisions with the Net Present Value Rule 7-1

Chapter 8   Introduction to Risk, Return, and the Opportunity Cost of Capital 8-1

Chapter 9   Risk and Return 9-1

Chapter 10   Capital Budgeting and Risk 10-1

Chapter 11   Project Analysis 11-1

Chapter 12   Investment, Strategy, and Economic Rents 12-1

Chapter 13   Agency problems, Management Compensation, and the Measurement of Performance 13-1

Chapter 14   Efficient Markets and Behavioral Finance 14-1

Chapter 15   An Overview of Corporate Financing 15-1

Chapter 16   How Corporations Issue Securities 16-1

Chapter 17   Payout Policy 17-1

Chapter 18   Does Debt Policy Matter 18-1

Chapter 19   How Much Should a Firm Borrow? 19-1

Chapter 20   Financing and Valuation 20-1

Chapter 21   Understanding Options 21-1

Chapter 22   Valuing Options 22-1

Chapter 23   Real Options 23-1

Chapter 24   Credit Risk and the Value of Corporate Debt 24-1

Chapter 25   The Many Different Kinds of Debt 25-1

Chapter 26   Leasing 26-1

Chapter 27   Managing Risk 27-1

Chapter 28   Managing International Risks 28-1

Chapter 29   Financial Analysis and Planning 29-1

Chapter 30   Working Capital Management 30-1

Chapter 31   Short-Term Financial Planning 31-1

Chapter 32   Mergers 32-1

Chapter 33   Corporate Restructuring 33-1

Chapter 34   Governance and Corporate Control Around the World 34-1

CHAPTER 2

Present Values, the Objectives of the Firm, and Corporate Governance

Answers to Practice Questions

9. The face value of the treasury security is $1,000. If this security earns 5%, then in one year we will receive $1,050. Thus:

$$NPV = C_0 + [C_1/(1 + r)] = -\$1000 + (\$1050/1.05) = 0$$

This is not a surprising result because 5% is the opportunity cost of capital, i.e., 5% is the return available in the capital market. If any investment earns a rate of return equal to the opportunity cost of capital, the NPV of that investment is zero.

10. $NPV = -\$1,300,000 + (\$1,500,000/1.10) = +\$63,636$

Since the NPV is positive, you would construct the motel.
Alternatively, we can compute r as follows:

$r = (\$1,500,000/\$1,300,000) - 1 = 0.1538 = 15.38\%$

Since the rate of return is greater than the cost of capital, you would construct the motel.

11.

Investment	NPV	Return
(1)	$-10,000 + \dfrac{18,000}{1.20} = \$5,000$	$\dfrac{18,000 - 10,000}{10,000} = 0.80 = 80.0\%$
(2)	$-5,000 + \dfrac{9,000}{1.20} = \$2,500$	$\dfrac{9,000 - 5,000}{5,000} = 0.80 = 80.0\%$
(3)	$-5,000 + \dfrac{5,700}{1.20} = -\$250$	$\dfrac{5,700 - 5,000}{5,000} = 0.14 = 14.0\%$
(4)	$-2,000 + \dfrac{4,000}{1.20} = \$1,333.33$	$\dfrac{4,000 - 2,000}{2,000} = 1.00 = 100.0\%$

a. Investment 1, because it has the highest NPV.

b. Investment 1, because it maximizes shareholders' wealth.

12. a. $NPV = (-\$50,000 + \$20,000) + (\$38,000/1.05) = \$6,190.48$

b. $NPV = (-\$50,000 + \$20,000) + (\$38,000/1.10) = \$4,545.45$

In Part (a), the NPV is higher than the NPV of the office building ($5,000); therefore, we should accept E. Coli's offer. In Part (b), the NPV is less than the NPV of the office building, so we should not accept the offer.

You can also think of this in another way. The true opportunity cost of the land is what you could sell it for, i.e., $56,190 (or $54,545). At $56,190, the office building has a negative NPV. At $54,545, the office building has a positive NPV.

13. a. $NPV = -\$1,000,000 + [(\$1,000,000 \times 1.05)/1.05] = \$0$

b. $NPV = -\$1,000,000 + [(\$1,000,000 \times 1.09)/1.10] = -\$9,090.91$

The correct discount rate is 10% because this is the appropriate rate for an investment with the level of risk inherent in Norman's nephew's restaurant. The NPV is negative because Norman will not earn enough to compensate for the risk.

c. $NPV = -\$1,000,000 + [(\$1,000,000 \times 1.12)/1.12] = \$0$

d. $NPV = -\$1,000,000 + (\$1,100,000/1.12) = -\$17,857.14$

Norman should invest in either the risk-free government securities or the risky stock market, depending on his tolerance for risk. Correctly priced securities always have an NPV = 0.

14. a. Expected rate of return on project =

$$\frac{\$1,100,000 - \$1,000,000}{\$1,000,000} = 0.05 = 5.0\%$$

This is equal to the return on the government securities.

b. Expected rate of return on project =

$$\frac{\$1,090,000 - \$1,000,000}{\$1,000,000} = 0.09 = 9.0\%$$

This is less than the correct 10% rate of return for restaurants with similar risk.

c. Expected rate of return on project =

$$\frac{\$1,120,000 - \$1,000,000}{\$1,000,000} = 0.12 = 12.0\%$$

This is equal to the rate of return in the stock market.

d.   Expected rate of return on project =

$$\frac{\$1,100,000 - \$1,000,000}{\$1,000,000} = 0.10 = 10.0\%$$

This is less than the return in the equally risky stock market.

15. $$NPV = -\$1,600,000 + \left[\frac{\$1,100,000 + (\$600,000 \times 1.12)}{1.12}\right] = -\$17,857.14$$

The rate at which Norman can borrow does not reflect the opportunity cost of the investments. Norman is still investing $1,000,000 at 10% while the opportunity cost of capital is 12%.

16.   The investment's positive NPV will be reflected in the price of Scaled Composites stock. In order to derive a cash flow from her investment that will allow her to spend more today, Ms. Espinoza can sell some of her shares at the higher price or she can borrow against the increased value of her holdings.

17.

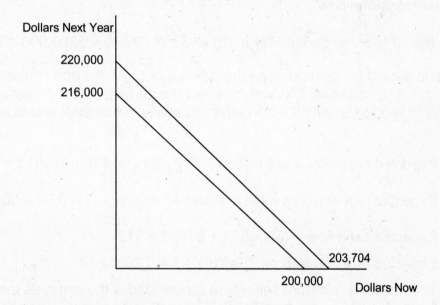

a.   Let x = the amount that Casper should invest now. Then ($200,000 – x) is the amount he will consume now, and (1.08x) is the amount he will consume next year. Since Casper wants to consume exactly the same amount each period:

         200,000 – x = 1.08x

Solving, we find that x = $96,153.85 so that Casper should invest $96,153.85 now, he should spend ($200,000 – $96,153.85) = $103,846.15 now, and he should spend (1.08 × $96,153.85) = $103,846.15 next year.

b. Since Casper can invest $200,000 at 10% risk-free, he can consume as much as ($200,000 × 1.10) = $220,000 next year. The present value of this $220,000 is: ($220,000/1.08) = $203,703.70

Therefore Casper can consume as much as $203,703.70 now by first investing $200,000 at 10% and then borrowing, at the 8% rate, against the $220,000 available next year. If we use the $203,703.70 as the available consumption now, and again let x = the amount that Casper should invest now, we can then solve the following for x:

$$\$203,703.70 - x = 1.08x$$

$$x = \$97,934.47$$

Therefore, Casper should invest $97,934.47 now at 8%, he should spend ($203,703.70 − $97,934.47) = $105,769.23 now, and he should spend ($97,934.47 × 1.08) = $105,769.23 next year.

[Note that this approach leads to the result that Casper borrows $203,703.70 at 8% and then invests $97,934.47 at 8%. We could simply say that he should borrow ($203,703.70 − $97,934.47) = $105,769.23 at 8% against the $220,000 available next year. This is the amount that he will consume now.]

c. The NPV of the opportunity in (b) is: $203,703.70 − $200,000 = $3,703.70

18. The value should fall by more than the amount of any fines and settlement payments. The additional loss would reflect the damage to the financial institution's reputation which would affect its ability to hire staff and to attract customers.

19. a. Expected cash flow = ($8 million + $12 million + $16 million)/3 = $12 million

b. Expected rate of return = ($12 million/$8 million) − 1 = 0.50 = 50%

c. Expected cash flow = ($8 + $12 + $16)/3 = $12

Expected rate of return = ($12/$10) − 1 = 0.20 = 20%

The net cash flow from selling the tanker load is the same as the payoff from one million shares of Stock Z in each state of the world economy. Therefore, the risk of each of these cash flows is the same.

d. NPV = −$8,000,000 + ($12,000,000/1.20) = +$2,000,000

The project is a good investment because the NPV is positive. Investors would be prepared to pay as much as $10,000,000 for the project, which costs $8,000,000.

Challenge Questions

20.   a.   Expected cash flow (Project B) = ($4 million + $6 million + $8 million)/3

                   Expected cash flow (Project B) = $6 million

                   Expected cash flow (Project C) = ($5 million + $5.5 million + $6 million)/3

                   Expected cash flow (Project C) = $5.5 million

    b.   Expected rate of return (Stock X) = ($110/$95.65) −1 = 0.15 = 15.0%

                   Expected rate of return (Stock Y) = ($44/$40) −1 = 0.10 = 10.0%

                   Expected rate of return (Stock Z) = ($12/$10) −1 = 0.20 = 20.0%

    c.

	Percentage Differences	
	Slump v. Normal	Boom v. Normal
Project B	4/6 = 66.67%	8/6 = 133.33%
Project C	5/5.5 = 90.91%	6/5.5 = 109.09%
Stock X	80/110 = 72.73%	140/110 = 127.27%
Stock Y	40/44 = 90.91%	48/44 = 109.09%
Stock Z	8/12 = 66.67%	16/12 = 133.33%

                   Project B has the same risk as Stock Z, so the cost of capital for Project B is 20%. Project C has the same risk as Stock Y, so the cost of capital for Project C is 10%.

    d.   NPV (Project B) = −$5,000,000 + ($6,000,000/1.20) = 0

                   NPV (Project C) = −$5,000,000 + ($5,500,000/1.10) = 0

    e.   The two projects will add nothing to the total market value of the company's shares.

CHAPTER 3

How to Calculate Present Values

Answers to Practice Questions

12.

a. $PV = \$100/1.01^{10} = \$90.53$

b. $PV = \$100/1.13^{10} = \$29.46$

c. $PV = \$100/1.25^{15} = \$3.52$

d. $PV = \$100/1.12 + \$100/1.12^2 + \$100/1.12^3 = \$240.18$

13.

a. $DF_1 = \dfrac{1}{1+r_1} = 0.905 \Rightarrow r_1 = 0.1050 = 10.50\%$

b. $DF_2 = \dfrac{1}{(1+r_2)^2} = \dfrac{1}{(1.105)^2} = 0.819$

c. $AF_2 = DF_1 + DF_2 = 0.905 + 0.819 = 1.724$

d. PV of an annuity = C × [Annuity factor at r% for t years]

Here:

$\$24.65 = \$10 \times [AF_3]$

$AF_3 = 2.465$

e. $AF_3 = DF_1 + DF_2 + DF_3 = AF_2 + DF_3$

$2.465 = 1.724 + DF_3$

$DF_3 = 0.741$

14. The present value of the 10-year stream of cash inflows is:

$$PV = \$170,000 \times \left[\frac{1}{0.14} - \frac{1}{0.14 \times (1.14)^{10}} \right] = \$886,739.66$$

Thus:

$NPV = -\$800,000 + \$886,739.66 = +\$86,739.66$

At the end of five years, the factory's value will be the present value of the five remaining $170,000 cash flows:

$$PV = \$170,000 \times \left[\frac{1}{0.14} - \frac{1}{0.14 \times (1.14)^5}\right] = \$583,623.76$$

15.

$$NPV = \sum_{t=0}^{10} \frac{C_t}{(1.12)^t} = -\$380,000 + \frac{\$50,000}{1.12} + \frac{\$57,000}{1.12^2} + \frac{\$75,000}{1.12^3} + \frac{\$80,000}{1.12^4} + \frac{\$85,000}{1.12^5}$$

$$+ \frac{\$92,000}{1.12^6} + \frac{\$92,000}{1.12^7} + \frac{\$80,000}{1.12^8} + \frac{\$68,000}{1.12^9} + \frac{\$50,000}{1.12^{10}} = \$23,696.15$$

16. a. Let S_t = salary in year t

$$PV = \sum_{t=1}^{30} \frac{S_t}{(1.08)^t} = \sum_{t=1}^{30} \frac{40,000\,(1.05)^{t-1}}{(1.08)^t} = \sum_{t=1}^{30} \frac{(40,000/1.05)}{(1.08/1.05)^t} = \sum_{t=1}^{30} \frac{38,095.24}{(1.0286)^t}$$

$$= 38,095.24 \times \left[\frac{1}{0.0286} - \frac{1}{0.0286 \times (1.0286)^{30}}\right] = \$760,379.21$$

b. PV(salary) x 0.05 = $38,018.96

Future value = $38,018.96 x (1.08)^{30} = $382,571.75

c.

$$PV = C \times \left[\frac{1}{r} - \frac{1}{r \times (1+r)^t}\right]$$

$$\$382,571.75 = C \times \left[\frac{1}{0.08} - \frac{1}{0.08 \times (1.08)^{20}}\right]$$

$$C = \$382,571.75 \bigg/ \left[\frac{1}{0.08} - \frac{1}{0.08 \times (1.08)^{20}}\right] = \$38,965.78$$

17.

Period		Present Value
0		−400,000.00
1	+100,000/1.12 =	+ 89,285.71
2	+200,000/1.12^2 =	+159,438.78
3	+300,000/1.12^3 =	+213,534.07
	Total = NPV =	$62,258.56

18. We can break this down into several different cash flows, such that the sum of these separate cash flows is the total cash flow. Then, the sum of the present values of the separate cash flows is the present value of the entire project. (All dollar figures are in millions.)

- Cost of the ship is $8 million
  PV = −$8 million

- Revenue is $5 million per year, operating expenses are $4 million. Thus, operating cash flow is $1 million per year for 15 years.

$$PV = \$1 \text{ million} \times \left[\frac{1}{0.08} - \frac{1}{0.08 \times (1.08)^{15}} \right] = \$8.559 \text{ million}$$

- Major refits cost $2 million each, and will occur at times t = 5 and t = 10.
  PV = (−$2 million)/1.08^5 + (−$2 million)/1.08^{10} = −$2.288 million

- Sale for scrap brings in revenue of $1.5 million at t = 15.
  PV = $1.5 million/1.08^{15} = $0.473 million

Adding these present values gives the present value of the entire project:

NPV = −$8 million + $8.559 million − $2.288 million + $0.473 million
NPV = −$1.256 million

19. a. PV = $100,000

b. PV = $180,000/1.12^5 = $102,136.83

c. PV = $11,400/0.12 = $95,000

d. $$PV = \$19,000 \times \left[\frac{1}{0.12} - \frac{1}{0.12 \times (1.12)^{10}} \right] = \$107,354.24$$

e. PV = $6,500/(0.12 − 0.05) = $92,857.14

Prize (d) is the most valuable because it has the highest present value.

20. Mr. Basset is buying a security worth $20,000 now. That is its present value. The unknown is the annual payment. Using the present value of an annuity formula, we have:

$$PV = C \times \left[\frac{1}{r} - \frac{1}{r \times (1+r)^t} \right]$$

$$\$20,000 = C \times \left[\frac{1}{0.08} - \frac{1}{0.08 \times (1.08)^{12}} \right]$$

$$C = \$20,000 \bigg/ \left[\frac{1}{0.08} - \frac{1}{0.08 \times (1.08)^{12}} \right] = \$2,653.90$$

21. Assume the Zhangs will put aside the same amount each year. One approach to solving this problem is to find the present value of the cost of the boat and then equate that to the present value of the money saved. From this equation, we can solve for the amount to be put aside each year.

$$PV(boat) = \$20,000/(1.10)^5 = \$12,418$$

$$PV(savings) = \text{Annual savings} \times \left[\frac{1}{0.10} - \frac{1}{0.10 \times (1.10)^5} \right]$$

Because PV(savings) must equal PV(boat):

$$\text{Annual savings} \times \left[\frac{1}{0.10} - \frac{1}{0.10 \times (1.10)^5} \right] = \$12,418$$

$$\text{Annual savings} = \$12,418 \bigg/ \left[\frac{1}{0.10} - \frac{1}{0.10 \times (1.10)^5} \right] = \$3,276$$

Another approach is to find the value of the savings at the time the boat is purchased. Because the amount in the savings account at the end of five years must be the price of the boat ($20,000) we can solve for the amount to be put aside each year. If x is the amount to be put aside each year, then:

$$x(1.10)^4 + x(1.10)^3 + x(1.10)^2 + x(1.10)^1 + x = \$20,000$$

$$x(1.464 + 1.331 + 1.210 + 1.10 + 1) = \$20,000$$

$$x(6.105) = \$20,000$$

$$x = \$\,3,276$$

22. The fact that Kangaroo Autos is offering "free credit" tells us what the cash payments are; it does not change the fact that money has time value. A 10% annual rate of interest is equivalent to a monthly rate of 0.83%:

$$r_{monthly} = r_{annual} / 12 = 0.10/12 = 0.0083 = 0.83\%$$

The present value of the payments to Kangaroo Autos is:

$$\$1,000 + \$300 \times \left[\frac{1}{0.0083} - \frac{1}{0.0083 \times (1.0083)^{30}} \right] = \$8,938$$

A car from Turtle Motors costs $9,000 cash. Therefore, Kangaroo Autos offers the better deal, i.e., the lower present value of cost.

23. The NPVs are:

at 5% $\Rightarrow$ NPV $= -\$170,000 - \dfrac{\$100,000}{1.05} + \dfrac{\$320,000}{(1.05)^2} = \$25,011$

at 10% $\Rightarrow$ NPV $= -\$170,000 - \dfrac{\$100,000}{1.10} + \dfrac{320,000}{(1.10)^2} = \$3,554$

at 15% $\Rightarrow$ NPV $= -\$170,000 - \dfrac{\$100,000}{1.15} + \dfrac{320,000}{(1.15)^2} = -\$14,991$

The figure below shows that the project has zero NPV at about 11%.

As a check, NPV at 11% is:

$$NPV = -\$170,000 - \frac{\$100,000}{1.11} + \frac{320,000}{(1.11)^2} = -\$371$$

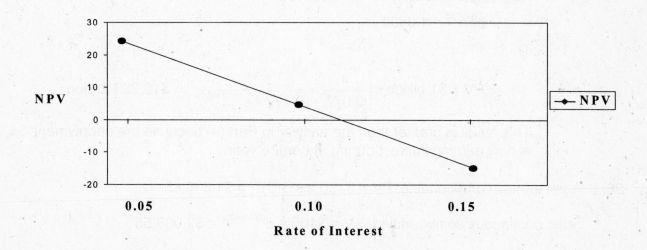

3-5

24. a. This is the usual perpetuity, and hence:

$$PV = \frac{C}{r} = \frac{\$100}{0.07} = \$1,428.57$$

b. This is worth the PV of stream (a) *plus* the immediate payment of $100:

PV = $100 + $1,428.57 = $1,528.57

c. The continuously compounded equivalent to a 7% annually compounded rate is approximately 6.77%, because:

$$e^{0.0677} = 1.0700$$

Thus:

$$PV = \frac{C}{r} = \frac{\$100}{0.0677} = \$1,477.10$$

Note that the pattern of payments in part (b) is more valuable than the pattern of payments in part (c). It is preferable to receive cash flows at the start of every year than to spread the receipt of cash evenly over the year; with the former pattern of payment, you receive the cash more quickly.

25. a. PV = $1 billion/0.08 = $12.5 billion

b. PV = $1 billion/(0.08 – 0.04) = $25.0 billion

c. $$PV = \$1 \text{ billion} \times \left[\frac{1}{0.08} - \frac{1}{0.08 \times (1.08)^{20}} \right] = \$9.818 \text{ billion}$$

d. The continuously compounded equivalent to an 8% annually compounded rate is approximately 7.7% , because:

$$e^{0.0770} = 1.0800$$

Thus:

$$PV = \$1 \text{ billion} \times \left[\frac{1}{0.077} - \frac{1}{0.077 \times e^{(0.077)(20)}} \right] = \$10.203 \text{ billion}$$

This result is greater than the answer in Part (c) because the endowment is now earning interest during the entire year.

26. With annual compounding: FV = $100 × (1.15)^{20} = $1,636.65

With continuous compounding: FV = $100 × e^{(0.15×20)} = $2,008.55

27. One way to approach this problem is to solve for the present value of:

　　(1) $100 per year for 10 years, and

　　(2) $100 per year in perpetuity, with the first cash flow at year 11.

If this is a fair deal, these present values must be equal, and thus we can solve for the interest rate (r).

The present value of $100 per year for 10 years is:

$$PV = \$100 \times \left[\frac{1}{r} - \frac{1}{(r) \times (1+r)^{10}} \right]$$

The present value, as of year 10, of $100 per year forever, with the first payment in year 11, is: $PV_{10} = \$100/r$

At t = 0, the present value of PV_{10} is:

$$PV = \left[\frac{1}{(1+r)^{10}} \right] \times \left[\frac{\$100}{r} \right]$$

Equating these two expressions for present value, we have:

$$\$100 \times \left[\frac{1}{r} - \frac{1}{(r) \times (1+r)^{10}} \right] = \left[\frac{1}{(1+r)^{10}} \right] \times \left[\frac{\$100}{r} \right]$$

Using trial and error or algebraic solution, we find that r = 7.18%.

28. Assume the amount invested is one dollar.
Let A represent the investment at 12%, compounded annually.
Let B represent the investment at 11.7%, compounded semiannually.
Let C represent the investment at 11.5%, compounded continuously.

After one year:

$$FV_A = \$1 \times (1 + 0.12)^1 \qquad = \$1.1200$$

$$FV_B = \$1 \times (1 + 0.0585)^2 \quad = \$1.1204$$

$$FV_C = \$1 \times e^{(0.115 \times 1)} \qquad = \$1.1219$$

After five years:

$$FV_A = \$1 \times (1 + 0.12)^5 \qquad = \$1.7623$$

$$FV_B = \$1 \times (1 + 0.0585)^{10} = \$1.7657$$

$$FV_C = \$1 \times e^{(0.115 \times 5)} \qquad = \$1.7771$$

After twenty years:

$$FV_A = \$1 \times (1 + 0.12)^{20} \quad = \$9.6463$$

$$FV_B = \$1 \times (1 + 0.0585)^{40} = \$9.7193$$

$$FV_C = \$1 \times e^{(0.115 \times 20)} \quad = \$9.9742$$

The preferred investment is C.

29. The total elapsed time is 113 years.

At 5%: $FV = \$100 \times (1 + 0.05)^{113} = \$24,797$

At 10%: $FV = \$100 \times (1 + 0.10)^{113} = \$4,757,441$

30. Because the cash flows occur every six months, we use a six-month discount rate, here 8%/2, or 4%. Thus:

$$PV = \$100,000 + \$100,000 \times \left[\frac{1}{0.04} - \frac{1}{0.04 \times (1.04)^9}\right] = \$843,533$$

31. a. Each installment is: \$9,420,713/19 = \$495,827

$$PV = \$495,827 \times \left[\frac{1}{0.08} - \frac{1}{0.08 \times (1.08)^{19}}\right] = \$4,761,724$$

b. If ERC is willing to pay \$4.2 million, then:

$$\$4,200,000 = \$495,827 \times \left[\frac{1}{r} - \frac{1}{r \times (1+r)^{19}}\right]$$

Using Excel or a financial calculator, we find that r = 9.81%.

32. a. $PV = \$70,000 \times \left[\frac{1}{0.08} - \frac{1}{0.08 \times (1.08)^8}\right] = \$402,264.73$

b.

Year	Beginning-of-Year Balance	Year-end Interest on Balance	Total Year-end Payment	Amortization of Loan	End-of-Year Balance
1	402,264.73	32,181.18	70,000.00	37,818.82	364,445.91
2	364,445.91	29,155.67	70,000.00	40,844.33	323,601.58
3	323,601.58	25,888.13	70,000.00	44,111.87	279,489.71
4	279,489.71	22,359.18	70,000.00	47,640.82	231,848.88
5	231,848.88	18,547.91	70,000.00	51,452.09	180,396.79
6	180,396.79	14,431.74	70,000.00	55,568.26	124,828.54
7	124,828.54	9,986.28	70,000.00	60,013.72	64,814.82
8	64,814.82	5,185.19	70,000.00	64,814.81	0.01

33. This is an annuity problem with the present value of the annuity equal to $2 million (as of your retirement date), and the interest rate equal to 8% with 15 time periods. Thus, your annual level of expenditure (C) is determined as follows:

$$PV = C \times \left[\frac{1}{r} - \frac{1}{r \times (1+r)^t} \right]$$

$$\$2,000,000 = C \times \left[\frac{1}{0.08} - \frac{1}{0.08 \times (1.08)^{15}} \right]$$

$$C = \$2,000,000 \bigg/ \left[\frac{1}{0.08} - \frac{1}{0.08 \times (1.08)^{15}} \right] = \$233,659$$

With an inflation rate of 4% per year, we will still accumulate $2 million as of our retirement date. However, because we want to spend a constant amount per year in real terms (R, constant for all t), the nominal amount (C_t) must increase each year. For each year t:

$$R = C_t / (1 + \text{inflation rate})^t$$

Therefore:

$$PV [\text{all } C_t] = PV [\text{all } R \times (1 + \text{inflation rate})^t] = \$2,000,000$$

$$R \times \left[\frac{(1+0.04)^1}{(1+0.08)^1} + \frac{(1+0.04)^2}{(1+0.08)^2} + \ldots + \frac{(1+0.04)^{15}}{(1+0.08)^{15}} \right] = \$2,000,000$$

$$R \times [0.9630 + 0.9273 + \ldots + 0.5677] = \$2,000,000$$

$$R \times 11.2390 = \$2,000,000$$

$$R = \$177,952$$

Thus $C_1 = (\$177,952 \times 1.04) = \$185,070$, $C_2 = \$192,473$, etc.

34. a.
$$PV = \$50,000 \times \left[\frac{1}{0.055} - \frac{1}{0.055 \times (1.055)^{12}} \right] = \$430,925.89$$

b. The annually compounded rate is 5.5%, so the semiannual rate is:
$$(1.055)^{(1/2)} - 1 = 0.0271 = 2.71\%$$

Since the payments now arrive six months earlier than previously:
$$PV = \$430,925.89 \times 1.0271 = \$442,603.98$$

35. In three years, the balance in the mutual fund will be:

$$FV = \$1,000,000 \times (1.035)^3 = \$1,108,718$$

The monthly shortfall will be: $15,000 - ($7,500 + $1,500) = $6,000

Annual withdrawals from the mutual fund will be: $6,000 \times 12 = $72,000

Assume the first annual withdrawal occurs three years from today, when the balance in the mutual fund will be $1,108,718. Treating the withdrawals as an annuity due, we solve for t as follows:

$$PV = C \times \left[\frac{1}{r} - \frac{1}{r \times (1+r)^t} \right] \times (1+r)$$

$$\$1,108,718 = \$72,000 \times \left[\frac{1}{0.035} - \frac{1}{0.035 \times (1.035)^t} \right] \times 1.035$$

Using Excel or a financial calculator, we find that t = 22.5 years.

Challenge Questions

36. a. Using the Rule of 72, the time for money to double at 12% is 72/12, or 6 years. More precisely, if x is the number of years for money to double, then:

$$(1.12)^x = 2$$

Using logarithms, we find:

$$x \, (\ln 1.12) = \ln 2$$

$$x = 6.12 \text{ years}$$

b. With continuous compounding for interest rate r and time period x:

$$e^{rx} = 2$$

Taking the natural logarithm of each side:

$$r \, x = \ln(2) = 0.693$$

Thus, if r is expressed as a percent, then x (the time for money to double) is: x = 69.3/(interest rate, in percent).

37. Spreadsheet exercise.

38. a. This calls for the growing perpetuity formula with a negative growth rate (g = –0.04):

$$PV = \frac{\$2 \text{ million}}{0.10 - (-0.04)} = \frac{\$2 \text{ million}}{0.14} = \$14.29 \text{ million}$$

b. The pipeline's value at year 20 (i.e., at t = 20), assuming its cash flows last forever, is:

$$PV_{20} = \frac{C_{21}}{r-g} = \frac{C_1(1+g)^{20}}{r-g}$$

With C_1 = $2 million, g = –0.04, and r = 0.10:

$$PV_{20} = \frac{(\$2 \text{ million}) \times (1-0.04)^{20}}{0.14} = \frac{\$0.884 \text{ million}}{0.14} = \$6.314 \text{ million}$$

Next, we convert this amount to PV today, and subtract it from the answer to Part (a):

$$PV = \$14.29 \text{ million} - \frac{\$6.314 \text{ million}}{(1.10)^{20}} = \$13.35 \text{ million}$$

CHAPTER 4

Valuing Bonds

Answers to Practice Questions

12. With annual coupon payments:

$$PV = 5 \times \left[\frac{1}{0.06} - \frac{1}{0.06 \times (1.06)^{10}} \right] + \frac{100}{(1.06)^{10}} = €92.64$$

13. With semi-annual coupon payments:

$$PV = 2.5 \times \left[\frac{1}{0.03} - \frac{1}{0.03 \times (1.03)^{20}} \right] + \frac{100}{(1.03)^{20}} = €92.56$$

14. a. $$PV = 275 \times \left[\frac{1}{0.026} - \frac{1}{0.026 \times (1.026)^{20}} \right] + \frac{10,000}{(1.026)^{20}} = \$10,231.64$$

   b.

Interest rate	PV of Interest	PV of Face value	PV of Bond
1.0%	$5,221.54	$9,050.63	$14,272.17
2.0%	4,962.53	8,195.44	13,157.97
3.0%	4,721.38	7,424.70	12,146.08
4.0%	4,496.64	6,729.71	11,226.36
5.0%	4,287.02	6,102.71	10,389.73
6.0%	4,091.31	5,536.76	9,628.06
7.0%	3,908.41	5,025.66	8,934.07
8.0%	3,737.34	4,563.87	8,301.21
9.0%	3,577.18	4,146.43	7,723.61
10.0%	3,427.11	3,768.89	7,196.00
11.0%	3,286.36	3,427.29	6,713.64
12.0%	3,154.23	3,118.05	6,272.28
13.0%	3,030.09	2,837.97	5,868.06
14.0%	2,913.35	2,584.19	5,497.54
15.0%	2,803.49	2,354.13	5,157.62

15. Purchase price for a 5-year government bond with 6% annual coupon, 4% yield:

$$PV = 6 \times \left[\frac{1}{0.04} - \frac{1}{0.04 \times (1.04)^{5}} \right] + \frac{100}{(1.04)^{5}} = €108.90$$

Purchase price for a 5-year government bond with 6% semi-annual coupon, 4% yield:

$$PV = 3 \times \left[\frac{1}{0.02} - \frac{1}{0.02 \times (1.02)^{10}} \right] + \frac{100}{(1.02)^{10}} = \$108.98$$

16. Purchase price for a 5-year government bond with 6% annual coupon, 3% yield:

$$PV = 6 \times \left[\frac{1}{0.03} - \frac{1}{0.03 \times (1.03)^{5}} \right] + \frac{100}{(1.03)^{5}} = €113.74$$

Purchase price for a 5-year government bond with 6% semi-annual coupon, 3% yield:

$$PV = 3 \times \left[\frac{1}{0.015} - \frac{1}{0.015 \times (1.015)^{10}} \right] + \frac{1,000}{(1.015)^{10}} = \$113.83$$

17. Purchase price for a 6-year government bond with 5 percent annual coupon:

$$PV = 50 \times \left[\frac{1}{0.03} - \frac{1}{0.03 \times (1.03)^{6}} \right] + \frac{1,000}{(1.03)^{6}} = \$1,108.34$$

Price one year later (yield = 3%):

$$PV = 50 \times \left[\frac{1}{0.03} - \frac{1}{0.03 \times (1.03)^{5}} \right] + \frac{1,000}{(1.03)^{5}} = \$1,091.59$$

Rate of return = [$50 + ($1,091.59 – $1,108.34)]/$1,108.34 = 3.00%

Price one year later (yield = 2%):

$$PV = 50 \times \left[\frac{1}{0.02} - \frac{1}{0.02 \times (1.02)^{5}} \right] + \frac{1,000}{(1.02)^{5}} = \$1,141.40$$

Rate of return = [$50 + ($1,141.40 – $1,108.34)]/$1,108.34 = 7.49%

18. The key here is to find a combination of these two bonds (i.e., a portfolio of bonds) that has a cash flow only at t = 6. Then, knowing the price of the portfolio and the cash flow at t = 6, we can calculate the 6-year spot rate.

We begin by specifying the cash flows of each bond and using these and their yields to calculate their current prices:

Investment	Yield	C_1	. . .	C_5	C_6	Price
6% bond	12%	60	. . .	60	1,060	$753.32
10% bond	8%	100	. . .	100	1,100	$1,092.46

From the cash flows in years one through five, the required portfolio consists of two 6% bonds minus 1.2 10% bonds, i.e., we should buy the equivalent of two 6% bonds and sell the equivalent of 1.2 10% bonds. This portfolio costs:

$$(\$753.32 \times 2) - (1.2 \times \$1,092.46) = \$195.68$$

The cash flow for this portfolio is equal to zero for years one through five and, for year 6, is equal to:

$$(1,060 \times 2) - (1.2 \times 1,100) = \$800$$

Thus:

$$\$195.68 \times (1 + r_6)^6 = 800$$

$$r_6 = 0.2645 = 26.45\%$$

19.   Downward sloping. This is because high coupon bonds provide a greater proportion of their cash flows in the early years. In essence, a high coupon bond is a 'shorter' bond than a low coupon bond of the same maturity.

20.   Using the general relationship between spot and forward rates, we have:

$$(1 + r_2)^2 = (1 + r_1) \times (1 + f_2) = 1.0600 \times 1.0640 \quad \Rightarrow r_2 = 0.0620 = 6.20\%$$

$$(1 + r_3)^3 = (1 + r_2)^2 \times (1 + f_3) = (1.0620)^2 \times 1.0710 \quad \Rightarrow r_3 = 0.0650 = 6.50\%$$

$$(1 + r_4)^4 = (1 + r_3)^3 \times (1 + f_4) = (1.0650)^3 \times 1.0730 \quad \Rightarrow r_4 = 0.0670 = 6.70\%$$

$$(1 + r_5)^5 = (1 + r_4)^4 \times (1 + f_5) = (1.0670)^4 \times 1.0820 \quad \Rightarrow r_5 = 0.0700 = 7.00\%$$

If the expectations hypothesis holds, we can infer—from the fact that the forward rates are increasing—that spot interest rates are expected to increase in the future.

21.   In order to lock in the currently existing forward rate for year five (f_5), the firm should:

- Borrow the present value of $100 million. Because this money will be received in four years, this borrowing is at the four-year spot rate: $r_4 = 6.70\%$
- Invest this amount for five years, at the five-year spot rate: $r_5 = 7.00\%$

Thus, the cash flows are:

Today: Borrow ($100 million/$1.0670^4$) = $77.151 million
                Invest $77.151 million for 5 years at 7.00%
                Net cash flow: Zero

In four years: Repay loan: ($77.151 million $\times 1.0670^4$) = $100 million dollars
                Net cash flow: –$100 million

In five years: Receive amount of investment:
                ($77.151 million $\times 1.0700^5$) = $108.208 million
                Net cash flow: +$108.2 million

Note that the cash flows from this strategy are exactly what one would expect from signing a contract today to invest $100 million in four years, for a time period of one year, at today's forward rate for year 5 (8.20%). With $108.2 million available, the firm can cover the payment of $107 million at t = 5.

22. We make use of the usual definition of the internal rate of return to calculate the yield to maturity for each bond.

5% Coupon Bond:

$$NPV = -920.70 + \frac{50}{(1+r)} + \frac{50}{(1+r)^2} + \frac{50}{(1+r)^3} + \frac{50}{(1+r)^4} + \frac{1050}{(1+r)^5} = 0$$

r = 0.06930 = 6.930%

7% Coupon Bond:

$$NPV = -1003.10 + \frac{70}{(1+r)} + \frac{70}{(1+r)^2} + \frac{70}{(1+r)^3} + \frac{70}{(1+r)^4} + \frac{1070}{(1+r)^5} = 0$$

r = 0.06925 = 6.925%

12% Coupon Bond:

$$NPV = -1209.20 + \frac{120}{(1+r)} + \frac{120}{(1+r)^2} + \frac{120}{(1+r)^3} + \frac{120}{(1+r)^4} + \frac{1120}{(1+r)^5} = 0$$

r = 0.06910 = 6.910%

Assuming that the default risk is the same for each bond, one might be tempted to conclude that the bond with the highest yield is the best investment. However, we know that the yield curve is rising (the spot rates are those found in Question 3) and that, because the bonds have different coupon rates, their durations are different.

5% Coupon Bond:

$$DUR = \frac{\dfrac{1(50)}{1.060} + \dfrac{2(50)}{1.062^2} + \dfrac{3(50)}{1.065^3} + \dfrac{4(50)}{1.067^4} + \dfrac{5(1050)}{1.070^5}}{920.70}$$

DUR = 4157.5 / 920.70 = 4.52 years

7% Coupon Bond:

$$DUR = \frac{\dfrac{1(70)}{1.060} + \dfrac{2(70)}{1.062^2} + \dfrac{3(70)}{1.065^3} + \dfrac{4(70)}{1.067^4} + \dfrac{5(1070)}{1.070^5}}{1003.10}$$

DUR = 4394.5 / 1003.10 = 4.38 years

12% Coupon Bond:

$$DUR = \frac{\dfrac{1(120)}{1.060} + \dfrac{2(120)}{1.062^2} + \dfrac{3(120)}{1.065^3} + \dfrac{4(120)}{1.067^4} + \dfrac{5(1120)}{1.070^5}}{1209.20}$$

$$DUR = 4987.1/1209.20 = 4.12 \text{ years}$$

Thus, the bond with the longest duration is also the bond with the highest yield to maturity. This is precisely what is expected, given that the yield curve is rising. We conclude that the bonds are equally attractive.

23.   a. & b.

Year	Discount Factor	Forward Rate
1	$1/1.05 = 0.952$	
2	$1/(1.054)^2 = 0.900$	$(1.054^2/1.05) - 1 = 0.0580 = 5.80\%$
3	$1/(1.057)^3 = 0.847$	$(1.057^3/1.054^2) - 1 = 0.0630 = 6.30\%$
4	$1/(1.059)^4 = 0.795$	$(1.059^4/1.057^3) - 1 = 0.0650 = 6.50\%$
5	$1/(1.060)^5 = 0.747$	$(1.060^5/1.059^4) - 1 = 0.0640 = 6.40\%$

c.   1.   5%, two-year note:

$$PV = \frac{\$50}{1.05} + \frac{\$1050}{(1.054)^2} = \$992.79$$

     2.   5%, five-year note:

$$PV = \frac{\$50}{1.05} + \frac{\$50}{(1.054)^2} + \frac{\$50}{(1.057)^3} + \frac{\$50}{(1.059)^4} + \frac{\$1050}{(1.060)^5} = \$959.34$$

     3.   10%, five-year note:

$$PV = \frac{\$100}{1.05} + \frac{\$100}{(1.054)^2} + \frac{\$100}{(1.057)^3} + \frac{\$100}{(1.059)^4} + \frac{\$1100}{(1.060)^5} = \$1,171.43$$

d.   First, we calculate the yield for each of the two bonds. For the 5% bond, this means solving for r in the following equation:

$$\$959.34 = \frac{\$50}{1+r} + \frac{\$50}{(1+r)^2} + \frac{\$50}{(1+r)^3} + \frac{\$50}{(1+r)^4} + \frac{\$1050}{(1+r)^5}$$

$$r = 0.05964 = 5.964\%$$

For the 10% bond:

$$\$1171.43 = \frac{\$100}{1+r} + \frac{\$100}{(1+r)^2} + \frac{\$100}{(1+r)^3} + \frac{\$100}{(1+r)^4} + \frac{\$1100}{(1+r)^5}$$

$$r = 0.05937 = 5.937\%$$

The yield depends upon both the coupon payment and the spot rate at the time of the coupon payment. The 10% bond has a slightly greater proportion of its total payments coming earlier, when interest rates are low, than does the 5% bond. Thus, the yield of the 10% bond is slightly lower.

e. The yield to maturity on a five-year zero coupon bond is the five-year spot rate, here 6.00%.

f. First, we find the price of the five-year annuity, assuming that the annual payment is $1:

$$PV = \frac{1}{1.05} + \frac{1}{(1.054)^2} + \frac{1}{(1.057)^3} + \frac{1}{(1.059)^4} + \frac{1}{(1.060)^5} = \$4.2417$$

Now we find the yield to maturity for this annuity:

$$4.2417 = \frac{1}{1+r} + \frac{1}{(1+r)^2} + \frac{1}{(1+r)^3} + \frac{1}{(1+r)^4} + \frac{1}{(1+r)^5}$$

$r = 0.05745 = 5.745\%$

g. The yield on the five-year Treasury note lies between the yield on a five-year zero-coupon bond and the yield on a 5-year annuity because the cash flows of the Treasury bond lie between the cash flows of these other two financial instruments. That is, the annuity has fixed, equal payments, the zero-coupon bond has one payment at the end, and the bond's payments are a combination of these.

24. A 6-year spot rate of 4.8 percent implies a negative forward rate:

$(1.048^6/1.06^5) - 1 = -0.010 = -1.0\%$

To make money, you could borrow $1,000 for 6 years at 4.8 percent and lend $990 for 5 years at 6 percent. The future value of the amount borrowed is:

$FV_6 = \$1,000 \times (1.048)^6 = \$1,324.85$

The future value of the amount loaned is:

$FV_5 = \$990 \times (1.06)^5 = \$1,324.84$

This ensures enough money to repay the loan by holding cash over from year 5 to year 6, and provides an immediate $10 inflow.

The minimum sensible rate satisfies the condition that the forward rate is 0%:

$(1 + r_6)^6/(1.06)^5 = 1.00$

This implies that $r_6 = 4.976$ percent.

25. a. Under the expectations theory, the expected spot rate equals the forward rate, which is equal to:

$(1.06^5/1.059^4) - 1 = 0.064 = 6.4$ percent

b. If investing in long-term bonds carries additional risk, then the expected spot rate is less than the forward rate of 6.4%.

26. In general, yield changes have the greatest impact on long-maturity, low-coupon bonds.

27. The duration is computed in the table below:

Year	C_t	PV @5.00%	Proportion of Total Value	Proportion of Total Value × Time
1	40.00	38.0952	0.03916	0.03916
2	40.00	36.2812	0.03730	0.07459
3	1040.00	898.3911	0.92354	2.77062
Totals		972.7675		2.88438

28. The calculations are shown in the tables below:

Year	C_t	$PV(C_t)$	Proportion of Total Value	Proportion of Total Value × Time	
1	80.00	76.19	0.070	0.070	
2	80.00	72.56	0.067	0.134	
3	1080.00	932.94	0.862	2.587	
4		0.00	0.000	0.000	
5		0.00	0.000	0.000	
6		0.00	0.000	0.000	
7		0.00	0.000	0.000	
8		0.00	0.000	0.000	
9		0.00	0.000	0.000	
10		0.00	0.000	0.000	
	V =	1081.70	1.000	2.792	= Duration (years)
Note:				2.659	= Volatility
Yield %	5.00				

Year	C_t	$PV(C_t)$	Proportion of Total Value	Proportion of Total Value × Time	
1	100.00	94.34	0.085	0.085	
2	100.00	89.00	0.080	0.161	
3	1100.00	923.58	0.834	2.503	
4		0.00	0.000	0.000	
5		0.00	0.000	0.000	
6		0.00	0.000	0.000	
7		0.00	0.000	0.000	
8		0.00	0.000	0.000	
9		0.00	0.000	0.000	
10		0.00	0.000	0.000	
	V =	1106.92	1.000	2.749	= Duration (years)
Note:				2.594	= Volatility
Yield %	6.00				

29. The duration of a perpetual bond is: [(1 + yield)/yield]
The duration of a perpetual bond with a yield of 5% is:

$$D_5 = 1.05/0.05 = 21 \text{ years}$$

The duration of a perpetual bond yielding 10% is:

$$D_{10} = 1.10/0.10 = 11 \text{ years}$$

Because the duration of a zero-coupon bond is equal to its maturity, the 15-year zero-coupon bond has a duration of 15 years.

Thus, comparing the 5% bond and the zero-coupon bond, the 5% bond has the longer duration. Comparing the 10% bond and the zero, the zero has a longer duration.

30. The duration of the contract is computed as follows:

Year	C_t	$PV(C_t)$	Proportion of Total Value	Proportion of Total Value × Time	
1	150,000	137,614.68	0.236	0.236	
2	150,000	126,252.00	0.216	0.433	
3	150,000	115,827.52	0.199	0.596	
4	150,000	106,263.78	0.182	0.729	
5	150,000	97,489.71	0.167	0.835	
	V =	583,447.69	1.000	2.828	= Duration (years)
Note:				2.595	= Volatility
Yield %	9.00				

Alternatively, the following formula can be used to compute the duration of a level annuity:

$$\frac{1+y}{y} - \frac{T}{(1+y)^T - 1} = \frac{1.09}{0.09} - \frac{5}{(1.09)^5 - 1} = 12.111 - 9.283 = 2.828 \text{ years}$$

The volatility is 2.595. This tells us that a 1% variation in the interest rate will cause the contract's value to change by 2.595%. On average, then, a 0.5% increase in yield will cause the contract's value to fall by 1.298%. The present value of the annuity is $583,447.69 so the value of the contract decreases by: $(0.01298 \times \$583,447.69) = \$7,573.15$

Challenge Questions

31.   Spreadsheet problem; answers will vary.

32.   Arbitrage opportunities can be identified by finding situations where the implied forward rates or spot rates are different.

We begin with the shortest-term bond, Bond G, which has a two-year maturity. Since G is a zero-coupon bond, we determine the two-year spot rate directly by finding the yield for Bond G. The yield is 9.5 percent, so the implied two-year spot rate (r_2) is 9.5 percent. Using the same approach for Bond A, we find that the three-year spot rate (r_3) is 10.0 percent.

Next we use Bonds B and D to find the four-year spot rate. The following position in these bonds provides a cash payoff only in year four:
a long position in two of Bond B and a short position in Bond D.
Cash flows for this position are:

$[(-2 \times \$842.30) + \$980.57] = -\$704.03$ today
$[(2 \times \$50) - \$100] = \$0$ in years 1, 2 and 3
$[(2 \times \$1050) - \$1100] = \$1000$ in year 4

We determine the four-year spot rate from this position as follows:

$$\$704.03 = \frac{\$1000}{(1 + r_4)^4}$$

$r_4 = 0.0917 = 9.17\%$

Next, we use r_2, r_3 and r_4 with one of the four-year coupon bonds to determine r_1. For Bond C:

$$\$1,065.28 = \frac{\$120}{1 + r_1} + \frac{\$120}{(1.095)^2} + \frac{\$120}{(1.100)^3} + \frac{\$1120}{(1.0917)^4} = \frac{\$120}{1 + r_1} + \$978.74$$

$r_1 = 0.3867 = 38.67\%$

Now, in order to determine whether arbitrage opportunities exist, we use these spot rates to value the remaining two four-year bonds. This produces the following results: for Bond B, the present value is $854.55, and for Bond D, the present value is $1,005.07. Since neither of these values equals the current market price of the respective bonds, arbitrage opportunities exist. Similarly, the spot rates derived above produce the following values for the three-year bonds: $1,074.22 for Bond E and $912.77 for Bond F.

33. We begin with the definition of duration as applied to a bond with yield r and an annual payment of C in perpetuity

$$DUR = \frac{\dfrac{1C}{1+r} + \dfrac{2C}{(1+r)^2} + \dfrac{3C}{(1+r)^3} + \cdots + \dfrac{tC}{(1+r)^t} + \cdots}{\dfrac{C}{1+r} + \dfrac{C}{(1+r)^2} + \dfrac{C}{(1+r)^3} + \cdots + \dfrac{C}{(1+r)^t} + \cdots}$$

We first simplify by dividing both the numerator and the denominator by C:

$$DUR = \frac{\dfrac{1}{(1+r)} + \dfrac{2}{(1+r)^2} + \dfrac{3}{(1+r)^3} + \cdots + \dfrac{t}{(1+r)^t} + \cdots}{\dfrac{1}{1+r} + \dfrac{1}{(1+r)^2} + \dfrac{1}{(1+r)^3} + \cdots + \dfrac{1}{(1+r)^t} + \cdots}$$

The denominator is the present value of a perpetuity of $1 per year, which is equal to (1/r). To simplify the numerator, we first denote the numerator S and then divide S by (1 + r):

$$\frac{S}{(1+r)} = \frac{1}{(1+r)^2} + \frac{2}{(1+r)^3} + \frac{3}{(1+r)^4} + \cdots + \frac{t}{(1+r)^{t+1}} + \cdots$$

Note that this new quantity [S/(1 + r)] is equal to the square of denominator in the duration formula above, that is:

$$\frac{S}{(1+r)} = \left(\frac{1}{1+r} + \frac{1}{(1+r)^2} + \frac{1}{(1+r)^3} + \cdots + \frac{1}{(1+r)^t} + \cdots \right)^2$$

Therefore:

$$\frac{S}{(1+r)} = \left(\frac{1}{r} \right)^2 \Rightarrow S = \frac{1+r}{r^2}$$

Thus, for a perpetual bond paying C dollars per year:

$$DUR = \frac{1+r}{r^2} \times \frac{1}{(1/r)} = \frac{1+r}{r}$$

34. We begin with the definition of duration as applied to a common stock with yield r and dividends that grow at a constant rate g in perpetuity:

$$DUR = \frac{\dfrac{1C(1+g)}{1+r} + \dfrac{2C(1+g)^2}{(1+r)^2} + \dfrac{3C(1+g)^3}{(1+r)^3} + \cdots + \dfrac{tC(1+g)^t}{(1+r)^t} + \cdots}{\dfrac{C(1+g)}{1+r} + \dfrac{C(1+g)^2}{(1+r)^2} + \dfrac{C(1+g)^3}{(1+r)^3} + \cdots + \dfrac{C(1+g)^t}{(1+r)^t} + \cdots}$$

We first simplify by dividing each term by [C(1 + g)]:

$$DUR = \frac{\dfrac{1}{1+r} + \dfrac{2(1+g)}{(1+r)^2} + \dfrac{3(1+g)^2}{(1+r)^3} + \cdots + \dfrac{t(1+g)^{t-1}}{(1+r)^t} + \cdots}{\dfrac{1}{1+r} + \dfrac{1+g}{(1+r)^2} + \dfrac{(1+g)^2}{(1+r)^3} + \cdots + \dfrac{(1+g)^{t-1}}{(1+r)^t} + \cdots}$$

The denominator is the present value of a growing perpetuity of $1 per year, which is equal to [1/(r – g)]. To simplify the numerator, we first denote the numerator S and then divide S by (1 + r):

$$\frac{S}{(1+r)} = \frac{1}{(1+r)^2} + \frac{2(1+g)}{(1+r)^3} + \frac{3(1+g)^2}{(1+r)^4} + \cdots + \frac{t(1+g)^{t-2}}{(1+r)^{t+1}} + \cdots$$

Note that this new quantity [S/(1 + r)] is equal to the square of denominator in the duration formula above, that is:

$$\frac{S}{(1+r)} = \left(\frac{1}{1+r} + \frac{1+g}{(1+r)^2} + \frac{(1+g)^2}{(1+r)^3} + \cdots + \frac{(1+g)^{t-1}}{(1+r)^t} + \cdots \right)^2$$

Therefore:

$$\frac{S}{(1+r)} = \left(\frac{1}{r-g} \right)^2 \Rightarrow S = \frac{1+r}{(r-g)^2}$$

Thus, for a perpetual bond paying C dollars per year:

$$DUR = \frac{1+r}{(r-g)^2} \times \frac{1}{[1/(r-g)]} = \frac{1+r}{r-g}$$

35. a. We make use of the one-year Treasury bill information in order to determine the one-year spot rate as follows:

$$\$93.46 = \frac{\$100}{1+r_1}$$

$$r_1 = 0.0700 = 7.00\%$$

The following position provides a cash payoff only in year two:

a long position in twenty-five two-year bonds and a short position in one one-year Treasury bill. Cash flows for this position are:

$$[(-25 \times \$94.92) + (1 \times \$93.46)] = -\$2,279.54 \text{ today}$$
$$[(25 \times \$4) - (1 \times \$100)] = \$0 \text{ in year 1}$$
$$(25 \times \$104) = \$2,600 \text{ in year 2}$$

We determine the two-year spot rate from this position as follows:

$$\$2,279.54 = \frac{\$2,600}{(1 + r_2)^2}$$

$$r_2 = 0.0680 = 6.80\%$$

The forward rate f_2 is computed as follows:

$$f_2 = [(1.0680)^2/1.0700] - 1 = 0.0660 = 6.60\%$$

The following position provides a cash payoff only in year three:

a long position in the three-year bond and a short position equal to (8/104) times a package consisting of a one-year Treasury bill and a two-year bond. Cash flows for this position are:

$$[(-1 \times \$103.64) + (8/104) \times (\$93.46 + \$94.92)] = -\$89.15 \text{ today}$$
$$[(1 \times \$8) - (8/104) \times (\$100 + \$4)] = \$0 \text{ in year 1}$$
$$[(1 \times \$8) - (8/104) \times \$104] = \$0 \text{ in year 2}$$
$$1 \times \$108 = \$108 \text{ in year 3}$$

We determine the three-year spot rate from this position as follows:

$$\$89.15 = \frac{\$108}{(1 + r_3)^3}$$

$$r_3 = 0.0660 = 6.60\%$$

The forward rate f_3 is computed as follows:

$$f_3 = [(1.0660)^3/(1.0680)^2] - 1 = 0.0620 = 6.20\%$$

b. We make use of the spot and forward rates to calculate the price of the 4 percent coupon bond:

The actual price of the bond ($950) is significantly greater than the price deduced using the spot and forward rates embedded in the prices of the other bonds ($931.01). Hence, a profit opportunity exists. In order to take advantage of this opportunity, one should sell the 4 percent coupon bond short and purchase the 8 percent coupon bond.

CHAPTER 5

The Value of Common Stocks

Answers to Practice Questions

14. Newspaper exercise, answers will vary

15.

	Expected Future Values		Present Values		
Horizon Period (H)	Dividend (DIV_t)	Price (P_t)	Cumulative Dividends	Future Price	Total
0		100.00		100.00	100.00
1	10.00	105.00	8.70	91.30	100.00
2	10.50	110.25	16.64	83.36	100.00
3	11.03	115.76	23.88	76.12	100.00
4	11.58	121.55	30.50	69.50	100.00
10	15.51	162.89	59.74	40.26	100.00
20	25.27	265.33	83.79	16.21	100.00
50	109.21	1,146.74	98.94	1.06	100.00
100	1,252.39	13,150.13	99.99	0.01	100.00

Assumptions
1. Dividends increase at 5% per year compounded.
2. Capitalization rate is 15%.

16. $P_A = \dfrac{DIV_1}{r} = \dfrac{\$10}{0.10} = \$100.00$

$P_B = \dfrac{DIV_1}{r - g} = \dfrac{\$5}{0.10 - 0.04} = \$83.33$

$P_C = \dfrac{DIV_1}{1.10^1} + \dfrac{DIV_2}{1.10^2} + \dfrac{DIV_3}{1.10^3} + \dfrac{DIV_4}{1.10^4} + \dfrac{DIV_5}{1.10^5} + \dfrac{DIV_6}{1.10^6} + \left(\dfrac{DIV_7}{0.10} \times \dfrac{1}{1.10^6}\right)$

$P_C = \dfrac{5.00}{1.10^1} + \dfrac{6.00}{1.10^2} + \dfrac{7.20}{1.10^3} + \dfrac{8.64}{1.10^4} + \dfrac{10.37}{1.10^5} + \dfrac{12.44}{1.10^6} + \left(\dfrac{12.44}{0.10} \times \dfrac{1}{1.10^6}\right) = \$104.50$

At a capitalization rate of 10%, Stock C is the most valuable.

For a capitalization rate of 7%, the calculations are similar.

The results are:

$P_A = \$142.86$
$P_B = \$166.67$
$P_C = \$156.48$

Therefore, Stock B is the most valuable.

17. a. $$P_0 = DIV_0 + \frac{DIV_1}{r-g} = \$1.35 + \frac{\$1.35 \times 1.0275}{0.095 - 0.0275} = \$21.90$$

b. First, compute the real discount rate as follows:

$$(1 + r_{nominal}) = (1 + r_{real}) \times (1 + \text{inflation rate})$$

$$1.095 = (1 + r_{real}) \times 1.0275$$

$$(1 + r_{real}) = (1.095/1.0275) - 1 = .0657 = 6.57\%$$

In real terms, g = 0. Therefore:

$$P_0 = DIV_0 + \frac{DIV_1}{r-g} = \$1.35 + \frac{\$1.35}{0.0657} = \$21.90$$

18. a. Plowback ratio = 1 − payout ratio = 1.0 − 0.5 = 0.5

Dividend growth rate = g= Plowback ratio × ROE = 0.5 × 0.14 = 0.07

Next, compute EPS_0 as follows:

ROE = EPS_0 /Book equity per share

0.14 = EPS_0 /\$50 $\Rightarrow$ EPS_0 = \$7.00

Therefore: DIV_0 = payout ratio × EPS_0 = 0.5 × \$7.00 = \$3.50

EPS and dividends for subsequent years are:

Year	EPS	DIV
0	\$7.00	\$7.00 × 0.5 = \$3.50
1	\$7.00 × 1.07 = \$7.4900	\$7.4900 × 0.5 = \$3.50 × 1.07 = \$3.7450
2	\$7.00 × 1.07^2 = \$8.0143	\$8.0143 × 0.5 = \$3.50 × 1.07^2 = \$4.0072
3	\$7.00 × 1.07^3 = \$8.5753	\$8.5753 × 0.5 = \$3.50 × 1.07^3 = \$4.2877
4	\$7.00 × 1.07^4 = \$9.1756	\$9.1756 × 0.5 = \$3.50 × 1.07^4 = \$4.5878
5	\$7.00 × 1.07^4 × 1.023 = \$9.3866	\$9.3866 × 0.5 = \$3.50 × 1.07^4 × 1.023 = \$4.6933

EPS and dividends for year 5 and subsequent years grow at 2.3% per year, as indicated by the following calculation:

Dividend growth rate = g = Plowback ratio × ROE = (1 − 0.08) × 0.115 = 0.023

b. $$P_0 = \frac{DIV_1}{1.115^1} + \frac{DIV_2}{1.115^2} + \frac{DIV_3}{1.115^3} + \frac{DIV_4}{1.115^4} + \left(\frac{DIV_5}{0.115} \times \frac{1}{1.115^4} \right)$$

$$= \frac{3.745}{1.115^1} + \frac{4.007}{1.115^2} + \frac{4.288}{1.115^3} + \frac{4.588}{1.115^4} + \left(\frac{4.693}{0.115 - 0.023} \times \frac{1}{1.10^4} \right) = \$45.65$$

The last term in the above calculation is dependent on the payout ratio and the growth rate after year 4.

19. a. $$r = \frac{DIV_1}{P_0} + g = \frac{8.5}{200} + 0.075 = 0.1175 = 11.75\%$$

b. g = Plowback ratio × ROE = (1 − 0.5) × 0.12 = 0.06 = 6.0%

The stated payout ratio and ROE are inconsistent with the security analysts' forecasts. With g = 6.0% (and assuming r remains at 11.75%) then:

$$P_0 = \frac{DIV_1}{r - g} = \frac{8.5}{0.1175 - 0.06} = 147.83 \text{ pesos}$$

20. a. If investors expected future oil prices to decline from what were then historically high levels in mid-2006, then investors' expectations were that future earnings of the major oil companies would be less than earnings being reported at that time. Since stock price is the present value of future cash flows to stockholders, stock prices in mid-2006 were based on lower expected earnings (and dividends) and were therefore low relative to earnings in prior periods.

  b. Newspaper or Internet exercise; answers will vary

21. Extremely high P/EPS ratios can be misleading for a number of reasons. In the case of Textron, the extremely high P/EPS of 63 resulted from a large one-time loss which reduced EPS below what it would otherwise have been, and (perhaps) below what investors expected Textron's EPS to be in the future.

A somewhat more common scenario resulting in an extremely high P/EPS ratio is a growth stock which investors expect will experience significant increases in earnings in the near term future. Mathematically, this is a result similar to Textron's, but the cause of the expected increase in future earnings and dividends is different.

22. The security analyst's forecast is wrong because it assumes a perpetual constant growth rate of 15% when, in fact, growth will continue for two years at this rate and then there will be no further growth in EPS or dividends.

The value of the company's stock is the present value of the expected dividend of $2.30 to be paid in 2017 plus the present value of the perpetuity of $2.65 beginning in 2018. Therefore, the actual expected rate of return is the solution for r in the following equation:

$$\$21.75 = \frac{\$2.30}{1+r} + \frac{\$2.65}{r(1+r)}$$

Solving algebraically (using the quadratic formula) or by trial and error, we find that: r = 0.1201 = 12.01%

23. a. <u>An Incorrect Application</u>. Hotshot Semiconductor's earnings and dividends have grown by 30 percent per year since the firm's founding ten years ago. Current stock price is $100, and next year's dividend is projected at $1.25. Thus:

$$r = \frac{DIV_1}{P_0} + g = \frac{1.25}{100} + 0.30 = 0.3125 = 31.25\%$$

This is *wrong* because the formula assumes perpetual growth; it is not possible for Hotshot to grow at 30 percent per year forever.

<u>A Correct Application</u>. The formula might be correctly applied to the Old Faithful Railroad, which has been growing at a steady 5 percent rate for decades. Its $EPS_1 = \$10$, $DIV_1 = \$5$, and $P_0 = \$100$. Thus:

$$r = \frac{DIV_1}{P_0} + g = \frac{5}{100} + 0.05 = 0.10 = 10.0\%$$

Even here, you should be careful not to blindly project past growth into the future. If Old Faithful hauls coal, an energy crisis could turn it into a growth stock.

b.   <u>An Incorrect Application</u>. Hotshot has current earnings of $5.00 per share. Thus:

$$r = \frac{EPS_1}{P_0} = \frac{5}{100} = 0.05 = 5.0\%$$

This is too low to be realistic. The reason P_0 is so high relative to earnings is not that r is low, but rather that Hotshot is endowed with valuable growth opportunities. Suppose PVGO = $60:

$$P_0 = \frac{EPS_1}{r} + PVGO$$

$$100 = \frac{5}{r} + 60$$

Therefore, r = 12.5%

<u>A Correct Application</u>. Unfortunately, Old Faithful has run out of valuable growth opportunities. Since PVGO = 0:

$$P_0 = \frac{EPS_1}{r} + PVGO$$

$$100 = \frac{10}{r} + 0$$

Therefore, r = 10.0%

24.   Share price $= \dfrac{EPS_1}{r} + \dfrac{NPV}{r - g}$

Therefore:

$$P_\alpha = \frac{EPS_{\alpha 1}}{r_\alpha} + \frac{NPV_\alpha}{(r_\alpha - 0.15)}$$

$$P_\beta = \frac{EPS_{\beta 1}}{r_\beta} + \frac{NPV_\beta}{(r_\beta - 0.08)}$$

The statement in the question implies the following:

$$\frac{NPV_\beta}{(r_\beta - 0.08)} \Big/ \left(\frac{EPS_{\beta 1}}{r_\beta} + \frac{NPV_\beta}{(r_\beta - 0.08)} \right) > \frac{NPV_\alpha}{(r_\alpha - 0.15)} \Big/ \left(\frac{EPS_{\alpha 1}}{r_\alpha} + \frac{NPV_\alpha}{(r_\alpha - 0.15)} \right)$$

Rearranging, we have:

$$\frac{NPV_\alpha}{(r_\alpha - 0.15)} \times \frac{r_\alpha}{EPS_{\alpha 1}} < \frac{NPV_\beta}{(r_\beta - 0.08)} \times \frac{r_\beta}{EPS_{\beta 1}}$$

a. $NPV_\alpha < NPV_\beta$, everything else equal.

b. $(r_\alpha - 0.15) > (r_\beta - 0.08)$, everything else equal.

c. $\dfrac{NPV_\alpha}{(r_\alpha - 0.15)} < \dfrac{NPV_\beta}{(r_\beta - 0.08)}$, everything else equal.

d. $\dfrac{r_\alpha}{EPS_{\alpha 1}} < \dfrac{r_\beta}{EPS_{\beta 1}}$, everything else equal.

25. a. Growth-Tech's stock price should be:

$$P = \frac{\$0.50}{(1.12)} + \frac{\$0.60}{(1.12)^2} + \frac{\$1.15}{(1.12)^3} + \left(\frac{1}{(1.12)^3} \times \frac{\$1.24}{(0.12 - 0.08)} \right) = \$23.81$$

b. The horizon value contributes:

$$PV(P_H) = \frac{1}{(1.12)^3} \times \frac{\$1.24}{(0.12 - 0.08)} = \$22.07$$

c. Without PVGO, P_3 would equal earnings for year 4 capitalized at 12 percent:

$$\frac{\$2.49}{0.12} = \$20.75$$

Therefore: PVGO = $31.00 − $20.75 = $10.25

d. The PVGO of $10.25 is lost at year 3. Therefore, the current stock price of $23.81 will decrease by:

$$\frac{\$10.25}{(1.12)^3} = \$7.30$$

The new stock price will be: $23.81 − $7.30 = $16.51

26. a. Here we can apply the standard growing perpetuity formula with $DIV_1 = \$4$, $g = 0.04$ and $P_0 = \$100$:

$$r = \frac{DIV_1}{P_0} + g = \frac{\$4}{\$100} + 0.04 = 0.08 = 8.0\%$$

The $4 dividend is 60 percent of earnings. Thus:

$EPS_1 = 4/0.6 = \$6.67$

Also:

$$P_0 = \frac{EPS_1}{r} + PVGO$$

$$\$100 = \frac{\$6.67}{0.08} + PVGO$$

$PVGO = \$16.63$

b. DIV_1 will decrease to: $0.20 \times 6.67 = \$1.33$

However, by plowing back 80 percent of earnings, CSI will grow by 8 percent per year for five years. Thus:

Year	1	2	3	4	5	6	7, 8 . . .
DIV_t	1.33	1.44	1.55	1.68	1.81	5.88	Continued growth at
EPS_t	6.67	7.20	7.78	8.40	9.07	9.80	4 percent

Note that DIV_6 increases sharply as the firm switches back to a 60 percent payout policy. Forecasted stock price in year 5 is:

$$P_5 = \frac{DIV_6}{r - g} = \frac{5.88}{0.08 - 0.04} = \$147$$

Therefore, CSI's stock price will increase to:

$$P_0 = \frac{1.33}{1.08} + \frac{1.44}{1.08^2} + \frac{1.55}{1.08^3} + \frac{1.68}{1.08^4} + \frac{1.81 + 147}{1.08^5} = \$106.21$$

27. Internet exercise; answers will vary depending on time period.

28.   a.   First, we use the following Excel spreadsheet to compute net income (or dividends) for 2006 through 2010:

	2006	2007	2008	2009	2010
Production (million barrels)	1.8000	1.6740	1.5568	1.4478	1.3465
Price of oil/barrel	65	60	55	50	52.5
Costs/barrel	25	25	25	25	25
Revenue	117,000,000	100,440,000	85,625,100	72,392,130	70,690,915
Expenses	45,000,000	41,850,000	38,920,500	36,196,065	33,662,340
Net Income (= Dividends)	72,000,000	58,590,000	46,704,600	36,196,065	37,028,574

Next, we compute the present value of the dividends to be paid in 2007, 2008 and 2009:

$$P_0 = \frac{58,590,000}{1.09} + \frac{46,704,600}{1.09^2} + \frac{36,196,065}{1.09^3} = \$121,012,624$$

The present value of dividends to be paid in 2010 and subsequent years can be computed by recognizing that both revenues and expenses can be treated as growing perpetuities. Since production will decrease 7% per year while costs per barrel remain constant, the growth rate of expenses is: −7.0%

To compute the growth rate of revenues, we use the fact that production decreases 7% per year while the price of oil increases 5% per year, so that the growth rate of revenues is:

$$[1.05 \times (1 - 0.07)] - 1 = -0.0235 = -2.35\%$$

Therefore, the present value (in 2009) of revenues beginning in 2010 is:

$$PV_{2009} = \frac{70,690,915}{0.09 - (-0.0235)} = \$622,827,445$$

Similarly, the present value (in 2009) of expenses beginning in 2010 is:

$$PV_{2009} = \frac{33,662,340}{0.09 - (-0.07)} = \$210,389,625$$

Subtracting these present values gives the present value (in 2009) of net income, and then discounting back three years to 2006, we find that the present value of dividends paid in 2010 and subsequent years is: \$318,477,671

The total value of the company is:

$$\$121,012,624 + \$318,477,671 = \$439,490,295$$

Since there are 7,000,000 shares outstanding, the present value per share is:

$$\$439,490,295 / 7,000,000 = \$62.78$$

  b. $EPS_{2006} = \$72,000,000/7,000,000 = \$10.29$

$EPS/P = \$10.29/\$62.78 = 0.164$

29. Internet exercise; answers will vary depending on time period.

30. Internet exercise; answers will vary depending on time period.

31. [Note: In this problem, the long-term growth rate, in year 9 and all later years, should be 8%.]

The free cash flow for years 1 through 10 is computed in the following table:

	Year									
	1	2	3	4	5	6	7	8	9	10
Asset value	10.00	12.00	14.40	17.28	20.74	23.12	25.66	28.36	30.63	33.08
Earnings	1.20	1.44	1.73	2.07	2.49	2.77	3.08	3.40	3.68	3.97
Investment	2.00	2.40	2.88	3.46	2.38	2.54	2.69	2.27	2.45	2.65
Free cash flow	−0.80	−0.96	−1.15	−1.38	0.10	0.23	0.38	1.13	1.23	1.32
Earnings growth from previous period	20.0%	20.0%	20.0%	20.0%	20.0%	11.5%	11.0%	10.5%	8.0%	8.0%

Computing the present value of the free cash flows, following the approach from Section 5.5, we find that the present value of the free cash flows occurring in years 1 through 7 is:

$$PV = \frac{-0.80}{1.10^1} + \frac{-0.96}{1.10^2} + \frac{-1.15}{1.10^3} + \frac{-1.38}{1.10^4} + \frac{0.10}{1.10^5} + \frac{0.23}{1.10^6} + \frac{0.38}{1.10^7} = -\$2.94$$

The present value of the growing perpetuity that begins in year 8 is:

$$PV = \left(\frac{1}{(1.10)^7} \times \frac{1.1343}{(0.10 - 0.08)} \right) = \$29.10$$

Therefore, the present value of the business is:

$-\$2.94 + \$29.10 = \$26.16$ million

Challenge Questions

32. From the equation given in the problem, it follows that:

$$\frac{P_0}{BVPS} = \frac{ROE \times (1-b)}{r - (b \times ROE)} = \frac{1-b}{(r/ROE) - b}$$

Consider three cases:

ROE $< r \Rightarrow (P_0/BVPS) < 1$

ROE $= r \Rightarrow (P_0/BVPS) = 1$

ROE $> r \Rightarrow (P_0/BVPS) > 1$

Thus, as ROE increases, the price-to-book ratio also increases, and, when ROE = r, price-to-book equals one.

33. Assume the portfolio value given, $100 million, is the value as of the end of the first year. Then, assuming constant growth, the value of the contract is given by the first payment (0.5 percent of portfolio value) divided by $(r - g)$. Also:

$$r = \text{dividend yield} + \text{growth rate}$$

Hence:

$$r - \text{growth rate} = \text{dividend yield} = 0.05 = 5.0\%$$

Thus, the value of the contract, V, is:

$$V = \frac{0.005 \times \$100\,\text{million}}{0.05} = \$10\,\text{million}$$

For stocks with a 4 percent yield:

$$r - \text{growth rate} = \text{dividend yield} = 0.04 = 4.0\%$$

Thus, the value of the contract, V, is:

$$V = \frac{0.005 \times \$100\,\text{million}}{0.04} = \$12.5\,\text{million}$$

34. If existing stockholders buy newly issued shares to cover the $3.6 million financing requirement, then the value of Concatco equals the discounted value of the cash flows (as computed in Section 5.5): $18.8 million. Since the existing stockholders own 1 million shares, the value per share is $18.80.

Now suppose instead that the $3.6 million comes from new investors, who buy shares each year at a fair price. Since the new investors buy shares at a fair price, the value of the existing stockholders' shares must remain at $18.8 million. Since existing stockholders expect to earn 10% on their investment, the expected value of their shares in year 6 is:

$$\$18.8\,\text{million} \times (1.10)^6 = \$33.39\,\text{million}$$

The total value of the firm in year 6 is:

$$\$1.59\,\text{million} / (0.10 - 0.06) = \$39.75\,\text{million}$$

Compensation to new stockholders in year 6 is:

$$\$39.75\,\text{million} - \$33.39\,\text{million} = \$6.36\,\text{million}$$

Since existing stockholders own 1 million shares, then in year 6, new stockholders will own:

$$(\$6.36\,\text{million} / \$33.39\,\text{million}) \times 1,000,000 = 190,300\,\text{shares}$$

Share price in year 6 equals:

$$\$39.75\,\text{million} / 1.1903\,\text{million} = \$33.39$$

CHAPTER 6

Why Net Present Value Leads to
Better Investment Decisions than Other Criteria

Answers to Practice Questions

8.   a. $NPV_A = -\$1000 + \dfrac{\$1000}{(1.10)} = -\$90.91$

$NPV_B = -\$2000 + \dfrac{\$1000}{(1.10)} + \dfrac{\$1000}{(1.10)^2} + \dfrac{\$4000}{(1.10)^3} + \dfrac{\$1000}{(1.10)^4} + \dfrac{\$1000}{(1.10)^5} = +\$4{,}044.73$

$NPV_C = -\$3000 + \dfrac{\$1000}{(1.10)} + \dfrac{\$1000}{(1.10)^2} + \dfrac{\$1000}{(1.10)^4} + \dfrac{\$1000}{(1.10)^5} = +\$39.47$

    b.   Payback $_A$ = 1 year
                Payback $_B$ = 2 years
                Payback $_C$ = 4 years

    c.   A and B

    d. $PV_A = \dfrac{\$1000}{(1.10)^1} = \$909.09$

The present value of the cash inflows for Project A never recovers the initial outlay for the project, which is always the case for a negative NPV project.

The present values of the cash inflows for Project B are shown in the third row of the table below, and the cumulative net present values are shown in the fourth row:

C_0	C_1	C_2	C_3	C_4	C_5
−2,000.00	+1,000.00	+1,000.00	+4,000.00	+1,000.0	+1,000.00
−2,000.00	909.09	826.45	3,005.26	683.01	620.92
	−1,090.91	−264.46	2,740.80	3,423.81	4,044.73

Since the cumulative NPV turns positive between year two and year three, the discounted payback period is:

$$2 + \dfrac{264.46}{3{,}005.26} = 2.09 \text{ years}$$

The present values of the cash inflows for Project C are shown in the third row of the table below, and the cumulative net present values are shown in the fourth row:

C_0	C_1	C_2	C_3	C_4	C_5
−3,000.00	+1,000.00	+1,000.00	0.00	+1,000.00	+1,000.00
−3,000.00	909.09	826.45	0.00	683.01	620.92
	−2,090.91	−1,264.46	−1,264.46	−581.45	39.47

Since the cumulative NPV turns positive between year four and year five, the discounted payback period is:

$$4 + \frac{581.45}{620.92} = 4.94 \text{ years}$$

e. Using the discounted payback period rule with a cutoff of three years, the firm should accept only Project B.

9. a. When using the IRR rule, the firm must still compare the IRR with the opportunity cost of capital. Thus, even with the IRR method, one must specify the appropriate discount rate.

b. Risky cash flows should be discounted at a higher rate than the rate used to discount less risky cash flows. Using the payback rule is equivalent to using the NPV rule with a zero discount rate for cash flows before the payback period and an infinite discount rate for cash flows thereafter.

10.

	r = −17.44%	0.00%	10.00%	15.00%	20.00%	25.00%	45.27%
Year 0	−3,000.00	−3,000.00	−3,000.00	−3,000.00	−3,000.00	−3,000.00	−3,000.00	−3,000.00
Year 1	3,500.00	4,239.34	3,500.00	3,181.82	3,043.48	2,916.67	2,800.00	2,409.31
Year 2	4,000.00	5,868.41	4,000.00	3,305.79	3,024.57	2,777.78	2,560.00	1,895.43
Year 3	−4,000.00	−7,108.06	−4,000.00	−3,005.26	−2,630.06	−2,314.81	−2,048.00	−1,304.76
PV =	−0.31	500.00	482.35	437.99	379.64	312.00	−0.02

The two IRRs for this project are (approximately): −17.44% and 45.27% Between these two discount rates, the NPV is positive.

11. a. The figure on the next page was drawn from the following points:

	Discount Rate		
	0%	10%	20%
NPV_A	+20.00	+4.13	−8.33
NPV_B	+40.00	+5.18	−18.98

b. From the graph, we can estimate the IRR of each project from the point where its line crosses the horizontal axis:

$IRR_A = 13.1\%$ and $IRR_B = 11.9\%$

c. The company should accept Project A if its NPV is positive and higher than that of Project B; that is, the company should accept Project A if the discount rate is greater than 10.7% (the intersection of NPV_A and NPV_B on the graph below) and less than 13.1%.

d. The cash flows for (B – A) are:

$$C_0 = \$\ 0$$
$$C_1 = -\$60$$
$$C_2 = -\$60$$
$$C_3 = +\$140$$

Therefore:

	Discount Rate		
	0%	10%	20%
NPV_{B-A}	+20.00	+1.05	–10.65

$IRR_{B-A} = 10.7\%$

The company should accept Project A if the discount rate is greater than 10.7% and less than 13.1%. As shown in the graph, for these discount rates, the IRR for the incremental investment is less than the opportunity cost of capital.

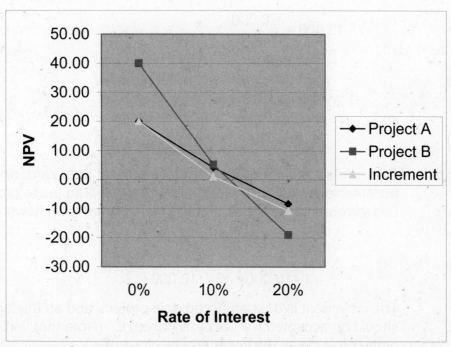

12. a. Because Project A requires a larger capital outlay, it is possible that Project A has both a lower IRR and a higher NPV than Project B. (In fact, NPV_A is greater than NPV_B for all discount rates less than 10 percent.) Because the goal is to maximize shareholder wealth, NPV is the correct criterion.

b. To use the IRR criterion for mutually exclusive projects, calculate the IRR for the incremental cash flows:

	C_0	C_1	C_2	IRR
A – B	–200	+110	+121	10%

Because the IRR for the incremental cash flows exceeds the cost of capital, the additional investment in A is worthwhile.

c. $NPV_A = -\$400 + \dfrac{\$250}{1.09} + \dfrac{\$300}{(1.09)^2} = \$81.86$

$NPV_B = -\$200 + \dfrac{\$140}{1.09} + \dfrac{\$179}{(1.09)^2} = \$79.10$

13.   Use incremental analysis:

	C_1	C_2	C_3
Current arrangement	–250,000	–250,000	+650,000
Extra shift	–550,000	+650,000	0
Incremental flows	–300,000	+900,000	–650,000

The IRRs for the incremental flows are (approximately): 21.13% *and* 78.87% If the cost of capital is between these rates, Titanic should work the extra shift.

14.   a. $PI_D = \dfrac{-10,000 + \dfrac{20,000}{1.10}}{-(-10,000)} = \dfrac{8,182}{10,000} = 0.82$

$PI_E = \dfrac{-20,000 + \dfrac{35,000}{1.10}}{-(-20,000)} = \dfrac{11,818}{20,000} = 0.59$

b.   Each project has a Profitability Index greater than zero, and so both are acceptable projects. In order to choose between these projects, we must use incremental analysis. For the incremental cash flows:

$PI_{E-D} = \dfrac{-10,000 + \dfrac{15,000}{1.10}}{-(-10,000)} = \dfrac{3,636}{10,000} = 0.36$

The increment is thus an acceptable project, and so the larger project should be accepted, i.e., accept Project E. (Note that, in this case, the better project has the lower profitability index.)

15.   Using the fact that Profitability Index = (Net Present Value/Investment), we find:

Project	Profitability Index
1	0.22
2	–0.02
3	0.17
4	0.14
5	0.07
6	0.18
7	0.12

Thus, given the budget of $1 million, the best the company can do is to accept Projects 1, 3, 4, and 6.

If the company accepted *all* positive NPV projects, the market value (compared to the market value under the budget limitation) would increase by the NPV of Project 5 plus the NPV of Project 7: $7,000 + $48,000 = $55,000
Thus, the budget limit costs the company $55,000 in terms of its market value.

Challenge Questions

16. The IRR is the discount rate which, when applied to a project's cash flows, yields NPV = 0. Thus, it does not represent an opportunity cost. However, if each project's cash flows could be invested at that project's IRR, then the NPV of each project would be zero because the IRR would then be the opportunity cost of capital for each project. The discount rate used in an NPV calculation is the opportunity cost of capital. Therefore, it is true that the NPV rule does assume that cash flows are reinvested at the opportunity cost of capital.

17. Note: There was an error in the 1st printing of this text, this problem should refer to Practice Question 10.
   a.

$$C_0 = -3{,}000 \qquad\qquad C_0 = -3{,}000$$
$$C_1 = +3{,}500 \qquad\qquad C_1 = +3{,}500$$
$$C_2 = +4{,}000 \qquad C_2 + PV(C_3) = +4{,}000 - 3{,}571.43 = 428.57$$
$$C_3 = -4{,}000 \qquad\qquad MIRR = 27.84\%$$

   b. $$xC_1 + \frac{xC_2}{1.12} = -\frac{C_3}{1.12^2}$$

$$(1.12^2)(xC_1) + (1.12)(xC_2) = -C_3$$

$$(x)[(1.12^2)(C_1) + (1.12C_2)] = -C_3$$

$$x = \frac{-C_3}{(1.12^2)(C_1) + (1.12C_2)}$$

$$x = \frac{4{,}000}{(1.12^2)(3{,}500) + (1.12)(4{,}000)} = 0.45$$

$$C_0 + \frac{(1-x)C_1}{(1+IRR)} + \frac{(1-x)C_2}{(1+IRR)^2} = 0$$

$$-3{,}000 + \frac{(1-0.45)(3{,}500)}{(1+IRR)} + \frac{(1-0.45)(4{,}000)}{(1+IRR)^2} = 0$$

Now, find MIRR using either trial and error or the IRR function (on a financial calculator or Excel). We find that MIRR = 23.53%.

It is not clear that either of these modified IRRs is at all meaningful. Rather, these calculations seem to highlight the fact that MIRR really has no economic meaning.

18. Maximize: $NPV = 6{,}700x_W + 9{,}000x_X + 0X_Y - 1{,}500x_Z$

subject to: $10{,}000x_W + 0x_X + 10{,}000x_Y + 15{,}000x_Z \leq 20{,}000$

$10{,}000x_W + 20{,}000x_X - 5{,}000x_Y - 5{,}000x_Z \leq 20{,}000$

$0x_W - 5{,}000x_X - 5{,}000x_Y - 4{,}000x_Z \leq 20{,}000$

$0 \leq x_W \leq 1$

$0 \leq x_X \leq 1$

$0 \leq x_Z \leq 1$

Using Excel Spreadsheet Add-in Linear Programming Module:

Optimized NPV = $13,450

with $x_W = 1$; $x_X = 0.75$; $x_Y = 1$ and $x_Z = 0$

If financing available at t = 0 is $21,000:

Optimized NPV = $13,500

with $x_W = 1$; $x_X = (23/30)$; $x_Y = 1$ and $x_Z = (2/30)$

Here, the shadow price for the constraint at t = 0 is $50, the increase in NPV for a $1,000 increase in financing available at t = 0.

In this case, the program viewed x_Z as a viable choice even though the NPV of Project Z is negative. The reason for this result is that Project Z provides a positive cash flow in periods 1 and 2.

If the financing available at t = 1 is $21,000:

Optimized NPV = $13,900

with $x_W = 1$; $x_X = 0.8$; $x_Y = 1$ and $x_Z = 0$

Hence, the shadow price of an additional $1,000 in t =1 financing is $450.

CHAPTER 7

Making Investment Decisions with
The Net Present Value Rule

Answers to Practice Questions

10. See the table below. We begin with the cash flows given in the text, Table 7.6, line 8, and utilize the following relationship from Chapter 4:

Real cash flow = nominal cash flow/$(1 + \text{inflation rate})^t$

Here, the nominal rate is 20%, the expected inflation rate is 10%, and the real rate is given by the following:

$$(1 + r_{nominal}) = (1 + r_{real}) \times (1 + \text{inflation rate})$$
$$1.20 = (1 + r_{real}) \times (1.10)$$
$$r_{real} = 0.0909 = 9.09\%$$

As can be seen in the table, the NPV is unchanged (to within a rounding error).

	Year 0	Year 1	Year 2	Year 3	Year 4	Year 5	Year 6	Year 7
Net Cash Flows (Nominal)	–12,600	–1,484	2,947	6,323	10,534	9,985	5,757	3,269
Net Cash Flows (Real)	–12,600	–1,349	2,436	4,751	7,195	6,200	3,250	1,678

NPV of Real Cash Flows (at 9.09%) = $3,804

11. No, this is not the correct procedure. The opportunity cost of the land is its value in its best use, so Mr. North should consider the $45,000 value of the land as an outlay in his NPV analysis of the funeral home.

12. Investment in net working capital arises as a forecasting issue only because accrual accounting recognizes sales when made, not when cash is received (and costs when incurred, not when cash payment is made). If cash flow forecasts recognize the exact timing of the cash flows, then there is no need to also include investment in net working capital.

13. If the $50,000 is expensed at the end of year 1, the value of the tax shield is:

$$\frac{0.35 \times \$50,000}{1.05} = \$16,667$$

If the $50,000 expenditure is capitalized and then depreciated using a five-year MACRS depreciation schedule, the value of the tax shield is:

$$[0.35 \times \$50,000] \times \left(\frac{0.20}{1.05} + \frac{0.32}{1.05^2} + \frac{0.192}{1.05^3} + \frac{0.1152}{1.05^4} + \frac{0.1152}{1.05^5} + \frac{0.0576}{1.05^6} \right) = \$15,306$$

If the cost can be expensed, then the tax shield is larger, so that the after-tax cost is smaller.

14. a. $NPV_A = -\$100,000 + \sum_{t=1}^{5} \dfrac{\$26,000}{1.08^t} = \$3,810$

$NPV_B = -\text{Investment} + PV(\text{after-tax cash flow}) + PV(\text{depreciation tax shield})$

$NPV_B = -\$100,000 + \sum_{t=1}^{5} \dfrac{\$26,000 \times (1-0.35)}{1.08^t} +$

$[0.35 \times \$100,000] \times \left[\dfrac{0.20}{1.08} + \dfrac{0.32}{1.08^2} + \dfrac{0.192}{1.08^3} + \dfrac{0.1152}{1.08^4} + \dfrac{0.1152}{1.08^5} + \dfrac{0.0576}{1.08^6} \right]$

$NPV_B = -\$4,127$

Another, perhaps more intuitive, way to do the Company B analysis is to first calculate the cash flows at each point in time, and then compute the present value of these cash flows:

	t = 0	t = 1	t = 2	t = 3	t = 4	t = 5	t = 6
Investment	100,000						
Cash Inflow		26,000	26,000	26,000	26,000	26,000	
Depreciation		20,000	32,000	19,200	11,520	11,520	5,760
Taxable Income		6,000	–6,000	6,800	14,480	14,480	–5,760
Tax		2,100	–2,100	2,380	5,068	5,068	–2,016
Cash Flow	–100,000	23,900	28,100	23,620	20,932	20,932	2,016

NPV (at 8%) = –\$4,127

b. $IRR_A = 9.43\%$

$IRR_B = 6.39\%$

Effective tax rate $= 1 - \dfrac{0.0639}{0.0943} = 0.322 = 32.2\%$

15. **a.**

	TABLE 7.5 Tax payments on IM&C's guano project ($thousands)								
	No. of years depreciation	7							
	Tax rate (percent)	35							
						Period			
		0	**1**	**2**	**3**	**4**	**5**	**6**	**7**
	MACRS %		14.29	24.49	17.49	12.49	8.93	8.92	13.38
	Tax depreciation		1,429	2,449	1,749	1,249	893	892	1,338
	(MACRS% × depreciable investment)								
1.	Sales	0	523	12,887	32,610	48,901	35,834	19,717	0
2.	Cost of goods sold	0	837	7,729	19,552	29,345	21,492	11,830	0
3.	Other costs	4,000	2,200	1,210	1,331	1,464	1,611	1,772	0
4.	Tax depreciation	0	1,429	2,449	1,749	1,249	893	892	1,338
5.	Pretax profits	−4,000	−3,943	1,499	9,978	16,843	11,838	5,223	611
6.	Tax	−1,400	−1,380	525	3,492	5,895	4,143	1,828	214

	TABLE 7.6 IM&C's guano project – revised cash flow analysis with MACRS depreciation ($thousands)								
						Period			
		0	**1**	**2**	**3**	**4**	**5**	**6**	**7**
1.	Sales	0	523	12,887	32,610	48,901	35,834	19,717	0
2.	Cost of goods sold	0	837	7,729	19,552	29,345	21,492	11,830	0
3.	Other costs	4,000	2,200	1,210	1,331	1,464	1,611	1,772	0
4.	Tax	−1,400	−1,380	525	3,492	5,895	4,143	1,828	214
5.	Cash flow from operations	−2,600	−1,134	3,423	8,235	12,197	8,588	4,287	−214
6.	Change in working capital		−550	−739	−1,972	−1,629	1,307	1,581	2,002
7.	Capital investment and disposal	−10,000	0	0	0	0	0	0	1,949
8.	Net cash flow (5+6+7)	−12,600	−1,684	2,684	6,263	10,568	9,895	5,868	3,737
9.	Present value	−12,600	−1,403	1,864	3,624	5,096	3,977	1,965	1,043
	Net present value =	3,566							
	Cost of capital (percent)	20							

b.

TABLE 7.1 IM&C's guano project – projections ($thousands) reflecting inflation and straight line depreciation

					Period				
		0	1	2	3	4	5	6	7
1.	Capital investment	15,000							−1,949
2.	Accumulated depn.		2,417	4,833	7,250	9,667	12,083	14,500	0
3.	Year-end book value	15,000	12,583	10,167	7,750	5,333	2,917	500	0
4.	Working capital		550	1,289	3,261	4,890	3,583	2,002	0
5.	Total book value (3 + 4)		13,133	11,456	11,011	10,223	6,500	2,502	0
6.	Sales		523	12,887	32,610	48,901	35,834	19,717	
7.	Cost of goods sold		837	7,729	19,552	29,345	21,492	11,830	
8.	Other costs	4,000	2,200	1,210	1,331	1,464	1,611	1,772	
9.	Depreciation		2,417	2,417	2,417	2,417	2,417	2,417	0
10.	Pretax profit	−4,000	−4,931	1,531	9,310	15,675	10,314	3,698	1,449
11.	Tax	−1,400	−1,726	536	3,259	5,486	3,610	1,294	507
12.	Profit after tax (10 − 11)	−2,600	−3,205	995	6,052	10,189	6,704	2,404	942
	Notes:								
	No. of years depreciation				6				
	Assumed salvage value in depreciation calculation				500				
	Tax rate (percent)				35				

TABLE 7.2 IM&C's guano project – initial cash flow analysis with straight-line depreciation ($thousands)

					Period				
		0	1	2	3	4	5	6	7
1	Sales	0	523	12,887	32,610	48,901	35,834	19,717	0
2	Cost of goods sold	0	837	7,729	19,552	29,345	21,492	11,830	0
3	Other costs	4,000	2,200	1,210	1,331	1,464	1,611	1,772	0
4	Tax	−1,400	−1,726	536	3,259	5,486	3,610	1,294	507
5	Cash flow from operations	−2,600	−788	3,412	8,468	12,606	9,121	4,821	−507
6	Change in working capital		−550	−739	−1,972	−1,629	1,307	1,581	2,002
7	Capital investment and disposal	−15,000	0	0	0	0	0	0	1,949

8	Net cash flow (5+6+7)	−17,600	−1,338	2,673	6,496	10,977	10,428	6,402	3,444
9	Present value	−17,600	−1,206	2,169	4,750	7,231	6,189	3,423	1,659
	Net present value =	6,614							
	Cost of capital (percent)	11							

c.

						Period			
		0	1	2	3	4	5	6	7
1.	Capital investment	15,000							−1,949
2.	Accumulated depn.		2,417	4,833	7,250	9,667	12,083	14,500	0
3.	Year-end book value	15,000	12,583	10,167	7,750	5,333	2,917	500	0
4.	Working capital		605	1,418	3,587	5,379	3,941	2,202	0
5.	Total book value (3 + 4)		13,188	11,585	11,337	10,712	6,858	2,702	0
6.	Sales		575	14,176	35,871	53,791	39,417	21,689	
7.	Cost of goods sold		921	8,502	21,507	32,280	23,641	13,013	
8.	Other costs	4,000	2,200	1,210	1,331	1,464	1,611	1,772	
9.	Depreciation		2,417	2,417	2,417	2,417	2,417	2,417	0
10.	Pretax profit	−4,000	−4,962	2,047	10,616	17,631	11,749	4,487	1,449
11.	Tax	−1,400	−1,737	716	3,716	6,171	4,112	1,570	507
12.	Profit after tax (10 − 11)	−2,600	−3,225	1,331	6,900	11,460	7,637	2,917	942
	Notes:								
	No. of years depreciation				6				
	Assumed salvage value in depreciation calculation				500				
	Tax rate (percent)				35				

TABLE 7.1 IM&C's guano project – projections ($thousands) reflecting inflation and straight line depreciation

TABLE 7.2 IM&C's guano project – initial cash flow analysis with straight-line depreciation ($thousands)

						Period			
		0	1	2	3	4	5	6	7
1	Sales	0	575	14,176	35,871	53,791	39,417	21,689	0
2	Cost of goods sold	0	921	8,502	21,507	32,280	23,641	13,013	0
3	Other costs	4,000	2,200	1,210	1,331	1,464	1,611	1,772	0
4	Tax	−1,400	−1,737	716	3,716	6,171	4,112	1,570	507
5	Cash flow from operations	−2,600	−809	3,747	9,317	13,877	10,053	5,333	−507
6	Change in working capital		−605	−813	−2,169	−1,792	1,438	1,739	2,202
7	Capital investment and disposal	−15,000	0	0	0	0	0	0	1,949
8	Net cash flow (5+6+7)	−17,600	−1,414	2,934	7,148	12,085	11,491	7,072	3,644
9	Present value	−17,600	−1,274	2,382	5,227	7,961	6,819	3,781	1,755
	Net present value =	9,051							
	Cost of capital (percent)	11							

16. Assume the following:
   a. The firm will manufacture widgets for at least 10 years.
   b. There will be no inflation or technological change.
   c. The 15% cost of capital is appropriate for all cash flows and is a real, after-tax rate of return.
   d. All operating cash flows occur at the end of the year.

   Note: Since purchasing the lids can be considered a one-year 'project,' the two projects have a common chain life of 10 years.

   Compute NPV for each project as follows:

   $$NPV(purchase) = -\sum_{t=1}^{10} \frac{(\$2 \times 200{,}000) \times (1-0.35)}{1.15^t} = -\$1{,}304{,}880$$

   $$NPV(make) = -\$150{,}000 - \$30{,}000 - \sum_{t=1}^{10} \frac{(\$1.50 \times 200{,}000) \times (1-0.35)}{1.15^t}$$

   $$+[0.35 \times \$150{,}000] \times \left[\frac{0.1429}{1.15^1} + \frac{0.2449}{1.15^2} + \frac{0.1749}{1.15^3} + \frac{0.1249}{1.15^4} + \right.$$

   $$\left. \frac{0.0893}{1.15^5} + \frac{0.0893}{1.15^6} + \frac{0.0893}{1.15^7} + \frac{0.0445}{1.15^8} \right] + \frac{\$30{,}000}{1.15^{10}} = -\$1{,}118{,}328$$

   Thus, the widget manufacturer should make the lids.

17. a. *Capital Expenditure*
      1. If the spare warehouse space will be used now or in the future, then the project should be credited with these benefits.
      2. Charge opportunity cost of the land and building.

3. The salvage value at the end of the project should be included.

Research and Development

1. Research and development is a sunk cost.

Working Capital

1. Will additional inventories be required as volume increases?
2. Recovery of inventories at the end of the project should be included.
3. Is additional working capital required due to changes in receivables, payables, etc.?

Revenue

1. Revenue forecasts assume prices (and quantities) will be unaffected by competition, a common and critical mistake.

Operating Costs

1. Are percentage labor costs unaffected by increase in volume in the early years?
2. Wages generally increase faster than inflation. Does Reliable expect continuing productivity gains to offset this?

Overhead

1. Is "overhead" truly incremental?

Depreciation

1. Depreciation is not a cash flow, but the ACRS deprecation does affect tax payments.
2. ACRS depreciation is fixed in nominal terms. The real value of the depreciation tax shield is reduced by inflation.

Interest

1. It is bad practice to deduct interest charges (or other payments to security holders). Value the project as if it is all equity-financed.

Tax

1. See comments on ACRS depreciation and interest.
2. If Reliable has profits on its remaining business, the tax loss should not be carried forward.

Net Cash Flow

1. See comments on ACRS depreciation and interest.

2. Discount rate should reflect project characteristics; in general, it is *not* equivalent to the company's borrowing rate.

b.
1. Potential use of warehouse.
2. Opportunity cost of building.
3. Other working capital items.
4. More realistic forecasts of revenues and costs.
5. Company's ability to use tax shields.
6. Opportunity cost of capital.

c. The table on the next page shows a sample NPV analysis for the project. The analysis is based on the following assumptions:

1. *Inflation*: 10% per year.

2. *Capital Expenditure:* $8 million for machinery; $5 million for market value of factory; $2.4 million for warehouse extension (we assume that it is eventually needed or that electric motor project and surplus capacity cannot be used in the interim). We assume salvage value of $3 million in real terms less tax at 35%.

3. *Working Capital*: We assume inventory in year t is 9.1% of expected revenues in year (t + 1). We also assume that receivables *less* payables, in year t, is equal to 5% of revenues in year t.

4. *Depreciation Tax Shield*: Based on 35% tax rate and 5-year ACRS class. This is a simplifying and probably inaccurate assumption; i.e., not all the investment would fall in the 5-year class. Also, the factory is currently owned by the company and may already be partially depreciated. We assume the company can use tax shields as they arise.

5. *Revenues*: Sales of 2,000 motors in 2007, 4,000 motors in 2008, and 10,000 motors thereafter. The unit price is assumed to decline from $4,000 (real) to $2,850 when competition enters in 2009. The latter is the figure at which new entrants' investment in the project would have NPV = 0.

6. *Operating Costs*: We assume direct labor costs decline progressively from $2,500 per unit in 2007, to $2,250 in 2008 and to $2,000 in real terms in 2009 and after.

7. *Other Costs*: We assume true incremental costs are 10% of revenue.

8. *Tax:* 35% of revenue less costs.

9. *Opportunity Cost of Capital*: Assumed 20%.

	2006	2007	2008	2009	2010	2011
Capital Expenditure	−15,400					
Changes in Working Capital						
Inventories	−801	−961	−1,690	−345	380	−418
Receivables – Payables		−440	−528	−929	−190	−209
Depreciation Tax Shield		1,078	1,725	1,035	621	621
Revenues		8,800	19,360	37,934	41,727	45,900
Operating Costs		−5,500	−10,890	−26,620	−29,282	−32,210
Other costs		−880	−1,936	−3,793	−4,173	−4,590
Tax		−847	−2,287	−2,632	−2,895	−3,185
Net Cash Flow	−16,201	1,250	3,754	4,650	5,428	5,909

	2012	2013	2014	2015	2016	2017
Capital Expenditure					5,058	
Changes in Working						
Inventories	−459	−505	−556	−612	6,727	
Receivables – Payables	−229	−252	−278	−306	−336	3,696
Depreciation Tax Shield	310					
Revenues	50,489	55,538	61,092	67,202	73,922	
Operating Costs	−35,431	−38,974	−42,872	−47,159	−51,875	
Other costs	−5,049	−5,554	−6,109	−6,720	−7,392	
Tax	−3,503	−3,854	−4,239	−4,663	−5,129	
Net Cash Flow	6,128	6,399	7,038	7,742	20,975	3,696

NPV (at 20%) = $5,991

18. The table below shows the real cash flows. The NPV is computed using the real rate, which is computed as follows:

$$(1 + r_{nominal}) = (1 + r_{real}) \times (1 + \text{inflation rate})$$
$$1.09 = (1 + r_{real}) \times (1.03)$$
$$r_{real} = 0.0583 = 5.83\%$$

	t = 0	t = 1	t = 2	t = 3	t = 4	t = 5	t = 6	t = 7	t = 8
Investment	−35,000.0								15,000.0
Savings		8,580.0	8,580.0	8,580.0	8,580.0	8,580.0	8,580.0	8,580.0	8,580.0
Insurance		−1,200.0	−1,200.0	−1,200.0	−1,200.0	−1,200.0	−1,200.0	−1,200.0	−1,200.0
Fuel		1,053.0	1,053.0	1,053.0	1,053.0	1,053.0	1,053.0	1,053.0	1,053.0
Net Cash Flow	−35,000.0	8,433.0	8,433.0	8,433.0	8,433.0	8,433.0	8,433.0	8,433.0	23,433.0

NPV (at 5.83%) = $27,254.2

19.

	t = 0	t = 1	t = 2	t = 3	t = 4	t = 5	t = 6	t = 7	t = 8
Sales		4,200.0	4,410.0	4,630.5	4,862.0	5,105.1	5,360.4	5,628.4	5,909.8
Manufacturing Costs		3,780.0	3,969.0	4,167.5	4,375.8	4,594.6	4,824.4	5,065.6	5,318.8
Depreciation		120.0	120.0	120.0	120.0	120.0	120.0	120.0	120.0
Rent		100.0	104.0	108.2	112.5	117.0	121.7	126.5	131.6
Earnings Before Taxes		200.0	217.0	234.8	253.7	273.5	294.3	316.3	339.4
Taxes		70.0	76.0	82.2	88.8	95.7	103.0	110.7	118.8
Cash Flow – Operations		250.0	261.1	272.6	284.9	297.8	311.3	325.6	340.6
Working Capital	350.0	420.0	441.0	463.1	486.2	510.5	536.0	562.8	0.0
Increase in W.C.	350.0	70.0	21.0	22.1	23.1	24.3	25.5	26.8	−562.8
Initial Investment	1,200.0								
Sale of Plant									400.0
Tax on Sale									56.0
Net Cash Flow	−1,550.0	180.0	240.1	250.5	261.8	273.5	285.8	298.8	1,247.4

NPV(at 12%) = $85.8

20. [Note: Section 7.2 provides several different calculations of pre-tax profit and taxes, based on different assumptions; the solution below is based on Table 7.6 in the text.]

See the table below. With full usage of the tax losses, the NPV of the tax payments is $4,779. With tax losses carried forward, the NPV of the tax payments is $5,741. Thus, with tax losses carried forward, the project's NPV decreases by $962, so that the value to the company of using the deductions immediately is $962.

	t = 0	t = 1	t = 2	t = 3	t = 4	t = 5	t = 6	t = 7
Pretax Profit	−4,000	−4,514	748	9,807	16,940	11,579	5,539	1,949
Full usage of tax losses immediately (Table 7.6)	−1,400	−1,580	262	3,432	5,929	4,053	1,939	682
NPV (at 20%) = $4,779								
Tax loss carry-forward	0	0	0	714	5,929	4,053	1,939	682
NPV (at 20%) = $5,741								

21. In order to solve this problem, we calculate the equivalent annual cost for each of the two alternatives. (All cash flows are in thousands.)

Alternative 1 – Sell the new machine: If we sell the new machine, we receive the cash flow from the sale, pay taxes on the gain, and pay the costs associated with keeping the old machine. The present value of this alternative is:

$$PV_1 = 50 - [0.35(50 - 0)] - 20 - \frac{30}{1.12} - \frac{30}{1.12^2} - \frac{30}{1.12^3} - \frac{30}{1.12^4} - \frac{30}{1.12^5}$$
$$+ \frac{5}{1.12^5} - \frac{0.35(5 - 0)}{1.12^5} = -\$93.80$$

The equivalent annual cost for the five-year period is computed as follows:

$PV_1 = EAC_1 \times$ [annuity factor, 5 time periods, 12%]

$-93.80 = EAC_1 \times [3.605]$

$EAC_1 = -26.02$, or an equivalent annual cost of $26,020

Alternative 2 – Sell the old machine: If we sell the old machine, we receive the cash flow from the sale, pay taxes on the gain, and pay the costs associated with keeping the new machine. The present value of this alternative is:

$$PV_2 = 25 - [0.35(25 - 0)] - \frac{20}{1.12} - \frac{20}{1.12^2} - \frac{20}{1.12^3} - \frac{20}{1.12^4} - \frac{20}{1.12^5}$$
$$- \frac{20}{1.12^5} - \frac{30}{1.12^6} - \frac{30}{1.12^7} - \frac{30}{1.12^8} - \frac{30}{1.12^9} - \frac{30}{1.12^{10}}$$
$$+ \frac{5}{1.12^{10}} - \frac{0.35(5 - 0)}{1.12^{10}} = -\$127.51$$

The equivalent annual cost for the ten-year period is computed as follows:

$PV_2 = EAC_2 \times$ [annuity factor, 10 time periods, 12%]

$-127.51 = EAC_2 \times [5.650]$

$EAC_2 = -22.57$, or an equivalent annual cost of $22,570

Thus, the least expensive alternative is to sell the old machine because this alternative has the lowest equivalent annual cost.

One key assumption underlying this result is that, whenever the machines have to be replaced, the replacement will be a machine that is as efficient to operate as the new machine being replaced.

22. The current copiers have net cost cash flows as follows:

Year	Before-Tax Cash Flow	After-Tax Cash Flow	Net Cash Flow
1	−2,000	$(−2,000 \times .65) + (.35 \times .0893 \times 20,000)$	−674.9
2	−2,000	$(−2,000 \times .65) + (.35 \times .0892 \times 20,000)$	−675.6
3	−8,000	$(−8,000 \times .65) + (.35 \times .0893 \times 20,000)$	−4,574.9
4	−8,000	$(−8,000 \times .65) + (.35 \times .0445 \times 20,000)$	−4,888.5
5	−8,000	$(−8,000 \times .65)$	−5,200.0
6	−8,000	$(−8,000 \times .65)$	−5,200.0

These cash flows have a present value, discounted at 7%, of −$15,857. Using the annuity factor for 6 time periods at 7% (4.767), we find an equivalent annual cost of $3,326. Therefore, the copiers should be replaced only when the equivalent annual cost of the replacements is less than $3,326.

When purchased, the new copiers will have net cost cash flows as follows:

Year	Before-Tax Cash Flow	After-Tax Cash Flow	Net Cash Flow
0	−25,000	−25,000	−25,000.0
1	−1,000	$(−1,000 \times .65) + (.35 \times .1429 \times 25,000)$	600.4
2	−1,000	$(−1,000 \times .65) + (.35 \times .2449 \times 25,000)$	1,492.9
3	−1,000	$(−1,000 \times .65) + (.35 \times .1749 \times 25,000)$	880.4
4	−1,000	$(−1,000 \times .65) + (.35 \times .1249 \times 25,000)$	442.9
5	−1,000	$(−1,000 \times .65) + (.35 \times .0893 \times 25,000)$	131.4
6	−1,000	$(−1,000 \times .65) + (.35 \times .0892 \times 25,000)$	130.5
7	−1,000	$(−1,000 \times .65) + (.35 \times .0893 \times 25,000)$	131.4
8	−1,000	$(−1,000 \times .65) + (.35 \times .0445 \times 25,000)$	−260.6

These cash flows have a present value, discounted at 7%, of −$21,967. The decision to replace must also take into account the resale value of the machine, as well as the associated tax on the resulting gain (or loss).

Consider three cases:

a. The book (depreciated) value of the existing copiers is now $6,248. If the existing copiers are replaced now, then the present value of the cash flows is:

$$−21,967 + 8,000 − [0.35 \times (8,000 − 6,248)] = −\$14,580$$

Using the annuity factor for 8 time periods at 7% (5.971), we find that the equivalent annual cost is $2,442.

b.   Two years from now, the book (depreciated) value of the existing copiers will be $2,678. If the existing copiers are replaced two years from now, then the present value of the cash flows is:

$$(-674.9/1.07^1) + (-675.6/1.07^2) + (-21,967/1.07^2) +$$

$$\{3,500 - [0.35 \times (3,500 - 2,678)]\}/1.07^2 = -\$17,602$$

Using the annuity factor for 10 time periods at 7% (7.024), we find that the equivalent annual cost is $2,506.

c.   Six years from now, both the book value and the resale value of the existing copiers will be zero. If the existing copiers are replaced six years from now, then the present value of the cash flows is:

$$-15,857 + (-21,967/1.07^6) = -\$30,495$$

Using the annuity factor for 14 time periods at 7% (8.745), we find that the equivalent annual cost is $3,487.

The copiers should be replaced immediately.

23.   a.

	Year 1	Year 2	Year 3	Year 4	Year 5	Year 6	Year 7	Year 8	Year 9	Year 10	Year 11
MACRS Percent	10.00%	18.00%	14.40%	11.52%	9.22%	7.37%	6.55%	6.55%	6.56%	6.55%	3.29%
MACRS Depr.	40.00	72.00	57.60	46.08	36.88	29.48	26.20	26.20	26.24	26.20	13.16
Tax Shield	15.60	28.08	22.46	17.97	14.38	11.50	10.22	10.22	10.23	10.22	5.13
Present Value (at 7%) = $114.57 million											

The equivalent annual cost of the depreciation tax shield is computed by dividing the present value of the tax shield by the annuity factor for 25 years at 7%:

Equivalent annual cost = $114.57 million/11.654 = $9.83 million

The equivalent annual cost of the capital investment is:

$34.3 million – $9.83 million = $24.47 million

b.   The extra cost per gallon (after tax) is:

$24.47 million/900 million gallons = $0.0272 per gallon

The pre-tax charge = $0.0272/0.65 = $0.0418 per gallon

24.   a. $PV_A = 40,000 + \dfrac{10,000}{1.06} + \dfrac{10,000}{1.06^2} + \dfrac{10,000}{1.06^3}$

$PV_A = \$66,730$ (Note that this is a cost.)

$PV_B = 50,000 + \dfrac{8,000}{1.06} + \dfrac{8,000}{1.06^2} + \dfrac{8,000}{1.06^3} + \dfrac{8,000}{1.06^4}$

$PV_B = \$77,721$ (Note that this is a cost.)

Equivalent annual cost (EAC) is found by:

$PV_A = EAC_A \times$ [annuity factor, 6%, 3 time periods]

$66,730 = EAC_A \times 2.673$

$EAC_A = \$24,964$ per year rental

$PV_B = EAC_B \times$ [annuity factor, 6%, 4 time periods]

$77,721 = EAC_B \times 3.465$

$EAC_B = \$22,430$ per year rental

   b.   Annual rental is $24,964 for Machine A and $22,430 for Machine B. Borstal should buy Machine B.

   c.   The payments would increase by 8% per year. For example, for Machine A, rent for the first year would be $24,964; rent for the second year would be ($24,964 × 1.08) = $26,961; etc.

25.   Because the cost of a new machine now decreases by 10% per year, the rent on such a machine also decreases by 10% per year. Therefore:

$PV_A = 40,000 + \dfrac{9,000}{1.06} + \dfrac{8,100}{1.06^2} + \dfrac{7,290}{1.06^3}$

$PV_A = \$61,820$ (Note that this is a cost.)

$PV_B = 50,000 + \dfrac{7,200}{1.06} + \dfrac{6,480}{1.06^2} + \dfrac{5,832}{1.06^3} + \dfrac{5,249}{1.06^4}$

$PV_B = \$71,614$ (Note that this is a cost.)

Equivalent annual cost (EAC) is found as follows:

$PV_A = EAC_A \times$ [annuity factor, 6%, 3 time periods]

$61,820 = EAC_A \times 2.673$

$EAC_A = \$23,128$, a reduction of 7.35%

$$PV_B = EAC_B \times [\text{annuity factor, 6\%, 4 time periods}]$$

$$71,614 = EAC_B \times 3.465$$

$$EAC_B = \$20,668, \text{ a reduction of } 7.86\%$$

26. With a 6-year life, the equivalent annual cost (at 8%) of a new jet is:

$$\$1,100,000/4.623 = \$237,941$$

If the jet is replaced at the end of year 3 rather than year 4, the company will incur an incremental cost of $237,941 in year 4. The present value of this cost is:

$$\$237,941/1.08^4 = \$174,894$$

The present value of the savings is: $\displaystyle\sum_{t=1}^{3} \frac{80,000}{1.08^t} = \$206,168$

The president should allow wider use of the present jet because the present value of the savings is greater than the present value of the cost.

Challenge Questions

27. a.

	Year 0	Year 1	Year 2	Year 3	Year 4	Year 5	Year 6	Year 7
Pre-Tax Flows	−14,000	−3,064	3,209	9,755	16,463	14,038	7,696	3,951

IRR = 33.5%

Post-Tax Flows	−12,600	−1,630	2,381	6,205	10,685	10,136	6,110	3,444

IRR = 26.8%

Effective Tax Rate = 20.0%

    b.   If the depreciation rate is accelerated, this has no effect on the pretax IRR, but it increases the after-tax IRR. Therefore, the numerator decreases and the effective tax rate decreases.

            If the inflation rate increases, we would expect pretax cash flows to increase at the inflation rate, while after-tax cash flows increase at a slower rate. After-tax cash flows increase at a slower rate than the inflation rate because depreciation expense does not increase with inflation. Therefore, the numerator of T_E becomes proportionately larger than the denominator and the effective tax rate increases.

    c.
$$T_E = \frac{\dfrac{C}{I(1-T_C)} - \dfrac{C(1-T_C)}{I(1-T_C)}}{\dfrac{C}{I(1-T_C)}} = \left[\frac{C}{I(1-T_C)} - \frac{C}{I}\right]\left[\frac{I(1-T_C)}{C}\right] = 1-(1-T_C) = T_C$$

Hence, if the up-front investment is deductible for tax purposes, then the effective tax rate is equal to the statutory tax rate.

28.　a.　With a real rate of 6% and an inflation rate of 5%, the nominal rate, r, is determined as follows:

$$(1 + r) = (1 + 0.06) \times (1 + 0.05)$$
$$r = 0.113 = 11.3\%$$

For a three-year annuity at 11.3%, the annuity factor is: 2.4310
For a two-year annuity, the annuity factor is: 1.7057

For a three-year annuity with a present value of $28.37, the nominal annuity is: ($28.37/2.4310) = $11.67

For a two-year annuity with a present value of $21.00, the nominal annuity is: ($21.00/1.7057) = $12.31

These nominal annuities are not realistic estimates of equivalent annual costs because the appropriate rental cost (i.e., the equivalent annual cost) must take into account the effects of inflation.

　b.　With a real rate of 6% and an inflation rate of 25%, the nominal rate, r, is determined as follows:

$$(1 + r) = (1 + 0.06) \times (1 + 0.25)$$
$$r = 0.325 = 32.5\%$$

For a three-year annuity at 32.5%, the annuity factor is: 1.7542
For a two-year annuity, the annuity factor is: 1.3243

For a three-year annuity with a present value of $28.37, the nominal annuity is: ($28.37/1.7542) = $16.17
For a two-year annuity with a present value of $21.00, the nominal annuity is: ($21.00/1.3243) = $15.86

With an inflation rate of 5%, Machine A has the lower nominal annual cost ($11.67 compared to $12.31). With inflation at 25%, Machine B has the lower nominal annual cost ($15.86 compared to $16.17). Thus it is clear that inflation has a significant impact on the calculation of equivalent annual cost, and hence, the warning in the text to do these calculations in real terms. The rankings change because, at the higher inflation rate, the machine with the longer life (here, Machine A) is affected more.

29.　a.　The spreadsheet on the next two pages indicates that the NPV for the Mid-American wind farm investment is: –$87,271,675
By eliminating the tax in the spreadsheet, we find that the NPV is still negative: –$7,692,376
NPV becomes positive with a tax subsidy of approximately 3.5%.

　b.　Using the same spreadsheet, we can show that a capacity factor of 30% reduces NPV to: –$138,249,182

ESTIMATED NPV OF MIDAMERICAN ENERGY'S WINDFARM PROJECT IN THE ABSENCE OF ANY TAX BREAKS

PROJECT DATA

Capacity (megawatts)	360.5
Load factor	35%
Year 1 electricity price $/mWh	55.00
Year 1 maintenance & other costs ($)	18,900,000
Inflation	3.00%
Total capital cost ($)	386,000,000
MACRS years	20
Cost of capital	12.0%

Year	0	1	2	3	4	5	6
Capital cost	386,000,000						
Revenues		60,791,115	62,614,848	64,493,294	66,428,093	68,420,936	70,473,564
Maintenance & other costs		18,900,000	19,467,000	20,051,010	20,652,540	21,272,117	21,910,280
MACRS depreciation		14,475,000	27,869,200	25,784,800	23,854,800	22,040,600	20,380,800
Pretax profit		27,416,115	15,278,648	18,657,484	21,920,752	25,108,219	28,182,484
Tax		9,595,640	5,347,527	6,530,119	7,672,263	8,787,877	9,863,869
Cash flow	−386,000,000	32,295,475	37,800,321	37,912,165	38,103,289	38,360,942	38,699,414
PV	−386,000,000	28,835,245	30,134,185	26,985,130	24,215,329	21,767,029	19,606,328
NPV	−87,271,675						
MACRS depreciation (%)		3.75	7.22	6.68	6.18	5.71	5.28

Year	7	8	9	10	11	12	13	14
Capital cost								
Revenues	72,587,770	74,765,404	77,008,366	79,318,617	81,698,175	84,149,120	86,673,594	89,273,802
Maintenance & other costs	22,567,588	23,244,616	23,941,955	24,660,213	25,400,020	26,162,020	26,946,881	27,755,287
MACRS depreciation	18,875,400	17,447,200	17,215,600	17,215,600	17,215,600	17,215,600	17,215,600	17,215,600
Pretax profit	31,144,782	34,073,588	35,850,811	37,442,803	39,082,556	40,771,500	42,511,113	44,302,915
Tax	10,900,674	11,925,756	12,547,784	13,104,981	13,678,894	14,270,025	14,878,890	15,506,020
Cash flow	39,119,508	39,595,032	40,518,627	41,553,422	42,619,261	43,717,075	44,847,824	46,012,495
PV	17,695,679	15,991,769	14,611,423	13,379,090	12,252,019	11,221,084	10,277,964	9,415,068
NPV								
MACRS depreciation (%)	4.89	4.52	4.46	4.46	4.46	4.46	4.46	4.46

Year	15	16	17	18	19	20	21
Capital cost							
Revenues	91,952,016	94,710,576	97,551,894	100,478,450	103,492,804	106,597,588	0
Maintenance & other costs	28,587,946	29,445,584	30,328,952	31,238,820	32,175,985	33,141,264	0
MACRS depreciation	17,215,600	17,215,600	17,215,600	17,215,600	17,215,600	17,215,600	8,607,800
Pretax profit	46,148,470	48,049,392	50,007,342	52,024,030	54,101,219	56,240,724	−8,607,800
Tax	16,151,965	16,817,287	17,502,570	18,208,411	18,935,427	19,684,253	−3,012,730
Cash flow	47,212,106	48,447,705	49,720,372	51,031,220	52,381,392	53,772,070	3,012,730
PV	8,625,475	7,902,870	7,241,491	6,636,079	6,081,835	5,574,377	278,857
NPV							
MACRS depreciation (%)	4.46	4.46	4.46	4.46	4.46	4.46	2.23

CHAPTER 8

Introduction to Risk, Return, and The Opportunity Cost of Capital

Answers to Practice Questions

10. Recall from Chapter 4 that:

    $$(1 + r_{nominal}) = (1 + r_{real}) \times (1 + \text{inflation rate})$$

    Therefore:

    $$r_{real} = [(1 + r_{nominal})/(1 + \text{inflation rate})] - 1$$

    a. The real return on the stock market in each year was:

1929:	−14.7%
1930:	−23.7%
1931:	−38.0%
1932:	0.5%
1933:	56.5%

    b. From the results for Part (a), the average real return was: −3.89%

    c. The risk premium for each year was:

1929:	−19.3%
1930:	−30.7%
1931:	−45.0%
1932:	−10.9%
1933:	57.0%

    d. From the results for Part (c), the average risk premium was: −9.78%

    e. The standard deviation (σ) of the risk premium is calculated as follows:

    $$\sigma^2 = \left(\frac{1}{5-1}\right) \times [(-0.193 - (-0.0978))^2 + (-0.307 - (-0.0978))^2 + (-0.450 - (-0.0978))^2$$

    $$+ (-0.109 - (-0.0978))^2 + (0.570 - (-0.0978))^2] = 0.155739$$

    $$\sigma = \sqrt{0.155739} = 0.394637 = 39.46\%$$

11. Internet exercise; answers will vary.

12. a. A long-term United States government bond is always absolutely safe in terms of the dollars received. However, the price of the bond fluctuates as interest rates change and the rate at which coupon payments received can be invested also changes as interest rates change. And, of course, the payments are all in nominal dollars, so inflation risk must also be considered.

b. It is true that stocks offer higher long-run rates of return than do bonds, but it is also true that stocks have a higher standard deviation of return. So, which investment is preferable depends on the amount of risk one is willing to tolerate. This is a complicated issue and depends on numerous factors, one of which is the investment time horizon. If the investor has a short time horizon, then stocks are generally not preferred.

c. Unfortunately, 10 years is not generally considered a sufficient amount of time for estimating average rates of return. Thus, using a 10-year average is likely to be misleading.

13. The risk to Hippique shareholders depends on the market risk, or beta, of the investment in the black stallion. The information given in the problem suggests that the horse has very high unique risk, but we have no information regarding the horse's market risk. So, the best estimate is that this horse has a market risk about equal to that of other racehorses, and thus this investment is not a particularly risky one for Hippique shareholders.

14. In the context of a well-diversified portfolio, the only risk characteristic of a single security that matters is the security's contribution to the overall portfolio risk. This contribution is measured by beta. Lonesome Gulch is the safer investment for a diversified investor because its beta (+0.10) is lower than the beta of Amalgamated Copper (+0.66). For a diversified investor, the standard deviations are irrelevant.

15. $x_I = 0.60$ $\sigma_I = 0.10$
    $x_J = 0.40$ $\sigma_J = 0.20$

a. $\rho_{IJ} = 1$

$$\sigma_p^2 = [x_I^2\sigma_I^2 + x_J^2\sigma_J^2 + 2(x_I x_J \rho_{IJ}\sigma_I\sigma_J)]$$

$$= [(0.60)^2(0.10)^2 + (0.40)^2(0.20)^2 + 2(0.60)(0.40)(1)(0.10)(0.20)] = 0.0196$$

b. $\rho_{IJ} = 0.50$

$$\sigma_p^2 = [x_I^2\sigma_I^2 + x_J^2\sigma_J^2 + 2(x_I x_J \rho_{IJ}\sigma_I\sigma_J)]$$

$$= [(0.60)^2(0.10)^2 + (0.40)^2(0.20)^2 + 2(0.60)(0.40)(0.50)(0.10)(0.20)] = 0.0148$$

c. $\rho_{ij} = 0$

$$\sigma_p^2 = [x_I^2\sigma_I^2 + x_J^2\sigma_J^2 + 2(x_I x_J \rho_{IJ}\sigma_I\sigma_J)]$$

$$= [(0.60)^2(0.10)^2 + (0.40)^2(0.20)^2 + 2(0.60)(0.40)(0)(0.10)(0.20)] = 0.0100$$

16. a. Refer to Figure 8.13 in the text. With 100 securities, the box is 100 by 100. The variance terms are the diagonal terms, and thus there are 100 variance terms. The rest are the covariance terms. Because the box has (100 times 100) terms altogether, the number of covariance terms is:

$$100^2 - 100 = 9,900$$

Half of these terms (i.e., 4,950) are different.

b. Once again, it is easiest to think of this in terms of Figure 8.13. With 50 stocks, all with the same standard deviation (0.30), the same weight in the portfolio (0.02), and all pairs having the same correlation coefficient (0.40), the portfolio variance is:

$$\sigma^2 = 50(0.02)^2(0.30)^2 + [(50)^2 - 50](0.02)^2(0.40)(0.30)^2 = 0.03708$$

$$\sigma = 0.193 = 19.3\%$$

c. For a fully diversified portfolio, portfolio variance equals the average covariance:

$$\sigma^2 = (0.30)(0.30)(0.40) = 0.036$$

$$\sigma = 0.190 = 19.0\%$$

17. a. Refer to Figure 8.13 in the text. For each different portfolio, the relative weight of each share is [one divided by the number of shares (n) in the portfolio], the standard deviation of each share is 0.40, and the correlation between pairs is 0.30. Thus, for each portfolio, the diagonal terms are the same, and the off-diagonal terms are the same. There are n diagonal terms and $(n^2 - n)$ off-diagonal terms. In general, we have:

$$\text{Variance} = n(1/n)^2(0.4)^2 + (n^2 - n)(1/n)^2(0.3)(0.4)(0.4)$$

For one share: $\text{Variance} = 1(1)^2(0.4)^2 + 0 = 0.160000$

For two shares:

$$\text{Variance} = 2(0.5)^2(0.4)^2 + 2(0.5)^2(0.3)(0.4)(0.4) = 0.104000$$

The results are summarized in the second and third columns of the table below.

b. (Graphs are on the next page.) The underlying market risk that can not be diversified away is the second term in the formula for variance above:

$$\text{Underlying market risk} = (n^2 - n)(1/n)^2(0.3)(0.4)(0.4)$$

As n increases, $[(n^2 - n)(1/n)^2] = [(n-1)/n]$ becomes close to 1, so that the underlying market risk is: $[(0.3)(0.4)(0.4)] = 0.048$

c. This is the same as Part (a), except that all of the off-diagonal terms are now equal to zero. The results are summarized in the fourth and fifth columns of the table below.

No. of Shares	(Part a) Variance	(Part a) Standard Deviation	(Part c) Variance	(Part c) Standard Deviation
1	.160000	.400	.160000	.400
2	.104000	.322	.080000	.283
3	.085333	.292	.053333	.231
4	.076000	.276	.040000	.200
5	.070400	.265	.032000	.179
6	.066667	.258	.026667	.163
7	.064000	.253	.022857	.151
8	.062000	.249	.020000	.141
9	.060444	.246	.017778	.133
10	.059200	.243	.016000	.126

Graphs for Part (a):

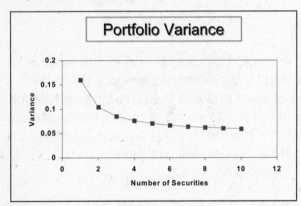

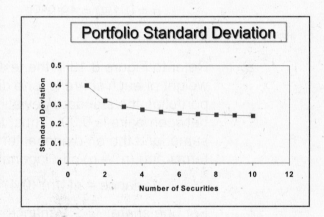

Graphs for Part (c):

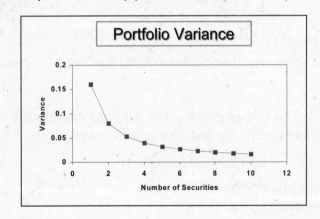

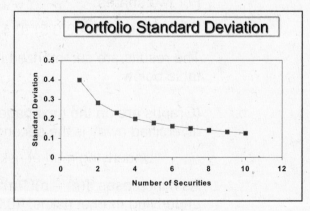

18. Internet exercise; answers will vary depending on time period.

19. The table below uses the format of Figure 8.13 in the text in order to calculate the portfolio variance. The portfolio variance is the sum of all the entries in the matrix. Portfolio variance equals: 0.0292516

	Alcan	BP	Deutsche	Fiat	Heineken	LVMH	Nestle
Alcan	0.0018002	0.0003792	0.0009669	0.0006528	0.0002085	0.0009959	0.0000669
BP	0.0003792	0.0006909	0.0004973	0.0003505	0.0001292	0.0003143	0.0001503
Deutsche	0.0009669	0.0004973	0.0018490	0.0011467	0.0002324	0.0010664	0.0002035
Fiat	0.0006528	0.0003505	0.0011467	0.0026302	0.0002142	0.0009539	0.0002629
Heineken	0.0002085	0.0001292	0.0002324	0.0002142	0.0006038	0.0003591	0.0002422
LVMH	0.0009959	0.0003143	0.0010664	0.0009539	0.0003591	0.0019612	0.0002706
Nestle	0.0000669	0.0001503	0.0002035	0.0002629	0.0002422	0.0002706	0.0003887

20. Internet exercise; answers will vary depending on time period.

21. "Safest" means lowest risk; in a portfolio context, this means lowest variance of return. Half of the portfolio is invested in Alcan stock, and half of the portfolio must be invested in one of the other securities listed. Thus, we calculate the portfolio variance for six different portfolios to see which is the lowest. The safest attainable portfolio is comprised of Alcan and Nestle.

Stocks	Portfolio Variance
BP	0.039806
Deutsche	0.068393
Fiat	0.070266
Heineken	0.034557
LVMH	0.070476
Nestle	0.028453

22. a. In general, we expect a stock's price to change by an amount equal to (beta × change in the market). Beta equal to –0.25 implies that, if the market rises by an extra 5%, the expected change in the stock's rate of return is –1.25%. If the market declines an extra 5%, then the expected change is +1.25%.

    b. "Safest" implies lowest risk. Assuming the well-diversified portfolio is invested in typical securities, the portfolio beta is approximately one. The largest reduction in beta is achieved by investing the $20,000 in a stock with a negative beta. Answer (iii) is correct.

23. Expected portfolio return = $x_A E[R_A] + x_B E[R_B]$ = 12% = 0.12

    Let $x_B = (1 - x_A)$

    $x_A (0.10) + (1 - x_A) (0.15) = 0.12 \Rightarrow x_A = 0.60$ and $x_B = 1 - x_A = 0.40$

Portfolio variance = $x_A^2\,\sigma_A^2 + x_B^2\,\sigma_B^2 + 2(x_A\,x_B\,\rho_{AB}\,\sigma_A\,\sigma_B)$

$\qquad = (0.60^2)(20^2) + (0.40^2)(40^2) + 2(0.60)(0.40)(0.50)(20)(40) = 592$

Standard deviation = $\sigma = \sqrt{592} = 24.33\%$

24. Internet exercise; answers will vary depending on time period.

Challenge Questions

25. a. In general:

$\qquad$ Portfolio variance = $\sigma_P^2 = x_1^2\sigma_1^2 + x_2^2\sigma_2^2 + 2x_1x_2\rho_{12}\sigma_1\sigma_2$

$\quad$ Thus:

$\qquad \sigma_P^2 = (0.5^2)(29.32^2)+(0.5^2)(29.27^2)+2(0.5)(0.5)(0.59)(29.32)(29.27)$

$\qquad \sigma_P^2 = 682.267$

$\qquad$ Standard deviation = $\sigma_P = 26.12\%$

b. We can think of this in terms of Figure 8.13 in the text, with three securities. One of these securities, T-bills, has zero risk and, hence, zero standard deviation. Thus:

$\qquad \sigma_P^2 = (1/3)^2(29.32^2)+(1/3)^2(29.27^2)+2(1/3)(1/3)(0.59)(29.32)(29.27)$

$\qquad \sigma_P^2 = 303.230$

$\qquad$ Standard deviation = $\sigma_P = 17.41\%$

Another way to think of this portfolio is that it is comprised of one-third T-Bills and two-thirds a portfolio which is half Dell and half Home Depot. Because the risk of T-bills is zero, the portfolio standard deviation is two-thirds of the standard deviation computed in Part (a) above:

$\qquad$ Standard deviation = $(2/3)(26.12) = 17.41\%$

c. With 50% margin, the investor invests twice as much money in the portfolio as he had to begin with. Thus, the risk is twice that found in Part (a) when the investor is investing only his own money:

$\qquad$ Standard deviation = $2 \times 26.12\% = 52.24\%$

d. With 100 stocks, the portfolio is well diversified, and hence the portfolio standard deviation depends almost entirely on the average covariance of the securities in the portfolio (measured by beta) and on the standard deviation of the market portfolio. Thus, for a portfolio made up of 100 stocks, each with beta = 1.25, the portfolio standard deviation is approximately: $1.25 \times 15\% = 18.75\%$

For stocks like Home Depot, it is: $1.53 \times 15\% = 22.95\%$

26. For a two-security portfolio, the formula for portfolio risk is:

$$\text{Portfolio variance} = x_1^2\sigma_1^2 + x_2^2\sigma_2^2 + 2x_1x_2\rho_{12}\sigma_1\sigma_2$$

If security one is Treasury bills and security two is the market portfolio, then σ_1 is zero, σ_2 is 20%. Therefore:

$$\text{Portfolio variance} = x_2^2\sigma_2^2 = x_2^2(0.20)^2$$

$$\text{Standard deviation} = 0.20x_2$$

$$\text{Portfolio expected return} = x_1(0.06) + x_2(0.06 + 0.85)$$

$$\text{Portfolio expected return} = 0.06x_1 + 0.145x_2$$

Portfolio	X_1	X_2	Expected Return	Standard Deviation
1	1.0	0.0	0.060	0.000
2	0.8	0.2	0.077	0.040
3	0.6	0.4	0.094	0.080
4	0.4	0.6	0.111	0.120
5	0.2	0.8	0.128	0.160
6	0.0	1.0	0.145	0.200

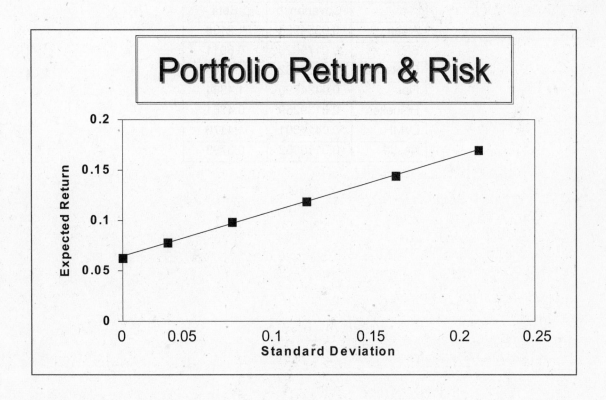

27. Internet exercise; answers will vary.

28. The matrix below displays the variance for each of the seven stocks along the diagonal and each of the covariances in the off-diagonal cells:

	Alcan	BP	Deutsche	Fiat	Heineken	LVMH	Nestle
Alcan	0.0882090	0.0185803	0.0473804	0.0319869	0.0102168	0.0487971	0.0032789
BP	0.0185803	0.0338560	0.0243690	0.0171746	0.0063296	0.0154008	0.0073637
Deutsche	0.0473804	0.0243690	0.0906010	0.0561907	0.0113898	0.0522536	0.0099691
Fiat	0.0319869	0.0171746	0.0561907	0.1288810	0.0104972	0.0467418	0.0128809
Heineken	0.0102168	0.0063296	0.0113898	0.0104972	0.0295840	0.0175956	0.0118680
LVMH	0.0487971	0.0154008	0.0522536	0.0467418	0.0175956	0.0961000	0.0132618
Nestle	0.0032789	0.0073637	0.0099691	0.0128809	0.0118680	0.0132618	0.0190440

The covariance of Alcan with the market portfolio ($\sigma_{Alcan, Market}$) is the mean of the seven respective covariances between Alcan and each of the seven stocks in the portfolio. (The covariance of Alcan with itself is the variance of Alcan.) Therefore, $\sigma_{Alcan, Market}$ is equal to the average of the seven covariances in the first row or, equivalently, the average of the seven covariances in the first column. Beta for Alcan is equal to the covariance divided by the market variance (see Practice Question 10). The covariances and betas are displayed in the table below:

	Covariance	Beta
Alcan	0.0354928	1.2134
BP	0.0175820	0.6011
Deutsche	0.0417362	1.4268
Fiat	0.0434790	1.4864
Heineken	0.0139259	0.4761
LVMH	0.0414501	1.4170
Nestle	0.0110952	0.3793

CHAPTER 9

Risk and Return

Answers to Practice Questions

8. a. False – investors demand higher expected rates of return on stocks with more nondiversifiable risk.

    b. False – a security with a beta of zero will offer the risk-free rate of return.

    c. False – the beta will be: $(1/3 \times 0) + (2/3 \times 1) = 0.67$

    d. True.

    e. True.

9. In the following solution, security one is Wal-Mart and security two is IBM. Then:

    $r_1 = 0.10 \qquad \sigma_1 = 0.198$

    $r_2 = 0.15 \qquad \sigma_2 = 0.297$

    Further, we know that for a two-security portfolio:

    $r_p = x_1 r_1 + x_2 r_2$

    $\sigma_p^2 = x_1^2 \sigma_1^2 + 2 x_1 x_2 \sigma_1 \sigma_2 \rho_{12} + x_2^2 \sigma_2^2$

    Therefore, we have the following results:

x_1	x_2	r_p	σ_p when $\rho = 0$	σ_p when $\rho = 1$	σ_p when $\rho = -1$
1.0	0.0	0.100	0.198	0.198	0.198
0.9	0.1	0.105	0.181	0.208	0.149
0.8	0.2	0.110	0.169	0.218	0.099
0.7	0.3	0.115	0.165	0.228	0.050
0.6	0.4	0.120	0.168	0.238	0.000
0.5	0.5	0.125	0.178	0.248	0.050
0.4	0.6	0.130	0.195	0.257	0.099
0.3	0.7	0.135	0.216	0.267	0.149
0.2	0.8	0.140	0.241	0.277	0.198
0.1	0.9	0.145	0.268	0.287	0.248
0.0	1.0	0.150	0.297	0.297	0.297

Correlation = 0

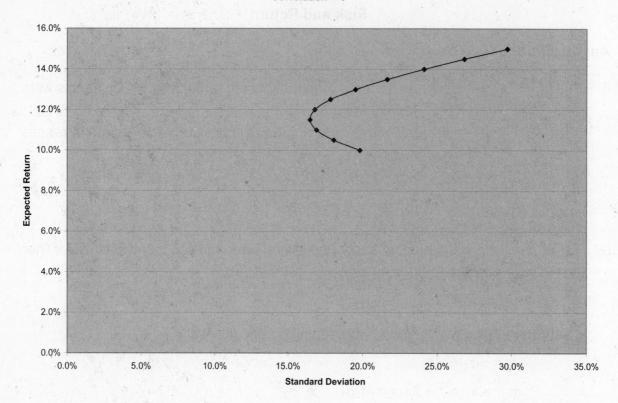

Correlation = 1

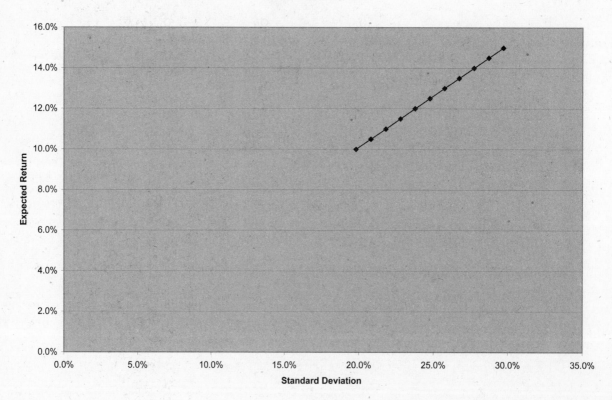

Correlation = -1

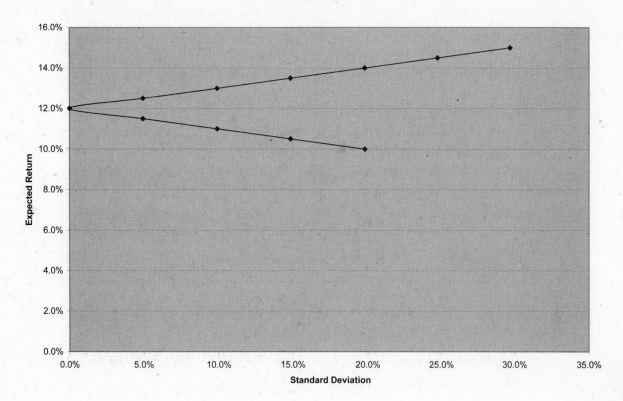

10. a.

Portfolio	r	σ
1	10.0%	5.1%
2	9.0	4.6
3	11.0	6.4

   b.   See the figure below. The set of portfolios is represented by the curved line. The five points are the three portfolios from Part (a) plus the following two portfolios: one consists of 100% invested in X and the other consists of 100% invested in Y.

   c.   See the figure below. The best opportunities lie along the straight line. From the diagram, the optimal portfolio of risky assets is portfolio 1, and so Mr. Harrywitz should invest 50 percent in X and 50 percent in Y.

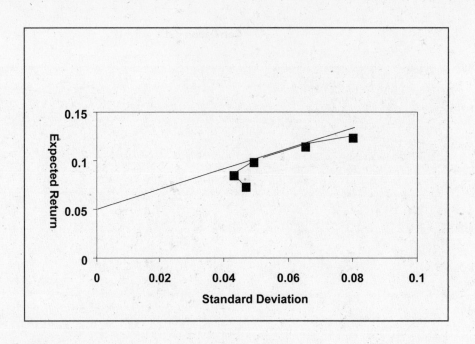

11.   a.   Expected return = $(0.6 \times 15) + (0.4 \times 20) = 17\%$

Variance = $(0.6^2 \times 20^2) + (0.4^2 \times 22^2) + 2(0.6)(0.4)(0.5)(20)(22) = 327.04$

Standard deviation = $327.04^{(1/2)} = 18.08\%$

    b.   Correlation coefficient = 0 $\Rightarrow$ Standard deviation = 14.88%

Correlation coefficient = –0.5 $\Rightarrow$ Standard deviation = 10.76%

    c.   His portfolio is better. The portfolio has a higher expected return *and* a lower standard deviation.

12.   Internet exercise; answers will vary depending on time period.

13.   Internet exercise; answers will vary depending on time period.

14.   Internet exercise; answers will vary depending on time period.

15.   a.

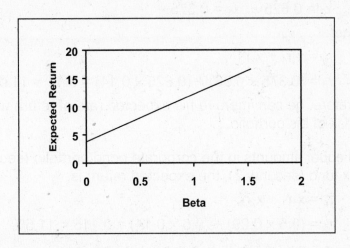

b.   Market risk premium = $r_m - r_f$ = 0.12 − 0.04 = 0.08 = 8.0%

c.   Use the security market line:

$$r = r_f + \beta(r_m - r_f)$$

$$r = 0.04 + [1.5 \times (0.12 - 0.04)] = 0.16 = 16.0\%$$

d.   For any investment, we can find the opportunity cost of capital using the security market line. With β = 0.8, the opportunity cost of capital is:

$$r = r_f + \beta(r_m - r_f)$$

$$r = 0.04 + [0.8 \times (0.12 - 0.04)] = 0.104 = 10.4\%$$

The opportunity cost of capital is 10.4% and the investment is expected to earn 9.8%. Therefore, the investment has a negative NPV.

e.   Again, we use the security market line:

$$r = r_f + \beta(r_m - r_f)$$

$$0.112 = 0.04 + \beta(0.12 - 0.04) \Rightarrow \beta = 0.9$$

16.   Internet exercise; answers will vary depending on time period.

17.   Internet exercise; answers will vary.

18.   a.   Percival's current portfolio provides an expected return of 9% with an annual standard deviation of 10%. First we find the portfolio weights for a combination of Treasury bills (security 1: standard deviation = 0%) and the index fund (security 2: standard deviation = 16%) such that portfolio standard deviation is 10%. In general, for a two security portfolio:

$$\sigma_P^2 = x_1^2\sigma_1^2 + 2x_1x_2\sigma_1\sigma_2\rho_{12} + x_2^2\sigma_2^2$$

$$(0.10)^2 = 0 + 0 + x_2^2(0.16)^2$$

$$x_2 = 0.625 \Rightarrow x_1 = 0.375$$

Further:

$$r_p = x_1 r_1 + x_2 r_2$$

$$r_p = (0.375 \times 0.06) + (0.625 \times 0.14) = 0.11 = 11.0\%$$

Therefore, he can improve his expected rate of return without changing the risk of his portfolio.

b. With equal amounts in the corporate bond portfolio (security 1) and the index fund (security 2), the expected return is:

$$r_p = x_1 r_1 + x_2 r_2$$

$$r_p = (0.5 \times 0.09) + (0.5 \times 0.14) = 0.115 = 11.5\%$$

$$\sigma_P^2 = x_1^2 \sigma_1^2 + 2x_1 x_2 \sigma_1 \sigma_2 \rho_{12} + x_2^2 \sigma_2^2$$

$$\sigma_P^2 = (0.5)^2(0.10)^2 + 2(0.5)(0.5)(0.10)(0.16)(0.10) + (0.5)^2(0.16)^2$$

$$\sigma_P^2 = 0.0097$$

$$\sigma_P = 0.985 = 9.85\%$$

Therefore, he can do even better by investing equal amounts in the corporate bond portfolio and the index fund. His expected return increases to 11.5% and the standard deviation of his portfolio decreases to 9.85%.

19. a. True. By definition, the factors represent macro-economic risks that cannot be eliminated by diversification.

b. False. The APT does not specify the factors.

c. True. Different researchers have proposed and empirically investigated different factors, but there is no widely accepted theory as to what these factors should be.

d. True. To be useful, we must be able to estimate the relevant parameters. If this is impossible, for whatever reason, the model itself will be of theoretical interest only.

20. Stock P: $r = 5\% + (1.0 \times 6.4\%) + [(-2.0) \times (-0.6\%)] + [(-0.2) \times 5.1\%] = 11.58\%$

Stock P^2: $r = 5\% + (1.2 \times 6.4\%) + [0 \times (-0.6\%)] + (0.3 \times 5.1\%) = 14.21\%$

Stock P^3: $r = 5\% + (0.3 \times 6.4\%) + [0.5 \times (-0.6\%)] + (1.0 \times 5.1\%) = 11.72\%$

21. a. Factor risk exposures:

b_1(Market) $= [(1/3) \times 1.0] + [(1/3) \times 1.2] + [(1/3) \times 0.3] = 0.83$

b_2(Interest rate) $= [(1/3) \times (-2.0)] + [(1/3) \times 0] + [(1/3) \times 0.5] = -0.50$

b_3(Yield spread) $= [(1/3) \times (-0.2)] + [(1/3) \times 0.3] + [(1/3) \times 1.0] = 0.37$

b. $r_P = 5\% + (0.83 \times 6.4\%) + [(-0.50) \times (-0.6\%)] + [0.37 \times 5.1\%] = 12.50\%$

22. $r_C = 5.0\% + (0.36 \times 7.6\%) + (0.23 \times 3.7\%) + (0.38 \times 5.2\%) = 10.56\%$

$r_F = 5.0\% + (2.00 \times 7.6\%) + (0.03 \times 3.7\%) + (1.10 \times 5.2\%) = 26.03\%$

$r_P = 5.0\% + (0.58 \times 7.6\%) + (-0.47 \times 3.7\%) + (-0.15 \times 5.2\%) = 6.89\%$

$r_M = 5.0\% + (0.89 \times 7.6\%) + (-0.07 \times 3.7\%) + (-1.17 \times 5.2\%) = 5.42\%$

Challenge Questions

23. In general, for a two-security portfolio:

$$\sigma_p^2 = x_1^2\sigma_1^2 + 2x_1x_2\sigma_1\sigma_2\rho_{12} + x_2^2\sigma_2^2$$

and:

$$x_1 + x_2 = 1$$

Substituting for x_2 in terms of x_1 and rearranging:

$$\sigma_p^2 = \sigma_1^2x_1^2 + 2\sigma_1\sigma_2\rho_{12}(x_1 - x_1^2) + \sigma_2^2(1 - x_1)^2$$

Taking the derivative of σ_p^2 with respect to x_1, setting the derivative equal to zero and rearranging:

$$x_1(\sigma_1^2 - 2\sigma_1\sigma_2\rho_{12} + \sigma_2^2) + (\sigma_1\sigma_2\rho_{12} - \sigma_2^2) = 0$$

Let Wal-Mart be security one ($\sigma_1 = 0.198$) and IBM be security two ($\sigma_2 = 0.297$). Substituting these numbers, along with $\rho_{12} = 0.35$, we have:

$$x_1 = 0.7841$$

Therefore:

$$x_2 = 0.2159$$

24. a. The ratio (expected risk premium/standard deviation) for each of the four portfolios is as follows:

        Portfolio A: (23.1 – 10.0)/56.0 = 0.234

        Portfolio B: (19.1 – 10.0)/36.1 = 0.252

        Portfolio C: (14.3 – 10.0)/17.8 = 0.242

        Portfolio D: (9.9 – 10.0)/10.6 = –0.009

Therefore, an investor should hold Portfolio B.

    b. The beta for Amazon relative to Portfolio B is equal to the ratio of the risk premium of Amazon to the risk premium of the portfolio times the beta of the portfolio:

$$[(23.1\% - 10.0\%)/(19.1\% - 10\%)] \times 1.0 = 1.440$$

Similarly, the betas for the remainder of the holdings are as follows:

$$\beta_{Amazon} = 1.440$$
$$\beta_{IBM} = 0.549$$
$$\beta_{Disney} = 0.374$$
$$\beta_{Micro} = 0.462$$
$$\beta_{Boeing} = 0.187$$
$$\beta_{Star} = 0.253$$
$$\beta_{Ex-M} = -0.231$$
$$\beta_{W-M} = 0.000$$
$$\beta_{Pfizer} = -0.220$$
$$\beta_{Heinz} = 0.066$$

c. If the interest rate is 5%, then Portfolio C becomes the optimal portfolio, as indicated by the following calculations:

Portfolio A: $(23.1 - 5.0)/56.0 = 0.323$

Portfolio B: $(19.1 - 5.0)/36.1 = 0.391$

Portfolio C: $(14.3 - 5.0)/17.8 = 0.522$

Portfolio D: $(9.9 - 5.0)/10.6 = 0.462$

The betas for the holdings in Portfolio C are:

$$\beta_{Amazon} = 1.946$$
$$\beta_{IBM} = 1.075$$
$$\beta_{Disney} = 0.903$$
$$\beta_{Micro} = 0.989$$
$$\beta_{Boeing} = 0.720$$
$$\beta_{Star} = 0.785$$
$$\beta_{Ex-M} = 0.312$$
$$\beta_{W-M} = 0.538$$
$$\beta_{Pfizer} = 0.323$$
$$\beta_{Heinz} = 0.620$$

25. Let r_x be the risk premium on investment X, let x_x be the portfolio weight of X (and similarly for Investments Y and Z, respectively).

a. $r_x = (1.75 \times 0.04) + (0.25 \times 0.08) = 0.09 = 9.0\%$

$r_y = [(-1.00) \times 0.04] + (2.00 \times 0.08) = 0.12 = 12.0\%$

$r_z = (2.00 \times 0.04) + (1.00 \times 0.08) = 0.16 = 16.0\%$

b. This portfolio has the following portfolio weights:

$$x_x = 200/(200 + 50 - 150) = 2.0$$
$$x_y = 50/(200 + 50 - 150) = 0.5$$
$$x_z = -150/(200 + 50 - 150) = -1.5$$

The portfolio's sensitivities to the factors are:

Factor 1: $(2.0 \times 1.75) + [0.5 \times (-1.00)] - (1.5 \times 2.00) = 0$

Factor 2: $(2.0 \times 0.25) + (0.5 \times 2.00) - (1.5 \times 1.00) = 0$

Because the sensitivities are both zero, the expected risk premium is zero.

c. This portfolio has the following portfolio weights:

$$x_x = 80/(80 + 60 - 40) = 0.8$$
$$x_y = 60/(80 + 60 - 40) = 0.6$$
$$x_z = -40/(80 + 60 - 40) = -0.4$$

The sensitivities of this portfolio to the factors are:

Factor 1: $(0.8 \times 1.75) + [0.6 \times (-1.00)] - (0.4 \times 2.00) = 0$

Factor 2: $(0.8 \times 0.25) + (0.6 \times 2.00) - (0.4 \times 1.00) = 1.0$

The expected risk premium for this portfolio is equal to the expected risk premium for the second factor, or 8 percent.

d. This portfolio has the following portfolio weights:

$$x_x = 160/(160 + 20 - 80) = 1.6$$
$$x_y = 20/(160 + 20 - 80) = 0.2$$
$$x_z = -80/(160 + 20 - 80) = -0.8$$

The sensitivities of this portfolio to the factors are:

Factor 1: $(1.6 \times 1.75) + [0.2 \times (-1.00)] - (0.8 \times 2.00) = 1.0$

Factor 2: $(1.6 \times 0.25) + (0.2 \times 2.00) - (0.8 \times 1.00) = 0$

The expected risk premium for this portfolio is equal to the expected risk premium for the first factor, or 4 percent.

e. The sensitivity requirement can be expressed as:

Factor 1: $(x_x)(1.75) + (x_y)(-1.00) + (x_z)(2.00) = 0.5$

In addition, we know that:

$$x_x + x_y + x_z = 1$$

With two linear equations in three variables, there is an infinite number of solutions. Two of these are:

1.　　$x_x = 0$　　　$x_y = 0.5$　　　$x_z = 0.5$

2.　　$x_x = 6/11$　　$x_y = 5/11$　　$x_z = 0$

The risk premiums for these two funds are:

$r_1 = 0 \times [(1.75 \times 0.04) + (0.25 \times 0.08)]$

　　　$+ (0.5) \times [(-1.00 \times 0.04) + (2.00 \times 0.08)]$

　　　$+ (0.5) \times [(2.00 \times 0.04) + (1.00 \times 0.08)] = 0.14 = 14.0\%$

$r_2 = (6/11) \times [(1.75 \times 0.04) + (0.25 \times 0.08)]$

　　　$+(5/11) \times [(-1.00 \times 0.04) + (2.00 \times 0.08)]$

　　　$+0 \times [(2.00 \times 0.04) + (1.00 \times 0.08)] = 0.104 = 10.4\%$

These risk premiums differ because, while each fund has a sensitivity of 0.5 to factor 1, they differ in their sensitivities to factor 2.

f.　　Because the sensitivities to the two factors are the same as in Part (b), one portfolio with zero sensitivity to each factor is given by:

$x_x = 2.0$　　　$x_y = 0.5$　　　$x_z = -1.5$

The risk premium for this portfolio is:

$(2.0 \times 0.08) + (0.5 \times 0.14) - (1.5 \times 0.16) = -0.01$

Because this is an example of a portfolio with zero sensitivity to each factor and a nonzero risk premium, it is clear that the Arbitrage Pricing Theory does not hold in this case.

A portfolio with a positive risk premium is:

$x_x = -2.0$　　　$x_y = -0.5$　　　$x_z = 1.5$

CHAPTER 10
Capital Budgeting and Risk

Answers to Practice Questions

9. a. $r_{equity} = r_f + \beta \times (r_m - r_f) = 0.04 + (1.5 \times 0.06) = 0.13 = 13\%$

    b. $r_{assets} = \dfrac{D}{V}r_{debt} + \dfrac{E}{V}r_{equity} = \left(\dfrac{\$4\text{million}}{\$10\text{million}} \times 0.04\right) + \left(\dfrac{\$6\text{million}}{\$10\text{million}} \times 0.13\right)$

    $r_{assets} = 0.094 = 9.4\%$

    c. The cost of capital depends on the risk of the project being evaluated. If the risk of the project is similar to the risk of the other assets of the company, then the appropriate rate of return is the company cost of capital. Here, the appropriate discount rate is 9.4%.

    d. $r_{equity} = r_f + \beta \times (r_m - r_f) = 0.04 + (1.2 \times 0.06) = 0.112 = 11.2\%$

    $r_{assets} = \dfrac{D}{V}r_{debt} + \dfrac{E}{V}r_{equity} = \left(\dfrac{\$4\text{million}}{\$10\text{million}} \times 0.04\right) + \left(\dfrac{\$6\text{million}}{\$10\text{million}} \times 0.112\right)$

    $r_{assets} = 0.0832 = 8.32\%$

10. a.
    $$\beta_{assets} = \left(\beta_{debt} \times \dfrac{D}{V}\right) + \left(\beta_{preferred} \times \dfrac{P}{V}\right) + \left(\beta_{common} \times \dfrac{C}{V}\right) =$$

    $$\left(0 \times \dfrac{\$100\text{million}}{\$439\text{million}}\right) + \left(0.20 \times \dfrac{\$40\text{million}}{\$439\text{million}}\right) \times \left(1.20 \times \dfrac{\$299\text{million}}{\$439\text{million}}\right) = 0.836$$

    b. $r = r_f + \beta \times (r_m - r_f) = 0.05 + (0.836 \times 0.06) = 0.10016 = 10.016\%$

11. Internet exercise; answers will vary.

12. Internet exercise; answers will vary.

13. a. The R^2 value for Alcan was 0.37, which means that 37% of total risk comes from movements in the market (i.e., market risk). Therefore, 63% of total risk is unique risk.

    The R^2 value for Canadian Pacific was 0.15, which means that 15% of total risk comes from movements in the market (i.e., market risk). Therefore, 85% of total risk is unique risk.

    b. The variance of Alcan is: $(29)^2 = 841$
    Market risk for Alcan: $0.37 \times 841 = 311.17$
    Unique risk for Alcan: $0.63 \times 841 = 529.83$

c. The t-statistic for β_{CP} is: 0.75/0.23 = 3.26

This is significant at the 1% level, so that the confidence level is 99%.

d. $r_{AL} = r_f + \beta_{AL} \times (r_m - r_f) = 0.05 + [1.58 \times (0.12 - 0.05)] = 0.1606 = 16.06\%$

e. $r_{AL} = r_f + \beta_{AL} \times (r_m - r_f) = 0.05 + [1.58 \times (0 - 0.05)] = -0.0290 = -2.90\%$

14. Internet exercise; answers will vary.

15. The total market value of outstanding debt is $300,000. The cost of debt capital is 8 percent. For the common stock, the outstanding market value is: $50 \times 10,000 = \$500,000$. The cost of equity capital is 15 percent. Thus, Lorelei's weighted-average cost of capital is:

$$r_{assets} = \left(\frac{300,000}{300,000 + 500,000}\right) \times 0.08 + \left(\frac{500,000}{300,000 + 500,000}\right) \times 0.15$$

$r_{assets} = 0.124 = 12.4\%$

16. a. $r_{BN} = r_f + \beta_{BN} \times (r_m - r_f) = 0.05 + (0.83 \times 0.07) = 0.1081 = 10.81\%$

$r_{IND} = r_f + \beta_{IND} \times (r_m - r_f) = 0.05 + (0.87 \times 0.07) = 0.1109 = 11.09\%$

b. No, we can not be confident that Burlington's true beta is not the industry average. The difference between β_{BN} and β_{IND} (0.04) is less than one standard error (0.19), so we cannot reject the hypothesis that $\beta_{BN} = \beta_{IND}$.

c. Burlington's beta might be different from the industry beta for a variety of reasons. For example, Burlington's business might be more cyclical than is the case for the typical firm in the industry. Or Burlington might have more fixed operating costs, so that operating leverage is higher. Another possibility is that Burlington has more debt than is typical for the industry so that it has higher financial leverage.

17. a. If you agree to the fixed price contract, operating leverage increases. Changes in revenue result in greater than proportionate changes in profit. If all costs are variable, then changes in revenue result in proportionate changes in profit. Business risk, measured by β_{assets}, also increases as a result of the fixed price contract. If fixed costs equal zero, then: $\beta_{assets} = \beta_{revenue}$. However, as PV(fixed cost) increases, β_{assets} increases.

b. With the fixed price contract:

PV(assets) = PV(revenue) − PV(fixed cost) − PV(variable cost)

$$PV(assets) = \frac{\$20\,million}{0.09} - (\$10\,million \times annuity\ factor\ 6\%, 10\,years) - \frac{\$10\,million}{(0.09) \times (1.09)^9}$$

PV(assets) = $97,462,710

Without the fixed price contract:

PV(assets) = PV(revenue) − PV(variable cost)

$$PV(assets) = \frac{\$20\text{million}}{0.09} - \frac{\$10\text{million}}{0.09}$$

PV(assets) = $111,111,111

18. a. The threat of a coup d'état means that the *expected* cash flow is less than $250,000. The threat could also increase the discount rate, but only if it increases market risk.

    b. The expected cash flow is: $(0.25 \times 0) + (0.75 \times 250,000) = \$187,500$

    Assuming that the cash flow is about as risky as the rest of the company's business:

    $$PV = \$187,500/1.12 = \$167,411$$

19. a. Expected daily production =

    $$(0.2 \times 0) + 0.8 \times [(0.4 \times 1,000) + (0.6 \times 5,000)] = 2,720 \text{ barrels}$$

    Expected annual cash revenues = $2,720 \times 365 \times \$15 = \$14,892,000$

    b. The possibility of a dry hole is a diversifiable risk and should not affect the discount rate. This possibility should affect forecasted cash flows, however. See Part (a).

20. The opportunity cost of capital is given by:

    $$r = r_f + \beta(r_m - r_f) = 0.05 + (1.2 \times 0.06) = 0.122 = 12.2\%$$

    Therefore:

    $CEQ_1 = 150(1.05/1.122) = 140.37$
    $CEQ_2 = 150(1.05/1.122)^2 = 131.37$
    $CEQ_3 = 150(1.05/1.122)^3 = 122.94$
    $CEQ_4 = 150(1.05/1.122)^4 = 115.05$
    $CEQ_5 = 150(1.05/1.122)^5 = 107.67$

    $a_1 = 140.37/150 = 0.9358$
    $a_2 = 131.37/150 = 0.8758$
    $a_3 = 122.94/150 = 0.8196$
    $a_4 = 115.05/150 = 0.7670$
    $a_5 = 107.67/150 = 0.7178$

From this, we can see that the a_t values decline by a constant proportion each year:

$$a_2/a_1 = 0.8758/0.9358 = 0.9358$$
$$a_3/a_2 = 0.8196/0.8758 = 0.9358$$
$$a_4/a_3 = 0.7670/0.8196 = 0.9358$$
$$a_5/a_4 = 0.7178/0.7670 = 0.9358$$

21.   a.   Using the Security Market Line, we find the cost of capital:

$$r = 0.07 + [1.5 \times (0.16 - 0.07)] = 0.205 = 20.5\%$$

Therefore:

$$PV = \frac{40}{1.205} + \frac{60}{1.205^2} + \frac{50}{1.205^3} = 103.09$$

b. $CEQ_1 = 40 \times (1.07/1.205) = 35.52$
$CEQ_2 = 60 \times (1.07/1.205)^2 = 47.31$
$CEQ_3 = 50 \times (1.07/1.205)^3 = 35.01$

c. $a_1 = 35.52/40 = 0.8880$
$a_2 = 47.31/60 = 0.7885$
$a_3 = 35.01/50 = 0.7002$

d.   Using a constant risk-adjusted discount rate is equivalent to assuming that a_t decreases at a constant compounded rate.

22.   At $t = 2$, there are two possible values for the project's NPV:

$$NPV_2 \text{ (if test is not successful)} = 0$$

$$NPV_2 \text{ (if test is successful)} = -5,000,000 + \frac{700,000}{0.12} = \$833,333$$

Therefore, at $t = 0$:

$$NPV_0 = -500,000 + \frac{(0.40 \times 0) + (0.60 \times 833,333)}{1.40^2} = -\$244,898$$

23.

	Ratio of σ's	Correlation	Beta
Argentina	2.36	0.5	1.18
Brazil	2.10	0.5	1.05
China	1.96	0.5	0.98
Egypt	1.49	0.5	0.75
India	1.80	0.5	0.90
Indonesia	1.71	0.5	0.86
Mexico	1.36	0.5	0.68
Sri Lanka	2.07	0.5	1.04
Turkey	2.96	0.5	1.48

The betas generally increase compared to those reported in Table 10.2 because the returns for these markets are now, in most cases, more highly correlated with the U.S. market. Thus, the contribution to overall market risk generally becomes greater.

24. The information could be helpful to a U.S. company considering international capital investment projects. By examining the beta estimates, such companies can evaluate the contribution to risk of the potential cash flows.

A German company would not find this information useful. The relevant risk depends on the beta of the country relative to the portfolio held by investors. German investors do not invest exclusively, or even primarily, in U.S. company stocks. They invest the major portion of their portfolios in German company stocks.

25. Internet exercise.

Challenge Questions

26. It is correct that, for a high beta project, you should discount *all* cash flows at a high rate. Thus, the higher the risk of the cash outflows, the less you should worry about them because, the higher the discount rate, the closer the present value of these cash flows is to zero. This result does make sense. It is better to have a series of payments that are high when the market is booming and low when it is slumping (i.e., a high beta) than the reverse.

The beta of an investment is independent of the sign of the cash flows. If an investment has a high beta for anyone paying out the cash flows, it must have a high beta for anyone receiving them. If the sign of the cash flows affected the discount rate, each asset would have one value for the buyer and one for the seller, which is clearly an impossible situation.

27. a. Since the risk of a dry hole is unlikely to be market-related, we can use the same discount rate as for producing wells. Thus, using the Security Market Line:

$$r_{nominal} = 0.06 + (0.9 \times 0.08) = 0.132 = 13.2\%$$

We know that:

$$(1 + r_{nominal}) = (1 + r_{real}) \times (1 + r_{inflation})$$

Therefore:

$$r_{real} = \frac{1.132}{1.04} - 1 = 0.0885 = 8.85\%$$

b. $$NPV_1 = -10\,million + \sum_{t=1}^{10} \frac{3\,million}{1.2885^t} = -10\,million + [(3\,million) \times (3.1914)]$$

$$NPV_1 = -\$425,800$$

$$NPV_2 = -10\text{million} + \sum_{t=1}^{15} \frac{2\text{million}}{1.2885^t} = -10\text{million} + [(2\text{million}) \times (3.3888)]$$

$$NPV_2 = -\$3,222,300$$

c. Expected income from Well 1: [(0.2 × 0) + (0.8 × 3 million)] = $2.4 million

Expected income from Well 2: [(0.2 × 0) + (0.8 × 2 million)] = $1.6 million

Discounting at 8.85 percent gives:

$$NPV_1 = -10\text{million} + \sum_{t=1}^{10} \frac{2.4\text{million}}{1.0885^t} = -10\text{million} + [(2.4\text{million}) \times (6.4602)]$$

$$NPV_1 = \$5,504,600$$

$$NPV_2 = -10\text{million} + \sum_{t=1}^{15} \frac{1.6\text{million}}{1.0885^t} = -10\text{million} + [(1.6\text{million}) \times (8.1326)]$$

$$NPV_2 = \$3,012,100$$

d. For Well 1, one can certainly find a discount rate (and hence a "fudge factor") that, when applied to cash flows of $3 million per year for 10 years, will yield the correct NPV of $5,504,600. Similarly, for Well 2, one can find the appropriate discount rate. However, these two "fudge factors" will be different. Specifically, Well 2 will have a smaller "fudge factor" because its cash flows are more distant. With more distant cash flows, a smaller addition to the discount rate has a larger impact on present value.

28. Internet exercise; answers will vary.

CHAPTER 11

Project Analysis

Answers to Practice Questions

8. We assume that the idea for a new obfuscator machine originates with a plant manager in the Deconstruction Division. (Keep in mind however that, in addition to bottom-up proposals, such as the obfuscator machine proposal, top-down proposals also originate with divisional managers and senior management.) Other steps in the capital budgeting process include the following:

    - Many large firms begin the process with forecasts of economic variables, such as inflation and GDP growth, as well as variables of particular interest to the industry, such as prices of raw materials and industry sales projections.

    - The plant manager, often in consultation with the division manager, prepares the proposal in the form of an appropriation request; the appropriation request typically includes an explanation of the need for the expenditure, detailed forecasts, discounted cash flow analysis and other supporting detail such as sensitivity analysis.

    - Depending on the size of the investment, the appropriation request is reviewed and approved by the divisional manager, senior management or, in the case of major expenditures, the board of directors.

    - The forecast expenditure is included as part of the annual capital budget, which is approved by top management and the board of directors.

    - Major cost over-runs typically require a supplementary appropriation request, which includes an explanation of the reason why the additional expenditure was not anticipated.

    - When the machine is finally up and running, most firms conduct a postaudit to identify problems and to assess forecast accuracy; the main purpose of the postaudit is to improve the process in the future.

9. a.
    $$NPV_F = -\$9,000 + \frac{\$6,000 \times (1-0.08)}{1.10} + \frac{\$5,000 \times (1-0.08)}{(1.10)^2} + \frac{\$4,000 \times (1-0.08)}{(1.10)^3}$$

    $$= \$2,584.67$$

    $$NPV_G = -\$9,000 + \frac{\$1,800 \times (1-0.08)}{0.10} = \$7,560$$

    b. $$NPV_F = -\$9,000 + \frac{\$6,000}{1.18} + \frac{\$5,000}{(1.18)^2} + \frac{\$4,000}{(1.18)^3} = \$2,110.19$$

    $$NPV_G = -\$9,000 + \frac{\$1,800}{0.18} = \$1,000$$

c. The 18% discount rate would give an approximation to the correct NPVs for projects with all (or most) of the inflows in the first year.

The present value of $1 to be received one year from now, discounted at 18% is: $0.8475

The present value of $1 × (1 − 0.08) (that is, $0.92) to be received one year from now, discounted at 10% is: $0.8364

The former calculation overstates the correct answer by approximately 1.3%. However, for cash flows five or ten years in to the future, discounting by 18% understates the correct present value by approximately 23% and 46%, respectively. The error increases substantially because the incorrect factor (i.e., 1.18) is compounded, causing the denominator of the present value calculation to be greatly overstated so that the present value is greatly understated.

10.

	Year 0	Years 1–10
Investment	¥15 B	
1. Revenue		¥44.000 B
2. Variable Cost		39.600 B
3. Fixed Cost		2.000 B
4. Depreciation		1.500 B
5. Pre-tax Profit		¥0.900 B
6. Tax @ 50%		0.450 B
7. Net Operating Profit		¥0.450 B
8. Operating Cash Flow		¥1.950 B

$$NPV = -¥15B + \sum_{t=1}^{10} \frac{¥1.950B}{1.10^t} = -¥3.02B$$

11. The spreadsheets show the following results:

	NPV		
	Pessimistic	Expected	Optimistic
Market Size	−1.17	3.43	8.04
Market Share	−10.39	3.43	17.26
Unit Price	−19.61	3.43	11.11
Unit Variable Cost	−11.93	3.43	11.11
Fixed Cost	−2.71	3.43	9.58

The principal uncertainties are market share, unit price, and unit variable cost.

12.   a.

	Year 0	Years 1–10
Investment	¥30 B	
1. Revenue		¥37.500 B
2. Variable Cost		26.000
3. Fixed Cost		3.000
4. Depreciation		3.000
5. Pre-tax Profit (1–2–3–4)		¥5.500
6. Tax		2.750
7. Net Operating Profit (5–6)		¥2.750
8. Operating Cash Flow (4+7)		5.750
	NPV =	+ ¥5.33 B

b.

Unit Sales (000's)	Inflows Revenues Yrs 1–10	Outflows Investment Yr 0	V. Costs Yr 1–10	F. Cost Yr 1–10	Taxes Yr 1–10	PV Inflows	PV Outflows	NPV
0	0.00	30.00	0.00	3.00	–3.00	0.00	–30.00	–30.00
100	37.50	30.00	26.00	3.00	2.75	230.42	–225.09	5.33
200	75.00	30.00	52.00	3.00	8.50	460.84	–420.18	40.66

Note that the break-even point can be found algebraically as follows:

$$NPV = \text{-Investment} + [(PVA_{10/10\%}) \times (t \times \text{Depreciation})] +$$
$$[\text{Quantity} \times (\text{Price} - \text{V.Cost}) - \text{F.Cost}] \times (1 - t) \times (PVA_{10/10\%})$$

Set NPV equal to zero and solve for Q:

$$Q = \frac{I - (PVA_{10/10\%} \times D \times t)}{(PVA_{10/10\%}) \times (P - V) \times (1 - t)} + \frac{F}{P - V}$$

$$= \frac{30{,}000{,}000{,}000 - 9{,}216{,}850{,}659}{6.144567 \times (375{,}000 - 260{,}000) \times 0.50} + \frac{3{,}000{,}000{,}000}{375{,}000 - 260{,}000}$$

$$= \frac{20{,}783{,}149{,}341}{353{,}313} + \frac{3{,}000{,}000{,}000}{115{,}000} = 58{,}824 + 26{,}087 = 84{,}911$$

Proof:

1. Revenue	¥31.84 B
2. Variable Cost	22.08
3. Fixed Cost	3.00
4. Depreciation	3.00
5. Pre-tax Profit	¥3.76 B
6. Tax	1.88
7. Net Profit	¥1.88
8. Operating Cash Flow	¥4.88

$$NPV = \sum_{t=1}^{10} \frac{4.88}{(1.10)^t} - 30 = 29.99 - 30 = -0.01$$
(difference due to rounding)

Break-Even

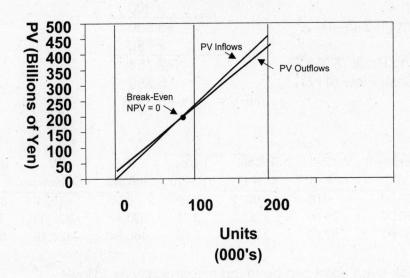

c.   The break-even point is the point where the present value of the cash flows, including the opportunity cost of capital, yields a zero NPV.

d.   To find the level of costs at which the project would earn zero profit, write the equation for net profit, set net profit equal to zero, and solve for variable costs:

$$Net\ Profit = (R - VC - FC - D) \times (1 - t)$$

$$0 = (37.5 - VC - 3.0 - 1.5) \times 0.50$$

$$VC = 33.0$$

This will yield zero profit.

Next, find the level of costs at which the project would have zero NPV. Using the data in Table 11.1, the equivalent annual cash flow yielding a zero NPV would be:

$$¥15\ B/PVA_{10/10\%} = ¥2.4412\ B$$

If we rewrite the cash flow equation and solve for the variable cost:

$$NCF = [(R - VC - FC - D) \times (1 - t)] + D$$

$$2.4412 = [(37.5 - VC - 3.0 - 1.5) \times 0.50] + 1.5$$

$$VC = 31.12$$

This will yield NPV = 0, assuming the tax credits can be used elsewhere in the company.

13. If Rustic replaces now rather than in one year, several things happen:
    i.   It incurs the equivalent annual cost of the $9 million capital investment.
    ii. It reduces manufacturing costs.

    For example, for the "Expected" case, analyzing "Sales" we have (all dollar figures in millions):

    i.   The economic life of the new machine is expected to be 10 years, so the equivalent annual cost of the new machine is:

        $9/5.6502 = $1.59

    ii. The reduction in manufacturing costs is:

        $0.5 \times $4 = $2.00

        Thus, the equivalent annual cost savings is:

        −$1.59 + $2.00 = $0.41

    Continuing the analysis for the other cases, we find:

	Equivalent Annual Cost Savings (Millions)		
	Pessimistic	Expected	Optimistic
Sales	0.01	0.41	1.21
Manufacturing Cost	−0.59	0.41	0.91
Economic Life	0.03	0.41	0.60

14. From the solution to Practice Question 13, we know that, in terms of potential negative outcomes, manufacturing cost is the key variable. Rustic should go ahead with the study, because the cost of the study is considerably less than the possible annual loss if the pessimistic manufacturing cost estimate is realized.

15. a. $$\text{Operating leverage} = \frac{\% \text{ change in operating income}}{\% \text{ change in sales}}$$

    For a 1% increase in sales, from 100,000 units to 101,000 units:

    $$\text{Operating leverage} = \frac{0.075/3}{0.375/37.5} = 2.50$$

    b. $$\text{Operating leverage} = 1 + \frac{\text{fixed cost} + \text{depreciation}}{\text{operating profit}}$$

    $$= 1 + \frac{(3.0 + 1.5)}{3.0} = 2.5$$

    c. $$\text{Operating leverage} = \frac{\% \text{ change in operating income}}{\% \text{ change in sales}}$$

For a 1% increase in sales, from 200,000 units to 202,000 units:

$$\text{Operating leverage} = \frac{(10.65-10.5)/10.5}{(75.75-75)/75} = 1.43$$

16.

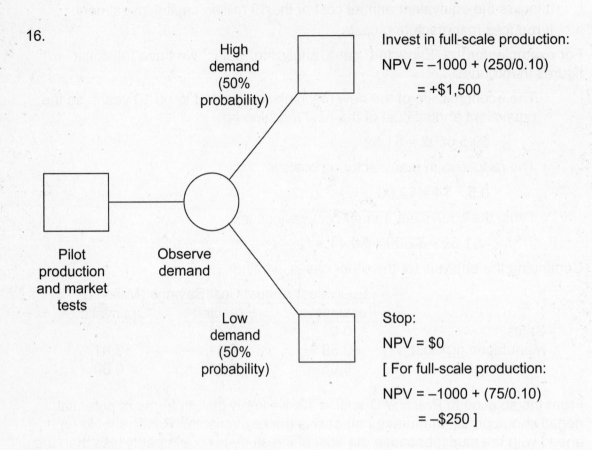

Pilot production and market tests

Observe demand

High demand (50% probability)

Invest in full-scale production:

NPV = –1000 + (250/0.10)

= +$1,500

Low demand (50% probability)

Stop:

NPV = $0

[For full-scale production:

NPV = –1000 + (75/0.10)

= –$250]

17.   Problem requires use of Excel program; answers will vary.

18.   a.   Timing option

b.   Expansion option

c.   Abandonment option

d.   Production option

e.   Expansion option

19.   a.   The expected value of the NPV for the plant is:

(0.5 × $140 million) + (0.5 × $50 million) – $100 million = –$5 million

Since the expected NPV is negative you would not build the plant.

b.   The expected NPV is now:

(0.5 × $140 million) + (0.5 × $90 million) – $100 million = +$15 million

Since the expected NPV is now positive, you would build the plant.

c.

Line is successful (50% probability)

Continue production:

NPV = $140 million − $100 million

= +$40 million

Build auto plant (Cost = $100 million)

Observe demand

Line is unsuccessful (50% probability)

Continue production:

NPV = $50 million − $100 million

= − $50 million

Sell plant:

NPV = $90 million − $100 million

= − $10 million

20. (See Figure 11.8, which is a revision of Figure 11.7 in the text.)

Which plane should we buy?
We analyze the decision tree by working backwards. So, for example, if we purchase the piston plane and demand is high:

- The NPV at t = 1 of the 'Expanded' branch is:

$$-150 + \frac{(0.8 \times 800) + (0.2 \times 100)}{1.08} = \$461$$

- The NPV at t = 1 of the 'Continue' branch is:

$$\frac{(0.8 \times 410) + (0.2 \times 180)}{1.08} = \$337$$

Thus, if we purchase the piston plane and demand is high, we should expand further at t = 1. This branch has the highest NPV.

Similarly, if we purchase the piston plane and demand is low:

- The NPV of the 'Continue' branch is:

$$\frac{(0.4 \times 220) + (0.6 \times 100)}{1.08} = \$137$$

- We can now use these results to calculate the NPV of the 'Piston' branch at t = 0:

$$-180 + \frac{(0.6) \times (100 + 461) + (0.4) \times (50 + 137)}{1.08} = \$201$$

- Similarly for the 'Turbo' branch, if demand is high, the expected cash flow at t = 1 is:

$$(0.8 \times 960) + (0.2 \times 220) = \$812$$

- If demand is low, the expected cash flow is:

$$(0.4 \times 930) + (0.6 \times 140) = \$456$$

- So, for the 'Turbo' branch, the combined NPV is:

$$NPV = -350 + \frac{(0.6 \times 150) + (0.4 \times 30)}{(1.08)} + \frac{(0.6 \times 812) + (0.4 \times 456)}{(1.08)^2} = \$319$$

Therefore, the company should buy the turbo plane.

In order to determine the value of the option to expand, we first compute the NPV without the option to expand:

$$NPV = -250 + \frac{(0.6 \times 100) + (0.4 \times 50)}{(1.08)} +$$

$$\frac{(0.6)[(0.8 \times 410) + (0.2 \times 180)] + (0.4)[(0.4 \times 220) + (0.6 \times 100)]}{(1.08)^2} = \$62.07$$

Therefore, the value of the option to expand is: $201 - $62 = $139

FIGURE 11.8

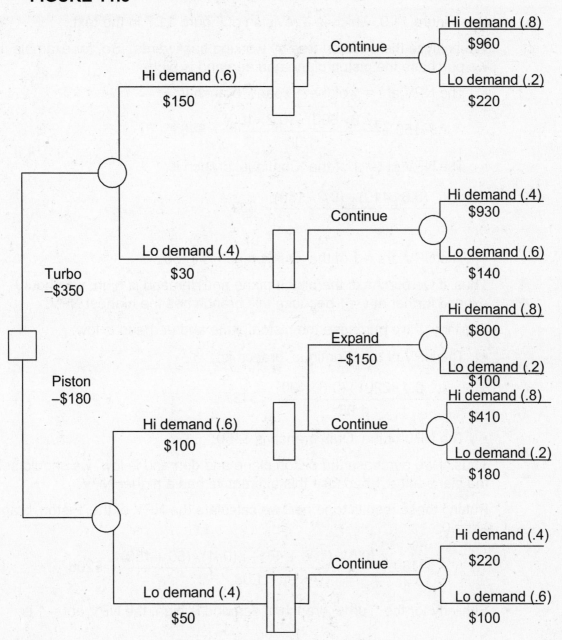

21. a. Ms. Magna should be prepared to sell either plane at t = 1 if the present value of the expected cash flows is less than the present value of selling the plane.

b. See Figure 11.9, which is a revision of Figure 11.7 in the text.

c. We analyze the decision tree by working backwards. So, for example, if we purchase the piston plane and demand is high:

- The NPV at t = 1 of the 'Expand' branch is:

$$-150 + \frac{(0.8 \times 800) + (0.2 \times 100)}{1.08} = \$461$$

- The NPV at t = 1 of the 'Continue' branch is:

$$\frac{(0.8 \times 410) + (0.2 \times 180)}{1.08} = \$337$$

- The NPV at t = 1 of the 'Quit' branch is $150.

Thus, if we purchase the piston plane and demand is high, we should expand further at t = 1 because this branch has the highest NPV.

Similarly, if we purchase the piston plane and demand is low:

- The NPV of the 'Continue' branch is:

$$\frac{(0.4 \times 220) + (0.6 \times 100)}{1.08} = \$137$$

- The NPV of the 'Quit' branch is $150

Thus, if we purchase the piston plane and demand is low, we should sell the plane at t = 1 because this alternative has a higher NPV.

Putting these results together, we calculate the NPV of the 'Piston' branch at t = 0:

$$-180 + \frac{(0.6) \times (100 + 461) + (0.4) \times (50 + 150)}{1.08} = \$206$$

- Similarly for the 'Turbo' branch, if demand is high, the NPV at t = 1 is:

$$\frac{(0.8 \times 960) + (0.2 \times 220)}{1.08} = \$752$$

- The NPV at t = 1 of 'Quit' is $500.

- If demand is low, the NPV at t = 1 of 'Quit' is $500.

- The NPV of 'Continue' is:

$$\frac{(0.4 \times 930) + (0.6 \times 140)}{1.08} = \$422$$

In this case, 'Quit' is better than 'Continue.' Therefore, for the 'Turbo' branch at t = 0, the NPV is:

$$-350 + \frac{0.6 \times (150 + 752) + 0.4 \times (30 + 500)}{1.08} = \$347$$

With the abandonment option, the turbo has the greater NPV, \$347 compared to \$206 for the piston.

d. The value of the abandonment option is different for the two different planes. For the piston plane, without the abandonment option, NPV at t = 0 is:

$$-180 + \frac{0.6 \times (100 + 461) + 0.4 \times (50 + 137)}{1.08} = \$201$$

Thus, for the piston plane, the abandonment option has a value of:

\$206 – \$201 = \$5

For the turbo plane, without the abandonment option, NPV at t = 0 is:

$$-350 + \frac{0.6 \times (150 + 752) + 0.4 \times (30 + 422)}{1.08} = \$319$$

For the turbo plane, the abandonment option has a value of:

\$347 – \$319 = \$28

FIGURE 11.9

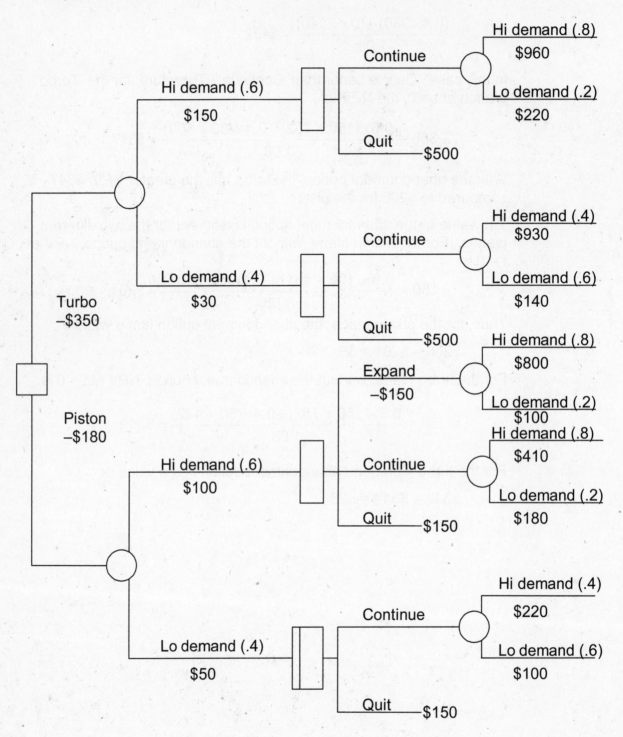

22. a. 1. Assume we open the mine at t = 0. Taking into account the distribution of possible future prices of gold over the next 3 years, we have:

$$NPV = -100,000 + \frac{1,000 \times [(0.5 \times 550) + (0.5 \times 450) - 460]}{1.10}$$

$$+ \frac{1,000 \times [(0.5^2) \times (600 + 500 + 500 + 400) - 460]}{1.10^2}$$

$$+ \frac{1,000 \times [(0.5^3) \times (650 + 550 + 550 + 550 + 450 + 450 + 450 + 350) - 460]}{1.10^3} = -\$526$$

Notice that the answer is the same if we simply assume that the price of gold remains at $500. This is because, at t = 0, the expected price for all future periods is $500.

Because this NPV is negative, we should not open the mine at t = 0. Further, we know that it does not make sense to plan to open the mine at any price less than or equal to $500 per ounce.

2. Assume we wait until t = 1 and then open the mine if the price is $550. At that point:

$$NPV = -\$100,000 + \sum_{t=1}^{3} \frac{1,000 \times (\$550 - \$460)}{1.10^t} = \$123,817$$

Since it is equally likely that the price will rise or fall by $50 from its level at the start of the year, then, at t = 1, if the price reaches $550, the expected price for all future periods is then $550. The NPV, at t = 0, of this NPV at t = 1 is:

$$\$123,817/1.10 = \$112,561$$

If the price rises to $550 at t = 1, we should open the mine at that time. The expected NPV of this strategy is:

$$(0.50 \times \$112,561) + (0.50 \times \$0) = \$56,280.5$$

b. 1. Suppose you open at t = 0, when the price is $500. At t = 2, there is a 0.25 probability that the price will be $400. Then, since the price at t = 3 cannot rise above the extraction cost, the mine should be closed. At t = 1, there is a 0.5 probability that the price will be $450. In that case, you face the following, where each branch has a probability of 0.5:

t = 1	t = 2	t = 3
		⇒ 550
	⇒ 500	
450		⇒ 450
	⇒ 400	⇒ Close mine

To check whether you should close the mine at t = 1, calculate the PV with the mine open:

$$PV = 0.5 \sum_{t=1}^{2} \frac{1,000 \times (\$500 - \$460)}{1.10^t} + 0.5 \frac{1,000 \times (\$400 - \$460)}{1.10} = \$7,438$$

Thus, if you open the mine when the price is $500, you should not close if the price is $450 at t = 1, but you should close if the price is $400 at t = 2. There is a 0.25 probability that the price will be $400 at t = 1, and then you will save an expected loss of $60,000 at t = 3. Thus, the value of the option to close is:

$$0.25 \times \frac{(1,000 \times \$60)}{1.10^3} = \$11,270$$

Now calculate the PV, at t = 1, for the branch with price equal to $550:

$$PV = \sum_{t=0}^{2} \frac{\$90,000}{1.10^t} = \$246,198$$

The expected PV at t = 1, with the option to close, is:

0.5 × [$7,438 + ($450 − $460) × 1,000] + (0.5 × $246,198) = $121,818

The NPV at t = 0, with the option to close, is:

NPV = $121,818/1.10 − 100,000 = $10,744

Therefore, opening the mine at t = 0 now has a positive NPV. We can verify this result by noting that the NPV from part (a) (without the option to abandon) is –$526, and the value of the option to abandon is $11,270 so that the NPV with the option to abandon is:

NPV = –$526 + $11,270 = 10,744

2. Now assume that we wait until t = 1 and then open the mine if the price is $550 at that time. For this strategy, the mine will be abandoned if price reaches $450 at t = 3 because the expected profit at t = 4 is:

[(450 − 460) × 1,000] = –$10,000

Thus, with this strategy, the value of the option to close is:

0.125 × ($10,000/1.10^4) = $854

Therefore, the NPV for this strategy is: $56,280.5 [the NPV for this strategy from part (a)] plus the value of the option to close:

NPV = $56,280.5 + $854 = $57,134.5

The option to close the mine increases the net present value for each strategy, but the optimal choice remains the same; that is, strategy 2 is still the preferable alternative because its NPV ($57,134.5) is still greater than the NPV for strategy 1 ($10,744).

23. Problem requires use of Crystal Ball software simulation; answers will vary.

CHAPTER 12

Investment, Strategy, and Economic Rents

Answers to Practice Questions

6. The 757 must be a zero-NPV investment for the marginal user. Unless Boeing can charge different prices to different users (which is precluded with a secondary market), Delta will earn economic rents if the 757 is particularly well suited to Delta's routes (and competition does not force Delta to pass the cost savings through to customers in the form of lower fares). Thus, the decision focuses on the issue of whether the plane is worth more in Delta's hands than in the hands of the marginal user.

   a. With a good secondary market and information on past changes in aircraft prices, it becomes somewhat more feasible to ignore cash flows beyond the first few years and to substitute the expected residual value of the plane.

   b. Past aircraft prices may be used to estimate systematic risk (see Chapter 9).

   c. The existence of a secondary market makes it more important to take note of the abandonment option.

7. The key question is: Will Gamma Airlines be able to earn economic rents on the Akron-Yellowknife route? The necessary steps include:

   a. Forecasting costs, including the cost of building and maintaining terminal facilities, all necessary training, advertising, equipment, etc.

   b. Forecasting revenues, which includes a detailed market demand analysis (what types of travelers are expected and what prices can be charged) as well as an analysis of the competition (if Gamma is successful, how quickly would competition spring up?).

   c. Calculating the net present value.

   The leasing market comes into play because it tells Gamma Airlines the opportunity cost of the planes, a critical component of costs.

   If the Akron-Yellowknife project is attractive and growth occurs at the Ulan Bator hub, Gamma Airlines should simply lease additional aircraft.

8. The price of $650 per ounce represents the discounted value of expected future gold prices. Hence, the present value of 1 million ounces produced 8 years from now should be: $650 × 1 million = $280 million

9. Interstate rail lines can be expected to generate economic rents when they have excess capacity that allows them to accommodate increased demand at low cost. For example, an economic expansion accompanied by high fuel costs would result in economic rents for interstate rail lines. Trucking companies have the flexibility to expand capacity relatively quickly, but high fuel costs ould tend to limit the ability of trucking companies to compete effectively with interstate rail lines that are relatively more fuel efficient.

10.   First, consider the sequence of events:

- At t = 0, the investment of $25,000,000 is made.
- At t = 1, production begins, so the first year of revenue and expenses is recorded at t = 2.
- At t = 6, the patent expires and competition may enter. Since it takes one year to achieve full production, competition is not a factor until t = 7. (This assumes the competition does not begin construction until the patent expires.)
- After t = 7, full competition will exist and thus any new entrant into the market for BGs will earn the 9% cost of capital.

Next, calculate the cash flows:

- At t = 0: –$25,000,000
- At t = 1: $0
- At t = 2, 3, 4, 5, 6: Sale of 200,000 units at $100 each, with costs of $65 each, yearly cash flow = $7,000,000.
- After t = 6, the NPV of new investment must be zero. Hence, to find the selling price per unit (P) solve the following for P:

$$0 = -25,000,000 + \frac{200,000 \times (P - 65)}{1.09^2} + \cdots + \frac{200,000 \times (P - 65)}{1.09^{12}}$$

Solving, we find P = $85.02 so that, for years t = 7 through t = 12, the yearly cash flow will be: [200,000 × ($85.02 – $65)] = $4,004,000.

Finally, the net present value (in millions):

$$NPV = -25 + \frac{7}{1.09^2} + \frac{7}{1.09^3} + \cdots + \frac{7}{1.09^6} + \frac{4.004}{1.09^7} + \cdots + \frac{4.004}{1.09^{12}}$$

NPV = $10.69 or $10,690,000

11.   The selling price after t = 6 now changes because the required investment is:

$25,000,000 \times (1 - 0.03)^5 = $21,468,351

After t = 5, the NPV of new investment must be zero, and hence the selling price per unit (P) is found by solving the following equation for P:

$$0 = -21,468,351 + \frac{200,000 \times (P - 65)}{1.09^2} + \cdots + \frac{200,000 \times (P - 65)}{1.09^{12}}$$

P = $82.19

Thus, for years t = 7 through t = 12, the yearly cash flow will be:

200,000 × ($82.19 – $65) = $3,438,000

Finally, the net present value (in millions) is:

$$NPV = -25 + \frac{7}{1.09^2} + \frac{7}{1.09^3} + \cdots + \frac{7}{1.09^6} + \frac{3.438}{1.09^7} + \cdots + \frac{3.438}{1.09^{12}}$$

NPV = $9.18 or $9,180,000

12. a. See the table below. The net present value is negative, so management should not proceed with the Polyzone project.

	t = 0	t = 1	t = 2	t = 3	t = 4	t = 5–10
Investment	100					
Production	0	0	40	80	80	80
Spread	1.20	1.20	1.20	1.20	1.20	0.95
Net Revenues	0	0	48	96	96	76
Prod. Costs	0	0	30	30	30	30
Transport	0	0	4	8	8	8
Other Costs	0	20	20	20	20	20
Cash Flow	−100	−20	−6	38	38	18

NPV (at 8%) = −$4.40

b. See the table below. The net present value is $40.40 million, and so the project is acceptable.

	t = 0	t = 1	t = 2	t = 3	t = 4	t = 5–10
Investment	100					
Production	0	40	80	80	80	80
Spread	1.20	1.20	1.20	1.20	1.10	0.95
Net Revenues	0	48	96	96	88	76
Prod. Costs	0	30	30	30	30	30
Transport	0	4	8	8	8	8
Other Costs	0	20	20	20	20	20
Cash Flow	−100	−6	38	38	30	18

NPV (at 8%) = $40.40

c. See the table below. The net present value is $18.64 million, and so the project is acceptable. However, the assumption that the technological advance will elude the competition for ten years seems questionable.

	t = 0	t = 1	t = 2	t − 3	t = 4	t = 5–10
Investment	100					
Production	0	0	40	80	80	80
Spread	1.20	1.20	1.20	1.20	1.10	0.95
Net Revenues	0	0	48	96	88	76
Prod. Costs	0	0	25	25	25	25
Transport	0	0	4	8	8	8
Other Costs	0	20	20	20	20	20
Cash Flow	−100	−20	−1	43	35	23

NPV (at 8%) = $18.64

13. There are four components that contribute to this project's NPV:

- The initial investment of $100,000.
- The depreciation tax shield. Depreciation expense is $20,000 per year for five years and is valued at the nominal rate of interest because it applies to nominal cash flows, i.e., earnings.
- The after-tax value of the increase in silver yield. Like gold, silver has low convenience yield and storage cost. (You can verify this by checking that the difference between the futures price and the spot price is approximately the interest saving from buying the futures contract.) We conclude, therefore, that the PV of silver delivered (with certainty) in the future is approximately today's spot price, and so there is no need to forecast the price of silver and then discount.
- The cost of operating the equipment. This cost is $80,000 per year for ten years and is valued at the real company cost of capital because we do not assume any future increase in cost due to inflation. We are concerned only with the after-tax cost.

$$NPV = -100,000 + \sum_{t=1}^{5} \frac{0.35 \times 20,000}{1.06^t} + (1-0.35) \times (10 \times 5,000 \times 20)$$

$$- \sum_{t=1}^{10} \frac{(1-0.35) \times 80,000}{1.08^t} = \$230,562$$

14. Assume we can ignore dividends paid on the stock market index. On June 30, 2011, each ticket must sell for $100 because this date marks the base period for the return calculation. At this price, investment in a ticket will offer the same return as investment in the index. On January 1, 2011, you know that each ticket will be worth $100 in 6 months. Therefore, on January 1, 2011, a ticket will be worth:

$100/(1.10)^{1/2} = \$95.35$

The price will be the same for a ticket based on the Dow Jones Industrial Average.

15. If available for immediate occupancy, the building would be worth $1 million. But because it will take the company one year to clear it out, the company will incur $200,000 in clean-up costs and will lose $80,000 net rent. Assume both rent *and* costs are spread evenly throughout the year. Thus (all dollar amounts are in thousands):

PV = 1,000 − PV(200 + 80) = 1,000 − (280 × 0.962) = 731

Since the selling price at each date is the present value of forecasted rents, the only effect of postponing the sale to year 2 is to postpone the sales commission. The commission is currently (0.05 × 1,000) = 50 and grows in line with property value. To estimate the growth rate of value, we can use the constant-growth model:

PV = 1,000 = 80/(0.08 – g) so that g = 0%

Thus, the commission in year 2 is: (50×1.00^2) and:

PV (commission) = $50 \times (1.00^2/1.08^2)$ = 43

The value of the warehouse, net of the sales commission, is:

731 – 43 = 688 or $688,000

Challenge Questions

16. a. The NPV of such plants is likely to be zero, because the industry is competitive and, after two years, no company will enjoy any technical advantages. The PV of each of these new plants would be $100,000 because the NPV is zero and the cost is $100,000.

b. The PV of revenue from such a plant is:

[100,000 tons × (Price – 0.85)]/0.10 = 100,000

Therefore, the price of polysyllabic acid will be $0.95 per ton.

c. At t = 2, the PV of the existing plant will be:

[100,000 tons × (0.95 – 0.90)]/0.10 = $50,000

Therefore, the existing plant would be scrapped at t = 2 as long as scrap value at that time exceeds $50,000.

d. No. Book value is irrelevant. NPV of the existing plant is negative after year 2.

e. Yes. Sunk costs are irrelevant. NPV of the existing plant is negative after year 2.

f. Phlogiston's project causes temporary excess capacity. Therefore, the price for the next two years must be such that the existing plant's owners will be indifferent between scrapping now and scrapping at the end of year 2. This allows us to solve for price in years 1 and 2.

Today's scrap value is $60,000. Also, today's scrap value is equal to the present value of future cash flows. Therefore:

$$\frac{100,000 \times (\text{Price} - 0.90)}{1.10} + \frac{100,000 \times (\text{Price} - 0.90)}{1.10^2} + \frac{57,900}{1.10^2} = 60,000$$

Solving, we find that the price is $0.97 per ton. Knowing this, we can calculate the PV of Phlogiston's new plant:

$$PV = 100,000 \times \left[\frac{0.97 - 0.85}{1.10} + \frac{0.97 - 0.85}{1.10^2} + \frac{0.95 - 0.85}{0.10 \times 1.10^2} \right] = \$103,471$$

17. Aircraft will be deployed in a manner that will minimize costs. This means that each aircraft will be used on the route for which it has the greatest comparative advantage. Thus, for example, for Part (a) of this problem, it is clear that Route X will be served with five A's and five B's, and that Route Y will be served with five B's and five C's. The remaining C-type aircraft will be scrapped.

The maximum price that anyone would pay for an aircraft is the present value of the total additional costs that would be incurred if that aircraft were withdrawn from service. Using the annuity factor for 5 time periods at 10 percent, we find the PV of the operating costs (all numbers are in millions):

Type	X	Y
A	5.7	5.7
B	9.5	7.6
C	17.1	13.3

Again, consider Part (a). The cost of using an A-type aircraft on Route X (Cost = Price of A + 5.7) must be equal to the cost of using a B-type aircraft on Route X (Cost = Price of B + 9.5). Also, the cost of using a B-type aircraft on Route Y (Price of B + 7.6) equals the cost of using a C-type on Route Y (Price of C + 13.3). Further, because five C-type aircraft are scrapped, the price of a C-type aircraft must be $1.0, the scrap value. Therefore, solving first for the price of B and then for the price of A, we find that the price of an A-type is $10.5 and the price of a B-type is $6.7. Using this approach, we have the following solutions:

	Usage			Aircraft Value (in millions)		
	X	Y	Scrap	A	B	C
a.	5A+5B	5B+5C	5C	$10.5	$6.7	$1.0
b.	10A	10B	10C	10.5	6.7	1.0
c.	10A	5A+5B	5B+10C	2.9	1.0	1.0
d.	10A	10A	10B+10C	2.9	1.0	1.0

18. a. $$\text{PV of 1-year-old plant} = \frac{43.33}{1.20} + \frac{58.33}{1.20^2} = \$76.62$$

$$\text{PV of 2-year-old plant} = \frac{58.33}{1.20} = \$48.61$$

b. Given that the industry is competitive, the investment in a new plant to produce bucolic acid must yield a zero NPV. First, we solve for the revenues (R) at which a new plant has zero NPV.

		0	1	2	3
1.	Initial investment	−100			
2.	Revenues net of tax		0.6R	0.6R	0.6R
3.	Operating costs net of tax		−30	−30	−30
4.	Depreciation tax shield		+40		
5.	Salvage value net of tax				+15

Therefore:

$$NPV = -100 + \frac{(0.6R-30+40)}{1.20} + \frac{(0.6R-30)}{1.20^2} + \frac{(0.6R-30+15)}{1.20^3} = 0$$

$$0 = -100 + 1.264R - 21.181$$

$$R = \$95.87$$

We can now use the new revenue to re-compute the present values from Part (a) above. (Recall that existing plants must use the original tax depreciation schedule.)

$$PV \text{ of } 1-year-old \text{ plant} = \frac{40.93}{1.20} + \frac{55.93}{1.20^2} = \$72.95$$

$$PV \text{ of } 2-year-old \text{ plant} = \frac{55.93}{1.20} = \$46.61$$

c. Existing 2-year-old plants have a net-of-tax salvage value of:

$$50 - [(0.4) \times (50.0 - 33.3)] = \$43.33$$

d. Solve again for revenues at which the new plant has zero NPV:

		0	1	2	3
1.	Initial investment	−100			
2.	Revenues		+R	+R	+R
3.	Operating costs		−50	−50	−50
4.	Salvage value				+25

$$NPV = -100 + \frac{(R-50)}{1.20} + \frac{(R-50)}{1.20^2} + \frac{(R-50+25)}{1.20^3} = 0$$

$$0 = -100 + 2.106R - 90.856$$

$$R = \$91$$

With revenues of $91:

$$PV \text{ of } 1-year-old \text{ plant} = \frac{41}{1.20} + \frac{66}{1.20^2} = \$80$$

$$PV \text{ of } 2-year-old \text{ plant} = \frac{66}{1.20} = \$55$$

CHAPTER 13

Agency Problems, Management Compensation, and the Measurement of Performance

Answers to Practice Questions

8. The typical compensation and incentive plans for top management include salary plus profit sharing and stock options. This is usually done to align as closely as possible the interests of the manager with the interests of the shareholders. These managers are usually responsible for corporate strategy and policies that can directly affect the future of the entire firm.

    Plant and divisional managers are usually paid a fixed salary plus a bonus based on accounting measures of performance. This is done because they are directly responsible for day-to-day performance and this valuation method provides an absolute standard of performance, as opposed to a standard that is relative to shareholder expectations. Further, it allows for the evaluation of junior managers who are only responsible for a small segment of the total corporate operation.

9. a. When paid a fixed salary without incentives to act in shareholders' best interest, managers often act sub-optimally.

    1. They may reduce their efforts to find and implement projects that add value.
    2. They may extract benefits-in-kind from the corporation in the form of a more lavish office, tickets to social events, overspending on expense accounts, etc.
    3. They may expand the size of the operation just for the prestige of running a larger company.
    4. They may choose second-best investments in order to reward existing employees, rather than the alternative that requires outside personnel but has a higher NPV.
    5. In order to maintain their comfortable jobs, managers may invest in safer rather than riskier projects.

    b. Tying the manager's compensation to EVA attempts to ensure that assets are deployed efficiently and that earned returns exceed the cost of capital. Hence, actions taken by the manager to shirk the duty of maximizing shareholder wealth generally result in a return that does not exceed the minimum required rate of return (cost of capital). The more the manager works in the interests of shareholders, the greater the EVA.

10. Shareholders are ultimately responsible for monitoring of top management of public U.S. corporations. However, unless there is a dominant shareholder (or a few major shareholders), monitoring is generally delegated to the board of directors elected by the shareholders. The board of directors of a large public company also retains an independent accounting firm to audit the

company's financial statements. In addition, lenders often monitor the company's management in order to protect lenders' interests in the loans they have extended; in the process, monitoring by lenders also protects stockholders' interests.

11. Since management effort is not observable, management compensation must in practice rely on results. The major problem introduced by rewarding results rather than effort is the fact that, in the corporate setting, results are a consequence of numerous factors, including the manger's efforts. It is generally very difficult, if not impossible, to precisely identify the extent to which a manager's efforts contributed to a particular outcome. Therefore, it is difficult to create the kinds of incentives that are most likely to reward the manager for her contribution, and therefore appropriately motivate the manager.

12. a. If a firm announces the hiring of a new manager who is expected to increase the firm's value, this information should be immediately reflected in the stock price. If the manager then performs as expected, there should not be much change in the share price since this performance has already been incorporated in the stock value.

    b. This could potentially be a very serious problem since the manager could lose money for reasons out of her control. One solution might be to index the price changes and then compare the actual raw material price paid with the indexed value. Another alternative would be to compare the performance with the performance of competitive firms.

    c. It is not necessarily an advantage to have a compensation scheme tied to stock returns. For example, in addition to the problem of expectations discussed in Part (a), there are numerous factors outside the manager's control, such as federal monetary policy or new environmental regulations. However, the stock price does tend to increase or decrease depending on whether the firm does or does not exceed the required cost of capital. To this extent, it is a measure of performance.

13. The issue to consider is which plan creates the most appropriate incentive structure in terms of aligning the CEO's motivations and compensation with those of the shareholders. In this regard, both plans have advantages and disadvantages. With stock-option package (a), the CEO will be compensated if the price of Androscoggin stock increases, regardless of whether the increase is a result of the CEO's actions or a consequence of a situation which is beyond the CEO's control (such as an increase in copper prices). On the other hand, with package (b), the CEO would be compensated if his actions lead to the result that Androscoggin stock outperforms the portfolio of copper-mining company shares; however, the Androscoggin CEO could also be rewarded if the CEOs of the other copper-mining companies performed poorly leading to the result that Androscoggin stock performs better than the lackluster average generated by the CEOs of the other companies.

14. a. EVA = Income earned – (Cost of capital x Investment)

   = $8.03m – (0.09 x $55.40m) = $3.04m

b. EVA = $8.03m – (0.09 x $95m) = –$0.52m

   The market value of the assets should be used to capture the true opportunity cost of capital.

15. EVA = Income earned – (Cost of capital x Investment)

   = $1.2m – [0.15 x ($4m + $2m + $8m)] = $1.2m – $2.1m = –$0.9m

16. a. False. The biases rarely wash out. For example, steady state income may not be much affected by investments in R & D but book asset value is understated. Thus, book profitability is too high, even in the steady state.

b. True. All biases in book profitability can be traced to accounting rules governing which assets are put on the balance sheet and the choice of book depreciation schedules.

17.

	Period		
	1	2	3
Net cash flow	0.00	78.55	78.55
PV at start of year	100.00	120.00	65.45
PV at end of year	120.00	65.45	0.00
Change in value during year	+20.00	–54.55	–65.45
Expected economic income	+20.00	+24.00	+13.10

18. The year-by-year book and economic profitability and rates of return are calculated in the table below. (We assume straight-line depreciation, $10 per year for years one through ten.)

Because a plant lasts for 10 years, 'steady state' for a mature company implies that we are operating ten plants, and every year we close one and begin construction on another. The total book income is $76.0, which is the same as the sum of the Book Income figures from the table (i.e., the sum of –$30.0, –$22.0, $16.0, etc.). Similarly, the total book investment is $550. Thus, the steady state book rate of return for a mature company producing Polyzone is: (76.0/550) = 13.82%. Note that this is considerably different from the economic rate of return, which is 8%.

	0	1	2	3	4	5
Investment	100.00					
Depreciation		10.00	10.00	10.00	10.00	10.00
Book Value – End of Year		90.00	80.00	70.00	60.00	50.00
Net Revenue	0.00	0.00	38.00	76.00	76.00	76.00
Production Costs	0.00	0.00	30.00	30.00	30.00	30.00
Transport & Other	0.00	20.00	20.00	20.00	20.00	20.00
Book Income		−30.00	−22.00	16.00	16.00	16.00
Book Rate of Return		−30.00%	−24.44%	20.00%	22.86%	26.67%
Cash Flow	−100.00	−20.00	−12.00	26.00	26.00	26.00
PV Start of Year		99.29	127.23	149.41	135.37	120.19
PV End of Year		127.23	149.41	135.37	120.19	103.81
Change in PV		27.94	22.18	−14.05	−15.17	−16.38
Economic Depreciation		−27.94	−22.18	14.05	15.17	16.38
Economic Income		7.94	10.18	11.95	10.83	9.62
Economic Rate of Return		8.00%	8.00%	8.00%	8.00%	8.00%

	6	7	8	9	10
Investment					
Depreciation	10.00	10.00	10.00	10.00	10.00
Book Value – End of Year	40.00	30.00	20.00	10.00	0.00
Net Revenue	76.00	76.00	76.00	76.00	76.00
Production Costs	30.00	30.00	30.00	30.00	30.00
Transport & Other	20.00	20.00	20.00	20.00	20.00
Book Income	16.00	16.00	16.00	16.00	16.00
Book Rate of Return	32.00%	40.00%	53.33%	80.00%	160.00%
Cash Flow	26.00	26.00	26.00	26.00	26.00
PV Start of Year	103.81	86.12	67.00	46.36	24.07
PV End of Year	86.12	67.00	46.36	24.07	0.00
Change in PV	−17.70	−19.11	−20.64	−22.29	−24.07
Economic Depreciation	17.70	19.11	20.64	22.29	24.07
Economic Income	8.30	6.89	5.36	3.71	1.93
Economic Rate of Return	8.00%	8.00%	8.00%	8.00%	8.00%

19.   a.   See table below. Straight-line depreciation would be $166.80 per year. Hence, economic depreciation in this case is accelerated, relative to straight-line depreciation.

b.   The true rate of return is found by dividing economic income by the start-of-period present value. As stated in the text, this will always be 10%. The book ROI is calculated in Panel B (using straight-line depreciation).

A.   Forecasted Book Income and ROI

Year

	1	2	3	4	5	6
Cash Flow	298.00	298.00	298.00	138.00	138.00	140.00
BV at start of year	1000.81	834.01	667.21	500.41	333.61	166.81
BV at end of year	834.01	667.21	500.41	333.61	166.81	0.01
Book depreciation	166.80	166.80	166.80	166.80	166.80	166.80
Book income	131.20	131.20	131.20	−28.80	−28.80	−26.80
Book ROI	0.1311	0.1573	0.1966	−0.0576	−0.0863	−0.1607
EVA	31.12	47.80	64.48	−78.84	−62.16	−43.48

B. Forecasted Economic Income and Rate of Return

Year

	1	2	3	4	5	6
Cash Flow	298.00	298.00	298.00	138.00	138.00	140.00
BV at start of year	1000.05	802.06	584.26	344.69	241.16	127.27
BV at end of year	802.06	584.26	344.69	241.16	125.27	0.00
Book depreciation	197.99	217.79	239.57	103.53	113.88	127.27
Book income	100.01	80.21	58.43	34.47	24.12	12.73
Book ROI	0.1000	0.1000	0.1000	0.1000	0.1000	0.1000
EVA	0.00	0.00	0.00	0.00	0.00	0.00

20. For a 10% expansion in book investment, ROI for Nodhead is given in the table below. When the steady-state growth rate is exactly equal to the economic rate of return (i.e., 10%), the economic rate of return and book ROI are the same.

Book Income for Assets Put in Place During Year	1	2	3	4	5	6
1	−66.80	33.20	83.20	131.20	131.20	131.20
2		−73.48	36.52	91.52	144.32	144.32
3			−80.83	40.17	100.67	158.75
4				−88.91	44.19	110.74
5					−97.80	48.61
6						−107.58
Total Book Inc:	−66.80	−40.28	38.89	173.98	322.58	486.04

Book Value for Assets Put in Place During Year	1	2	3	4	5	6
1	1000.81	834.01	667.21	500.41	333.61	166.81
2		1100.89	917.41	733.93	550.45	366.97
3			1210.98	1009.15	807.32	605.50
4				1332.08	1110.07	888.06
5					1465.29	1221.07
6						1611.81
Total BV:	1000.81	1934.90	2795.60	3575.57	4266.74	4860.22
Book ROI:	−0.067	−0.021	0.014	0.049	0.076	0.1000*

*This is the steady state rate of return.

21. Internet exercise; answers will vary.

Challenge Questions.

22.

	Year 1	Year 2	Year 3
Cash Flow	5.20	4.80	4.40
PV at start of year	12	8	4
PV at end of year	8	4	0
Change in PV	−4	−4	−4
Economic depreciation	4	4	4
Economic income	1.20	0.80	0.40
Economic rate of return	0.10	0.10	0.10
Book depreciation	4	4	4
Book income	1.20	0.80	0.40
Book rate of return	0.10	0.10	0.10

23. a. See table on next page. Note that economic depreciation is simply the change in market value, while book depreciation (per year) is:

$[19.69 - (0.2 \times 19.69)]/15 = 1.05$

Thus, economic depreciation is accelerated in this case, relative to book depreciation.

 b. See table on next page. Note that the book rate of return exceeds the true rate in only the first year.

c.   Because the economic return from investing in one airplane is 10% each year, the economic return from investing in a fixed number per year is also 10% each year. In order to calculate the book return, assume that we invest in one new airplane each year (the number of airplanes does not matter, just so long as it is the same each year). Then, book income will be (3.67 − 1.05) = 2.62 from the airplane in its first year, (3.00 − 1.95) = 1.95 from the airplane in its second year, etc., for a total book income of 15.21. Book value is calculated similarly: 19.69 for the airplane just purchased, 18.64 for the airplane that is one year old, etc., for a total book value of 185.09. Thus, the steady-state book rate of return is 8.22%, which understates the true (economic) rate of return (10%).

<u>Year</u>

	1	2	3	4	5	6	7	8
Market value	19.69	17.99	16.79	15.78	14.89	14.09	13.36	12.68
Economic		1.70	1.20	1.01	0.89	0.80	0.73	0.68
Cash flow		3.67	3.00	2.69	2.47	2.29	2.14	2.02
Economic income		1.97	1.80	1.68	1.58	1.49	1.41	1.34
Economic return		10.0%	10.0%	10.0%	10.0%	10.0%	10.0%	10.0%
Book value	19.69	18.64	17.59	16.54	15.49	14.44	13.39	12.34
Book depreciation		1.05	1.05	1.05	1.05	1.05	1.05	1.05
Book income		2.62	1.95	1.64	1.42	1.24	1.09	0.97
Book return		13.3%	10.5%	9.3%	8.6%	8.0%	7.5%	7.2%

<u>Year</u>

	9	10	11	12	13	14	15	16
Market value	12.05	11.46	10.91	10.39	9.91	9.44	9.01	8.59
Economic	0.63	0.59	0.55	0.52	0.48	0.47	0.43	0.42
Cash flow	1.90	1.80	1.70	1.61	1.52	1.46	1.37	1.32
Economic income	1.27	1.21	1.15	1.09	1.04	0.99	0.94	0.90
Economic return	10.0%	10.0%	10.0%	10.0%	10.0%	10.0%	10.0%	10.0%
Book value	11.29	10.24	9.19	8.14	7.09	6.04	4.99	3.94
Book depreciation	1.05	1.05	1.05	1.05	1.05	1.05	1.05	1.05
Book income	0.85	0.75	0.65	0.56	0.47	0.41	0.32	0.27
Book return	6.9%	6.6%	6.3%	6.1%	5.8%	5.8%	5.3%	5.4%

CHAPTER 14

Efficient Markets and Behavioral Finance

Answers to Practice Questions

9.   a.   An individual *can* do crazy things, but still not affect the efficiency of markets. The price of the asset in an efficient market is a consensus price as well as a marginal price. A nutty person can give assets away for free or offer to pay twice the market value. However, when the person's supply of assets or money runs out, the price will adjust back to its prior level (assuming there is no new, relevant information released by his action). If you are lucky enough to know such a person, you *will* receive a positive gain at the nutty investor's expense. You had better not count on this happening very often, though. Fortunately, an efficient market protects crazy investors in cases less extreme than the above. Even if they trade in the market in an "irrational" manner, they can be assured of getting a fair price since the price reflects all information.

     b.   Yes, and how many people have dropped a bundle? Or, more to the point, how many people have made a bundle only to lose it later? People can be lucky and some people can be very lucky; efficient markets do not preclude this possibility.

     c.   Investor psychology is a slippery concept, more often than not used to explain price movements that the individual invoking it cannot personally explain. Even if it exists, is there any way to make money from it? If investor psychology drives up the price one day, will it do so the next day also? Or will the price drop to a 'true' level? Almost no one can tell you beforehand what 'investor psychology' will do. Theories based on it have no content.

     d.   What good is a stable value when you can't buy or sell at that value because new conditions or information have developed which make the stable price obsolete? It is the market price, the price at which you can buy or sell today, which determines value.

10. a.   There is risk in almost everything you do in daily life. You could lose your job or your spouse, or suffer damage to your house from a storm. That doesn't necessarily mean you should quit your job, get a divorce, or sell your house. If we accept that our world is risky, then we must accept that asset values fluctuate as new information emerges. Moreover, if capital markets are functioning properly, then stock price changes will follow a random walk. The random walk of values is the *result* of rational investors coping with an uncertain world.

b. To make the example clearer, assume that everyone believes in the same chart. What happens when the chart shows a downward movement? Are investors going to be willing to hold the stock when it has an expected loss? Of course not. They start selling, and the price will decline until the stock is expected to give a positive return. The trend will 'self-destruct.'

c. Random-walk theory as applied to efficient markets means that fluctuations from the *expected* outcome are random. Suppose there is an 80 percent chance of rain tomorrow (because it rained today). Then the local umbrella store's stock price will respond *today* to the prospect of high sales tomorrow. The store's *sales* will not follow a random walk, but its stock price will, because each day the stock price reflects all that investors know about future weather and future sales.

11. One of the ways to think about market inefficiency is that it implies there is easy money to be made. The following appear to suggest market inefficiency:
   (d) strong form
   (e) weak form
   (f) semi-strong form

12. The estimates are first substituted in the market model. Then the result from this expected return equation is subtracted from the actual return for the month to obtain the abnormal return.

   Abnormal return (Intel) = Actual return − [(−0.87) + (2.02 × Market return)]

   Abnormal return (Conagra) = Actual return − [0.40 + (0.40 × Market return)]

13. One possible procedure is to first form groups of stocks with similar P/E ratios, adjusting for market risk (using either historical estimates of alpha or estimates based on the Capital Asset Pricing Model). Then determine whether the alpha of each group is significantly different from zero. Here are some things to look out for:
   a. Don't select samples of stock at the end of the period. You will have omitted the companies that went bankrupt.
   b. Include dividends in the actual rate of return. Low P/E stocks have high yields.
   c. Check that earnings are known on the date that you calculate P/E. Stocks whose earnings *subsequently* turned out high relative to price naturally perform better.
   d. Adjust for risk. Low P/E stocks tend to be more risky.
   e. You may need to disentangle the P/E effect from other effects, e.g., size or dividend yield.

14. The efficient market hypothesis does not imply that portfolio selection should be done with a pin. The manager still has three important jobs to do. First, she must make sure that the portfolio is well diversified. It should be noted that a large number of stocks is not enough to ensure diversification. Second, she

must make sure that the risk of the diversified portfolio is appropriate for the manager's clients. Third, she might want to tailor the portfolio to take advantage of special tax laws for pension funds. These laws may make it possible to increase the expected return of the portfolio without increasing risk.

15.   They are both under the illusion that markets are predictable and they are wasting their time trying to guess the market's direction. Remember the first lesson of market efficiency: Markets have no memory. The decision as to when to issue stock should be made without reference to 'market cycles.'

16.   The efficient-market hypothesis says that there is no easy way to make money. Thus, when such an opportunity seems to present itself, we should be very skeptical. For example:

- In the case of short- versus long-term rates, and borrowing short-term versus long-term, there are different risks involved. For example, suppose that we need the money long-term but we borrow short-term. When the short-term note is due, we must somehow refinance. However; this may not be possible, or may be possible only at a very high interest rate.

- In the case of Japanese versus United States interest rates, there is the risk that the Japanese yen - U.S. dollar exchange rate will change during the period of time for which we have borrowed.

17.   Some key points are as follows:

a.   Unidentified Risk Factor: From an economic standpoint, given the information available and the number of participants, it is hard to believe that any securities market in the U.S is not very efficient. Thus, the most likely explanation for the small-firm effect is that the model used to estimate expected returns is incorrect, and that there is some as-yet-unidentified risk factor.

b.   Coincidence: In statistical inference, we never prove an affirmative fact. The best we can do is to accept or reject a specified hypothesis with a given degree of confidence. Thus, no matter what the outcome of a statistical test, there is always a possibility, however slight, that the small-firm effect is simply the result of statistical chance or, in other words, a coincidence.

c.   Market Inefficiency: One key to market efficiency is the high level of competition among participants in the market. For small stocks, the level of competition is relatively low because major market participants (e.g., mutual funds and pension funds) are biased toward holding the securities of larger, well-known companies. Thus, it is likely that the market for small stocks is fundamentally different from the market for larger stocks and, hence, it is quite plausible that the small-firm effect is simply a reflection of market inefficiency.

18.   There are several ways to approach this problem, but all (when done correctly!) should give approximately the same answer. We have chosen to use the

regression analysis function of an electronic spreadsheet program to calculate the alpha and beta for each security. The regressions are in the following form:

Security return = alpha + (beta × market return) + error term

The results are:

	Alpha	Beta
Executive Cheese	−1.44	0.21
Paddington Beer	1.33	0.19

The abnormal return for Executive Cheese in February 2007 was:

$$-7.1 - [-1.44 + 0.21 \times (-0.5)] = -5.555\%$$

For Paddington Beer, the abnormal return was:

$$-14.1 - [1.33 + 0.19 \times (-0.5)] = -15.335\%$$

Thus, the average abnormal return of the two stocks during the month of the dividend announcement was −10.445%.

19. The market is most likely efficient. The government of Kuwait is not likely to have non-public information about the BP shares. Goldman Sachs is providing an intermediary service for which they should be remunerated. Stocks are bought by investors at (higher) ask prices and sold at (lower) bid prices. The spread between the two ($0.11) is revenue for the broker. In the U.S., at that time, a bid-ask spread of 1/8 ($0.125) was not uncommon. The 'profit' of $15 million reflects the size of the order more than any mispricing.

Challenge Questions

20. a. The probability that mutual fund X achieved superior performance in any one year is 0.50. The probability that mutual fund X achieved superior performance in each of the past ten years is:

$$0.5^{10} = 0.00097656$$

b. The probability that, out of 10,000 mutual funds, none of them obtained ten successive years of superior performance is:

$$(1 - 0.00097656)^{10,000} = 0.00005712$$

Therefore, the probability that at least one of the 10,000 mutual funds obtained ten successive years of superior performance is:

$$1 - 0.00005712 = 0.99994288$$

21. No, this does not follow. The decline in prices merely reflects the consensus market opinion about the seriousness of the country's difficulties. The stability after the announcement reflects the market's opinion of the nature of the assistance and its likelihood of success.

22. Internet exercise; answers will vary.

CHAPTER 15

An Overview of Corporate Financing

Answers to Practice Questions

6. a. Par value is $0.05 per share, which is computed as follows:

$439 million/8,784 million shares

   b. The shares were sold at an average price of:

[$439 million + $67,622 million]/8,784 million shares = $7.75

   c. The company has repurchased:

8,784 million – 7,361 million = 1,423 million shares

   d. Average repurchase price:

$39,323 million/1,423 million shares = $27.63 per share.

   e. The value of the net common equity is:

$439 million + $67,622 million + $37,608 million – $39,323 million

= $66,346 million

7. Internet exercise; answers will vary.

8. a. The day after the founding of Inbox:

Common shares ($0.10 par value)	$ 50,000
Additional paid-in capital	1,950,000
Retained earnings	0
Treasury shares	0
Net common equity	$2,000,000

   b. After 2 years of operation:

Common shares ($0.10 par value)	$ 50,000
Additional paid-in capital	1,950,000
Retained earnings	120,000
Treasury shares	0
Net common equity	$2,120,000

   c. After 3 years of operation:

Common shares ($0.10 par value)	$ 150,000
Additional paid-in capital	6,850,000
Retained earnings	370,000
Treasury shares	0
Net common equity	$7,370,000

9. a.

Common shares ($1.00 par value)	$1,008
Additional paid-in capital	5,076
Retained earnings	11,722
Treasury shares	(5,052)
Net common equity	$12,754

b.

Common shares ($1.00 par value)	$1,008
Additional paid-in capital	5,076
Retained earnings	11,722
Treasury shares	(5,752)
Net common equity	$12,054

10. One would expect that the voting shares have a higher price because they have an added benefit/responsibility that has value.

11. a.

Gross profits	$ 760,000
Interest	100,000
EBT	$ 660,000
Tax (at 35%)	231,000
Funds available to common shareholders	$ 429,000

b.

Gross profits (EBT)	$ 760,000
Tax (at 35%)	266,000
Net income	$ 494,000
Preferred dividend	80,000
Funds available to common shareholders	$ 414,000

12. Internet exercise; answers will vary.

13. a. Less valuable
    b. More valuable
    c. More valuable
    d. Less valuable

Challenge Questions

14. a. For majority voting, you must own or otherwise control the votes of a simple majority of the shares outstanding, i.e., one-half of the shares outstanding plus one. Here, with 200,000 shares outstanding, you must control the votes of 100,001 shares.

    b. With cumulative voting, the directors are elected in order of the total number of votes each receives. With 200,000 shares outstanding and five directors to be elected, there will be a total of 1,000,000 votes cast. To ensure you can elect at least one director, you must ensure that someone else can elect at most four directors. That is, you must have enough votes so that, even if the others split their votes evenly among five other candidates, the number of votes your candidate gets would be higher by one.

Let x be the number of votes controlled by you, so that others control (1,000,000 − x) votes. To elect one director:

$$x = \frac{1,000,000 - x}{5} + 1$$

Solving, we find x = 166,666.8 votes, or 33,333.4 shares. Because there are no fractional shares, we need 33,334 shares.

CHAPTER 16

How Corporations Issue Securities

Answers to Practice Questions

9. a. Zero-stage financing represents the savings and personal loans the company's principals raise to start a firm. First-stage and second-stage financing comes from funds provided by others (often venture capitalists) to supplement the founders' investment.

    b. An after-the-money valuation represents the estimated value of the firm after the first-stage financing has been received.

    c. Mezzanine financing comes from other investors, after the financing provided by venture capitalists.

    d. A road show is a presentation about the firm given to potential investors in order to gauge their reactions to a stock issue and to estimate the demand for the new shares.

    e. A best efforts offer is an underwriter's promise to sell as much as possible of a security issue.

    f. A qualified institutional buyer is a large financial institution which, under SEC Rule 144A, is allowed to trade unregistered securities with other qualified institutional buyers.

    g. Blue-sky laws are state laws governing the sale of securities within the state.

    h. A greenshoe option in an underwriting agreement gives the underwriter the option to increase the number of shares the underwriter buys from the issuing company.

10. a. Management's willingness to invest in Marvin's equity was a credible signal because the management team stood to lose everything if the new venture failed, and thus they signaled their seriousness. By accepting only part of the venture capital that would be needed, management was increasing its own risk and reducing that of First Meriam. This decision would be costly and foolish if Marvin's management team lacked confidence that the project would get past the first stage.

    b. Marvin's management agreed not to accept lavish salaries. The cost of management perks comes out of the shareholders' pockets. In Marvin's case, the managers *are* the shareholders.

11.	If he is bidding on under-priced stocks, he will receive only a portion of the shares he applies for. If he bids on under-subscribed stocks, he will receive his full allotment of shares, which no one else is willing to buy. Hence, on average, the stocks may be under-priced but once the weighting of all stocks is considered, it may not be profitable.

12.	Some possible reasons for cost differences:
a.	Large issues have lower proportionate costs.
b.	Debt issues have lower costs than equity issues.
c.	Initial public offerings involve more risk for underwriters than issues of seasoned stock. Underwriters demand higher spreads in compensation.

13.	There are several possible reasons why the issue costs for debt are lower than those of equity, among them:
- The cost of complying with government regulations may be lower for debt.
- The risk of the security is less for debt and hence the price is less volatile. This decreases the probability that the issue will be mis-priced and therefore decreases the underwriter's risk.

14.	a.	Inelastic demand implies that a large price reduction is needed in order to sell additional shares. This would be the case only if investors believe that a stock has no close substitutes (i.e., they value the stock for its unique properties).

b.	Price pressure may be inconsistent with market efficiency. It implies that the stock price falls when new stock is issued and subsequently recovers.

c.	If a company's stock is undervalued, managers will be reluctant to sell new stock, even if it means foregoing a good investment opportunity. The converse is true if the stock is overvalued. Investors know this and, therefore, mark down the price when companies issue stock. (Of course, managers of a company with undervalued stock become even more reluctant to issue stock because their actions can be misinterpreted.)

If (b) is the reason for the price fall, there should be a subsequent price recovery. If (a) is the reason, we would not expect a price recovery, but the fall should be greater for large issues. If (c) is the reason, the price fall will depend only on issue size (assuming the information is correlated with issue size).

15.	a.	Example: Before issue, there are 100 shares outstanding at $10 per share. The company sells 20 shares for cash at $5 per share. Company value increases by: (20 x $5) = $100. Thus, after issue, each share is worth:

$$\frac{(100 \times \$10) + \$100}{100 + 20} = \frac{\$1,100}{120} = \$9.17$$

Note that new shareholders gain: 20 × $4.17 = $83

Old shareholders lose: 100 × $0.83 = $83

b. Example: Before issue, there are 100 shares outstanding at $10 per share. The company makes a rights issue of 20 shares at $5 per share. Each right is worth:

$$\text{Value of right} = \frac{(\text{rights on price}) - (\text{issue price})}{N+1} = \frac{10-5}{6} = \$0.83$$

The new share price is $9.17. If a shareholder sells his right, he receives $0.83 cash and the value of each share declines by: $10 – $9.17 = $0.83 The shareholder's total wealth is unaffected.

16. a. €5 × (10,000,000/4) = €12.5 million

b. $$\text{Value of right} = \frac{(\text{rights on price}) - (\text{issue price})}{N+1} = \frac{6-5}{4+1} = €0.20$$

c. $$\text{Stock price} = \frac{(10,000,000 \times 6) + 12,500,000}{10,000,000 + 2,500,000} = €5.80$$

A stockholder who previously owned four shares had stocks with a value of: (4 × €6) = €24. This stockholder has now paid €5 for a fifth share so that the total value is: (€24 + €5) = €29. This stockholder now owns five shares with a value of: (5 × €5.80) = €29, so that she is no better or worse off than she was before.

d. The share price would have to fall to the issue price per share, or €5 per share. Firm value would then be: 10 million × €5 = €50 million

17. €12,500,000/€4 = 3,125,000 shares

10,000,000/3,125,000 = 3.20 rights per share

$$\text{Value of right} = \frac{(\text{rights on price}) - (\text{issue price})}{N+1} = \frac{6-4}{3.2+1} = €0.48$$

$$\text{Stock price} = \frac{(10,000,000 \times 6) + 12,500,000}{10,000,000 + 3,125,000} = €5.52$$

A stockholder who previously owned 3.2 shares had stocks with a value of: (3.2 × €6) = €19.20. This stockholder has now paid €4 for an additional share, so that the total value is: (€19.20 + €4) = €23.20. This stockholder now owns 4.2 shares with a value of: (4.2 × €5.52) = €23.18 (difference due to rounding).

18.   Before the general cash offer, the value of the firm's equity is:

$$10{,}000{,}000 \times €6 = €60{,}000{,}000$$

New financing raised (from Practice Question 16) is €12,500,000

Total equity after general cash offer = €60,000,000 + €12,500,000 = €72,500,000

Total new shares = €12,500,000/€4 = 3,125,000

Total shares after general cash offer = 10,000,000 + 3,125,000 = 13,125,000

Price per share after general cash offer = €72,500,000/13,125,000 = €5.5238

Existing shareholders have lost = €6.00 – €5.5238 = €0.4762 per share

Total loss for existing shareholders = €0.4762 × 10,000,000 = €4,762,000

New shareholders have gained = €5.5238 – €4.00 = €1.5238 per share

Total gain for new shareholders = €1.5238 × 3,125,000 = €4,761,875

Except for rounding error, we see that the gain for the new shareholders comes at the expense of the existing shareholders.

Challenge Questions

19.   a.   Venture capital companies prefer to advance money in stages because this approach provides an incentive for management to reach the next stage, and it allows First Meriam to check at each stage whether the project continues to have a positive NPV. Marvin is happy because it signals their confidence. With hindsight, First Meriam loses because it has to pay more for the shares at each stage.

        b.   The problem with this arrangement would be that, while Marvin would have an incentive to ensure that the option was exercised, it would not have the incentive to maximize the price at which it sells the new shares.

        c.   The right of first refusal could make sense if First Meriam was making a large up-front investment that it needed to be able to recapture in its subsequent investments. In practice, Marvin is likely to get the best deal from First Meriam.

20.   In a uniform-price auction, all successful bidders pay the same price. In a discriminatory auction, each successful bidder pays a price equal to his own bid. A uniform-price auction provides for the pooling of information from bidders and reduces the winner's curse.

21.   Pisa Construction's return on investment is 8%, whereas investors require a 10% rate of return. Pisa proposes a scenario in which 2,000 shares of common stock are issued at $40 per share, and the proceeds ($80,000) are then invested at 8%. Assuming that the 8% return is received in the form of a perpetuity, then the NPV for this scenario is computed as follows:

$$-\$80{,}000 + (0.08 \times \$80{,}000)/0.10 = -\$16{,}000$$

Share price would decline as a result of this project, not because the company sells shares for less than book value, but rather due to the fact that the NPV is negative.

Note that, if investors know price will decline as a consequence of Pisa's undertaking a negative NPV investment, Pisa will not be able to sell shares at $40 per share. Rather, after the announcement of the project, the share price will decline to:

$$(\$400,000 - \$16,000)/10,000 = \$38.40$$

Therefore, Pisa will have to issue: $80,000/$38.40 = 2,083 new shares
One can show that, if the proceeds of the stock issue are invested at 10%, then share price remains unchanged.

CHAPTER 17

Payout Policy

Answers to Practice Questions

8. Newspaper exercise; answers will vary depending on the stocks chosen.

9. a. Distributes a relatively low proportion of current earnings to offset fluctuations in operational cash flow; lower P/E ratio.

   b. Distributes a relatively high proportion of current earnings since the decline is unexpected; higher P/E ratio.

   c. Distributes a relatively low proportion of current earnings in order to offset anticipated declines in earnings; lower P/E ratio.

   d. Distributes a relatively low proportion of current earnings in order to fund expected growth; higher P/E ratio.

10. a. A t = 0 each share is worth $20. This value is based on the expected stream of dividends: $1 at t = 1, and increasing by 5% in each subsequent year. Thus, we can find the appropriate discount rate for this company as follows:

$$P_0 = \frac{DIV_1}{r - g}$$

$$\$20 = \frac{1}{r - 0.05} \Rightarrow r = 0.10 = 10.0\%$$

Beginning at t = 2, each share in the company will enjoy a perpetual stream of growing dividends: $1.05 at t = 2, and increasing by 5% in each subsequent year. Thus, the total value of the shares at t = 1 (after the t = 1 dividend is paid and after N new shares have been issued) is given by:

$$V_1 = \frac{\$1.05 \text{ million}}{0.10 - 0.05} = \$21 \text{ million}$$

If P_1 is the price per share at t = 1, then:

$$V_1 = P_1 \times (1,000,000 + N) = \$21,000,000$$

and:

$$P_1 \times N = \$1,000,000$$

From the first equation:

$$(1,000,000 \times P_1) + (N \times P_1) = \$21,000,000$$

Substituting from the second equation:

$$(1{,}000{,}000 \times P_1) + \$1{,}000{,}000 = \$21{,}000{,}000$$

so that $P_1 = \$20.00$

b.   With P_1 equal to $20, and $1,000,000 to raise, the firm will sell 50,000 new shares.

c.   The expected dividends paid at $t = 2$ are $1,050,000, increasing by 5% in each subsequent year. With 1,050,000 shares outstanding, dividends per share are: $1 at $t = 2$, increasing by 5% in each subsequent year. Thus, total dividends paid to old shareholders are: $1,000,000 at $t = 2$, increasing by 5% in each subsequent year.

d.   For the current shareholders:

$$PV(t = 0) = \frac{\$2{,}000{,}000}{1.10} + \frac{\$1{,}000{,}000}{(0.10 - 0.05) \times (1.10)} = \$20{,}000{,}000$$

11.   From Question 10, the fair issue price is $20 per share. If these shares are instead issued at $10 per share, then the new shareholders are getting a bargain, i.e., the new shareholders win and the old shareholders lose.

As pointed out in the text, any increase in cash dividend must be offset by a stock issue if the firm's investment and borrowing policies are to be held constant. If this stock issue cannot be made at a fair price, then shareholders are clearly not indifferent to dividend policy.

12.   The risk stems from the decision to not invest, and it is not a result of the form of financing. If an investor consumes the dividend instead of re-investing the dividend in the company's stock, she is also 'selling' a part of her stake in the company. In this scenario, she will suffer an equal opportunity loss if the stock price subsequently rises sharply.

13.   If the company does not pay a dividend:

Cash	0	0	Debt
Existing fixed assets	4,500	5,500 + NPV	Equity
New project	1,000 + NPV		
	$5,500 + NPV	$5,500 + NPV	

If the company pays a $1,000 dividend:

Cash	0	0	Debt
Existing fixed assets	4,500	1,000	Value of new stock
New project	1,000 + NPV	4,500 + NPV	Value of original stock
	$5,500 + NPV	$5,500 + NPV	

Because the new stockholders receive stock worth $1,000, the value of the original stock declines by $1,000, which exactly offsets the dividends.

14. One problem with this analysis is that it assumes the company's net profit remains constant even though the asset base of the company shrinks by 20%. That is, in order to raise the cash necessary to repurchase the shares, the company must sell assets. If the assets sold are representative of the company as a whole, we would expect net profit to decrease by 20% so that earnings per share and the P/E ratio remain the same. After the repurchase, the company will look like this next year:

Net profit:	$8 million
Number of shares:	0.8 million
Earnings per share:	$10
Price-earnings ratio:	20
Share price:	$200

15. a. If we ignore taxes and there is no information conveyed by the repurchase when the repurchase program is announced, then share price will remain at $80.

b. The regular dividend has been $4 per share, and so the company has $400,000 cash on hand. Since the share price is $80, the company will repurchase 5,000 shares.

c. Total asset value (before each dividend payment or stock repurchase) remains at $8,000,000. These assets earn $400,000 per year, under either policy.

Old Policy: The annual dividend is $4, which never changes, so the stock price (immediately prior to the dividend payment) will be $80 in all years.

New Policy: Every year, $400,000 is available for share repurchase. As noted above, 5,000 shares will be repurchased at t = 0. At t = 1, immediately prior to the repurchase, there will be 95,000 shares outstanding. These shares will be worth $8,000,000, or $84.21 per share. With $400,000 available to repurchase shares, the total number of shares repurchased will be 4,750. Using this reasoning, we can generate the following table:

Time	Shares Outstanding	Share Price	Shares Repurchased
t = 0	100,000	$80.00	5,000
t = 1	95,000	$84.21	4,750
t = 2	90,250	$88.64	4,513
t = 3	85,737	$93.31	4,287

Note that the stock price is increasing by 5.26% each year. This is consistent with the rate of return to the shareholders under the old policy, whereby every year assets worth $7,600,000 (the asset value immediately after the dividend) earn $400,000, or a return of 5.26%.

16. If markets are efficient, then a share repurchase is a zero-NPV investment. Suppose that the trade-off is between an investment in real assets or a share repurchase. Obviously, the shareholders would prefer a share repurchase to a negative-NPV project. The quoted statement seems to imply that firms have only negative-NPV projects available.

   Another possible interpretation is that managers have inside information indicating that the firm's stock price is too low. In this case, share repurchase is detrimental to those stockholders who sell and beneficial to those who do not. It is difficult to see how this could be beneficial to the firm, however.

17. a. This statement implicitly equates the cost of equity capital with the stock's dividend yield. If this were true, companies that pay no dividend would have a zero cost of equity capital, which is clearly not correct.

   b. One way to think of retained earnings is that, from an economic standpoint, the company earns money on behalf of the shareholders, who then immediately re-invest the earnings in the company. Thus, retained earnings do not represent free capital. Retained earnings carry the full cost of equity capital (although issue costs associated with raising new equity capital are avoided).

   c. If the tax on capital gains is less than that on dividends, the conclusion of this statement is correct; i.e., a stock repurchase is always preferred over dividends. This conclusion, however, is strictly because of taxes. Earnings per share is irrelevant.

18. a. Because this is a regular dividend, the announcement is not news to the stock market. Hence, the stock price will adjust only when the stock begins to trade without the dividend and, thus, the stock price will fall on the ex-dividend date.

   b. With no taxes, the stock price will fall by the amount of the dividend, here $1.

   c. With taxes on dividends but no taxes on capital gains, investors will require the same after-tax return from two comparable companies, one of which pays a dividend, the other, a capital gain of the same magnitude. The stock price will thus fall by the amount of the after-tax dividend, here:

      $1 \times (1 - 0.30) = 0.70.

   d. If dealers are taxed equally on capital gains and dividends, then they should not demand any extra return for holding stocks that pay dividends. Thus, if shareholders are able to freely trade securities

17-4

around the time of the dividend payment, there should be no tax effects associated with dividends.

19. a. If you own 100 shares at $100 per share, then your wealth is $10,000. After the dividend payment, each share will be worth $99 and your total wealth will be the same: 100 shares at $99 per share plus $100 in dividends, or $10,000.

   b. With no taxes, it does not matter how the company transfers wealth to the shareholders; that is, you are indifferent between a dividend and a share repurchase program. In either case, your total wealth will remain at $10,000.

20. *After-tax Return on Share A*: At t = 1, a shareholder in company A will receive a dividend of $10, which is subject to taxes of 30%. Therefore, the after-tax gain is $7. Since the initial investment is $100, the after-tax rate of return is 7%.

   After-tax Return on Share B: If an investor sells share B after 2 years, the price will be: $(100 \times 1.10^2) = \$121$. The capital gain of $21 is taxed at the 30% rate, and so the after-tax gain is $14.70. On an initial investment of $100, over a 2-year time period, this is an after-tax annual rate of return of 7.10%.

   If an investor sells share B after 10 years, the price will be: $(100 \times 1.10^{10}) = \$259.37$. The capital gain of $159.37 is taxed at the 30% rate, and so the after-tax gain is $111.56. On an initial investment of $100, over a 10-year time period, this is an after-tax annual rate of return of 7.78%.

21. a. (i) The tax-free investor should buy on the with-dividend date because the dividend is worth $1 and the price decrease is only $0.90.

   (ii) The dividend is worth only $0.60 to the taxable investor who is subject to a 40% marginal tax rate. Therefore, this investor should buy on the ex-dividend date.

   [Actually, the taxable investor's problem is a little more complicated. By buying at the ex-dividend price, this investor increases the capital gain that is eventually reported upon the sale of the asset. At most, however, this will cost: $(0.16 \times 0.90) = \$0.14$
   This is not enough to offset the tax on the dividend.]

   b. The marginal investor, by definition, must be indifferent between buying with-dividend or ex-dividend. If we let T represent the marginal tax rate on dividends, then the marginal tax rate on capital gains is (0.4T). In order for the net extra return from buying with-dividend (instead of ex-dividend) to be zero:

   –Extra investment + After-tax dividend + Reduction in capital gains tax = 0

Therefore, per dollar of dividend:

$$-0.85 + [(1 - T) \times 1.00] + [0.4T \times 0.85] = 0$$
$$T = 0.227 = 22.7\%$$

c.　We would expect the high-payout stocks to show the largest decline per dollar of dividends paid because these stocks should be held by investors in low, or perhaps even zero, marginal tax brackets.

d.　Some investors (e.g., pension funds and security dealers) are indifferent between $1 of dividends and $1 of capital gains. These investors should be prepared to buy any amount of stock with-dividend as long as the fall-off in price is fractionally less than the dividend. Elton and Gruber's result suggests that there must be some impediment to such tax arbitrage (e.g., transactions costs or IRS restrictions). But, in that case, it is difficult to interpret their result as indicative of marginal tax rates.

e.　The tax advantage to capital gains has been reduced. If investors are now indifferent between dividends and capital gains, we would expect that the payment of a $1 dividend would result in a $1 decrease in price.

22.　Even if the middle-of-the-road party is correct about the supply of dividends, we still do not know why investors wanted the dividends they got. So, it is difficult to be sure about the effect of the tax change. If there is some non-tax advantage to dividends that offsets the apparent tax disadvantage, then we would expect investors to demand more dividends after the government reduces the tax rate on dividends. If the apparent tax disadvantage were irrelevant because there were too many loopholes in the tax system, then the reduction in the tax rate on dividends would not affect the demand for dividends. In any case, the middle-of-the-roaders would argue that once companies adjusted the supply of dividends to the new equilibrium, dividend policy would again become irrelevant.

Challenge Questions

23.　Reducing the amount of earnings retained each year will, of course, reduce the growth rate of dividends. Also, the firm will have to issue new shares each year in order to finance company growth. Under the original dividend policy, we expect next year's stock price to be: (50×1.08) = $54. If N is the number of shares previously outstanding, the value of the company at t = 1 is (54N).

Under the new policy, n new shares will be issued at t = 1 to make up for the reduction in retained earnings resulting from the new policy. This decrease is: ($4 – $2) = $2 per original share, or an aggregate reduction of 2N. If P_1 is the price of the common stock at t = 1 under the new policy, then:

$$2N = nP_1$$

Also, because the total value of the company is unchanged:

$$54N = (N + n)P_1$$

Solving, we find that $P_1 = \$52$.

If g is the expected growth rate under the new policy and P_0 the price at t = 0, we have:

$$52 = (1 + g)P_0$$

and:

$$P_0 = \frac{4}{0.12 - g}$$

Substituting the second equation above for P_0 in the first equation and then solving, we find that g = 4% and $P_0 = \$50$, so that the current stock price is unchanged.

24. Assume that all taxpayers pay a 20% tax on dividend income and 10% tax on capital gains. Firm A pays no dividends but investors expect the price of Firm A stock to increase from $40 to $50 per share. Firm B pays a dividend of $5 per share and investors expect the price of Firm B stock to be $45 next year. Results for Firm A are:

Before-tax rate of return	$10/$40 = 25.00%
Tax on dividend at 20%	$0.00
Tax on capital gains at 10%	0.10 × $10.00 = $1.00
Total after-tax income (dividends plus capital gains less taxes)	$0 + $10 – $1 = $9.00
After-tax rate of return	$9/$40 = 22.50%

The price of Firm B stock today must adjust so as to provide an after-tax return equal to that of Firm A. Let X equal the current price of Firm B stock. Then, for Firm B:

Next year's price	$45.00
Dividend	$5.00
Today's stock price	X
Capital gain	$45 – X
Before-tax rate of return	[$5 + ($45 – X)]/X
Tax on dividend at 20%	0.20 × $5.00 = $1.00
Tax on capital gains at 10%	0.10 × ($45 – X)
Total after-tax income (dividends plus capital gains less taxes)	[$5 + ($45 – X)] – [$1 + 0.10 × ($45 – X)]

The price of Firm B stock adjusts so that the after-tax rate of return for Firm B is equal to 22.5%, the after-tax rate of return for Firm A. To find today's price for Firm A stock, solve the following for X:

$$\frac{[\$5 + (\$45 - X)] - \{\$1 + [0.10 \times (\$45 - X)]\}}{X} = 0.225 \Rightarrow X = \$39.56$$

25.   It is true that researchers have been consistent in finding a positive association between price-earnings multiples and payout ratios. But simple tests like this one do not isolate the effects of dividend policy, so the evidence is not convincing.

Suppose that King Coal Company, which customarily distributes half its earnings, suffers a strike that cuts earnings in half. The setback is regarded as temporary, however, so management maintains the normal dividend. The payout ratio for that year turns out to be 100 percent, not 50 percent.

The temporary earnings drop also affects King Coal's price-earnings ratio. The stock price may drop because of this year's disappointing earnings, but it does not drop to one-half its pre-strike value. Investors recognize the strike as temporary, and the ratio of price to this year's earnings increases. Thus, King Coal's labor troubles create both a high payout ratio and a high price-earnings ratio. In other words, they create a spurious association between dividend policy and market value. The same thing happens whenever a firm encounters temporary good fortune, or whenever reported earnings underestimate or overestimate the true long-run earnings on which both dividends and stock prices are based.

A second source of error is omission of other factors affecting both the firm's dividend policy and its market valuation. For example, we know that firms seek to maintain stable dividend rates. Companies whose prospects are uncertain therefore tend to be conservative in their dividend policies. Investors are also likely to be concerned about such uncertainty, so that the stocks of such companies are likely to sell at low multiples. Again, the result is an association between the price of the stock and the payout ratio, but it stems from the common association with risk and not from a market preference for dividends.

Another reason that earnings multiples may be different for high-payout and low-payout stocks is that the two groups may have different growth prospects. Suppose, as has sometimes been suggested, that management is careless in the use of retained earnings but exercises appropriately stringent criteria when spending external funds. Under such circumstances, investors would be correct to value stocks of high-payout firms more highly. But the reason would be that the companies have different investment policies. It would not reflect a preference for high dividends as such, and no company could achieve a lasting improvement in its market value simply by increasing its payout ratio.

26.   a.   The marginal investors are the institutions.

b.   Price of low-payout stock: $P_0 = \dfrac{\$20}{0.12} = \$166.67$

Price of medium-payout stock: $P_0 = \dfrac{\$10}{0.12} = \$83.33$

Price of high-payout stock: $$P_0 = \frac{\$30}{0.12} = \$250.00$$

c. For corporations, after-tax return is 12% for each type of stock.

For individuals, after-tax returns are:

For low-payout stock: $$\frac{(0.50 \times \$5) + (0.85 \times \$15)}{\$166.67} = 9.15\%$$

For medium-payout stock: $$\frac{(0.50 \times \$5) + (0.85 \times \$5)}{\$83.33} = 8.10\%$$

For high-payout stock: $$\frac{(0.50 \times \$30) + (0.85 \times \$0)}{\$250.00} = 6.00\%$$

For corporations, after-tax returns are:

For low-payout stock: $$\frac{(0.95 \times \$5) + (0.65 \times \$15)}{\$166.67} = 8.70\%$$

For medium-payout stock: $$\frac{(0.95 \times \$5) + (0.65 \times \$5)}{\$83.33} = 9.60\%$$

For high-payout stock: $$\frac{(0.95 \times \$30) + (0.65 \times \$0)}{\$250.00} = 11.40\%$$

d.

	Low Payout	Medium Payout	High Payout
Individuals	$80 billion		
Corporations			$10 billion
Institutions	$20 billion	$50 billion	$110 billion

CHAPTER 18

Does Debt Policy Matter?

Answers to Practice Questions

9. a. The two firms have equal value; let V represent the total value of the firm. Rosencrantz could buy one percent of Company B's equity and borrow an amount equal to:

$$0.01 \times (D_A - D_B) = 0.002V$$

This investment requires a net cash outlay of (0.007V) and provides a net cash return of:

$$(0.01 \times \text{Profits}) - (0.003 \times r_f \times V)$$

where r_f is the risk-free rate of interest on debt. Thus, the two investments are identical.

b. Guildenstern could buy two percent of Company A's equity and lend an amount equal to:

$$0.02 \times (D_A - D_B) = 0.004V$$

This investment requires a net cash outlay of (0.018V) and provides a net cash return of:

$$(0.02 \times \text{Profits}) - (0.002 \times r_f \times V)$$

Thus the two investments are identical.

c. The expected dollar return to Rosencrantz' original investment in A is:

$$(0.01 \times C) - (0.003 \times r_f \times V_A)$$

where C is the expected profit (cash flow) generated by the firm's assets. Since the firms are the same except for capital structure, C must also be the expected cash flow for Firm B. The dollar return to Rosencrantz' alternative strategy is:

$$(0.01 \times C) - (0.003 \times r_f \times V_B)$$

Also, the cost of the original strategy is $(0.007V_A)$ while the cost of the alternative strategy is $(0.007V_B)$.

If V_A is less than V_B, then the original strategy of investing in Company A would provide a larger dollar return at the same time that it would cost less than the alternative. Thus, no rational investor would invest in Company B if the value of Company A were less than that of Company B.

10. When a firm issues debt, it shifts its cash flow into two streams. MM's Proposition I states that this does not affect firm value if the investor can reconstitute a firm's cash flow stream by creating personal leverage or by undoing the effect of the firm's leverage by investing in both debt and equity.

It is similar with Carruther's cows. If the cream and skim milk go into the same pail, the cows have no special value. (If an investor holds both the debt and equity, the firm does not add value by splitting the cash flows into the two streams.) In the same vein, the cows have no special value if a dairy can costlessly split up whole milk into cream and skim milk. (Firm borrowing does not add value if investors can borrow on their own account.) Carruther's cows will have extra value if consumers want cream and skim milk and if the dairy cannot split up whole milk, or if it is costly to do so.

11. a. The market price of the stock is not affected by the announcement.

b. Since the market price of the shares is $10, the company can buy back:

$160 million/$10 = 16 million shares

c. After the change in capital structure, the market value of the firm is unchanged:

Equity + Debt = (9 million × $10) + $160 million = $250 million

d. After the change in structure, the debt ratio is:

Debt/(Debt + Equity) = $160 million/$250 million = 0.64

e. No one gains or loses. (See the answer to the next question.)

12. a. The market value of the firm's equity increases by $30 million, the amount of the decrease in the market value of the firm's existing debt. Therefore, the price of the stock increases to:

($150 million + $30 million)/15 million shares = $12

b. Since the market price of the shares is $12, the company can buy back:

$60 million/$12 = 5 million shares

c. After the change in capital structure, the market value of the firm is unchanged:

Equity + Debt = (10 million × $12) + $130 million = $250 million

d. After the change in structure, the debt ratio is:

Debt/(Debt + Equity) = $130 million/$250 million = 0.52

e. The investors in the existing debt lose $30 million while the shareholders gain this $30 million. The value of each share increases by:

$30 million/15 million shares = $2

13. The company cost of capital is:

$$r_A = (0.8 \times 0.12) + (0.2 \times 0.06) = 0.108 = 10.8\%$$

Under Proposition I, this is unaffected by capital structure changes. With the bonds remaining at the 6% default-risk free rate, we have:

Debt-Equity Ratio	r_E	r_A
0.00	0.108	0.108
0.10	0.113	0.108
0.50	0.132	0.108
1.00	0.156	0.108
2.00	0.204	0.108
3.00	0.252	0.108

See figure on next page.

14. This is not a valid objection. MM's Proposition II explicitly allows for the rates of return for both debt and equity to increase as the proportion of debt in the capital structure increases. The rate for debt increases because the debt-holders are taking on more of the risk of the firm; the rate for common stock increases because of increasing financial leverage. See Figure 18.2 and the accompanying discussion.

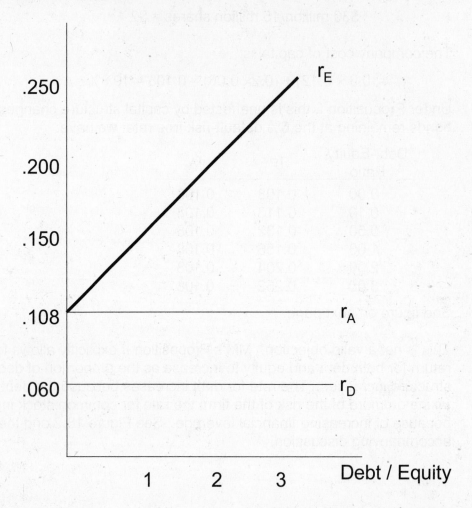

Rates of Return

.250 — r_E

.200

.150

.108 — r_A

.060 — r_D

$\qquad$ 1 $\qquad$ 2 $\qquad$ 3 $\qquad$ Debt / Equity

15.   a.   Under Proposition I, the firm's cost of capital (r_A) is not affected by the choice of capital structure. The reason the quoted statement seems to be true is that it does not account for the changing proportions of the firm financed by debt and equity. As the debt-equity ratio increases, it is true that both the cost of equity and the cost of debt increase, but a smaller proportion of the firm is financed by equity. The overall effect is to leave the firm's cost of capital unchanged.

       b.   Moderate borrowing does not significantly affect the probability of financial distress, but it does increase the variability (and market risk) borne by stockholders. This additional risk must be offset by a higher average return to stockholders.

16.   a.   If the opportunity were the firm's only asset, this would be a good deal. Stockholders would put up no money and, therefore, would have nothing to lose. However, rational lenders will not advance 100% of

the asset's value for an 8% promised return unless other assets are put up as collateral.

Sometimes firms find it convenient to borrow all the cash required for a particular investment. Such investments do not support all of the additional debt; lenders are protected by the firm's other assets too.

In any case, if firm value is independent of leverage, then any asset's contribution to firm value must be independent of how it is financed. Note also that the statement ignores the effect on the stockholders of an increase in financial leverage.

b. This is not an important reason for conservative debt levels. So long as MM's Proposition I holds, the company's overall cost of capital is unchanged despite increasing interest rates paid as the firm borrows more. (However, the increasing interest rates may signal an increasing probability of financial distress—and that can be important.)

17. Examples of such securities are given in the text and include unbundled stock units, preferred equity redemption cumulative stock and floating-rate notes. Note that, in order to succeed, such securities must both meet regulatory requirements and appeal to an unsatisfied clientele.

18. a. As leverage is increased, the cost of equity capital rises. This is the same as saying that, as leverage is increased, the ratio of the income after interest (which is the cash flow stockholders are entitled to) to the value of equity increases. Thus, as leverage increases, the ratio of the market value of the equity to income after interest decreases.

b. (i) Assume MM are correct. The market value of the firm is determined by the income of the firm, not how it is divided among the firm's security holders. Also, the firm's income before interest is independent of the firm's financing. Thus, both the value of the firm and the value of the firm's income before interest remain constant as leverage is increased. Hence, the ratio is a constant.

(ii) Assume the traditionalists are correct. The firm's income before interest is independent of leverage. As leverage increases, the firm's cost of capital first decreases and then increases; as a result, the market value of the firm first increases and then decreases. Thus, the ratio of the market value of the firm to firm income before interest first increases and then decreases, as leverage increases.

19. We begin with r_E and the capital asset pricing model:

$$r_E = r_f + \beta_E (r_m - r_f) = 0.10 + 1.5 (0.18 - 0.10) = 0.22 = 22.0\%$$

Similarly for debt:

$$r_D = r_f + \beta_D (r_m - r_f)$$

$$0.12 = 0.10 + \beta_D (0.18 - 0.10)$$

$$\beta_D = 0.25$$

Also, we know that:

$$r_A = \left(\frac{D}{D+E} \times r_D \right) + \left(\frac{E}{D+E} \times r_E \right) = (0.5 \times 0.12) + (0.5 \times 0.22) = 0.17 = 17.0\%$$

To solve for β_A, use the following:

$$\beta_A = \left(\frac{D}{D+E} \times \beta_D \right) + \left(\frac{E}{D+E} \times \beta_E \right) = (0.5 \times 0.25) + (0.5 \times 1.5) = 0.875$$

20. We know from Proposition I that the value of the firm will not change. Also, because the expected operating income is unaffected by changes in leverage, the firm's overall cost of capital will not change. In other words, r_A remains equal to 17% and β_A remains equal to 0.875. However, risk and, hence, the expected return for equity and for debt, will change. We know that r_D is 11%, so that, for debt:

$$r_D = r_f + \beta_D (r_m - r_f)$$

$$0.11 = 0.10 + \beta_D (0.18 - 0.10)$$

$$\beta_D = 0.125$$

For equity:

$$r_A = \left(\frac{D}{D+E} \times r_D \right) + \left(\frac{E}{D+E} \times r_E \right)$$

$$0.17 = (0.3 \times 0.11) + (0.7 \times r_E)$$

$$r_E = 0.196 = 19.6\%$$

Also:

$$r_E = r_f + \beta_E (r_m - r_f)$$

$$0.196 = 0.10 + \beta_E (0.18 - 0.10)$$

$$\beta_E = 1.20$$

21. [Note: In the following solution, we have assumed that $200 million of long-term bonds have been issued.]

   a. E = $55 \times 10 million = $550 million

   V = D + E = $200 million + $550 million = $750 million

   $$\frac{D}{V} = \frac{\$200 \text{million}}{\$750 \text{million}} = 0.267$$

$$\frac{E}{V} = \frac{\$550\text{million}}{\$750\text{million}} = 0.733$$

$$\text{After-tax WACC} = r_D(1-T_C)\frac{D}{V} + r_E\frac{E}{V}$$

$$= 0.07 \times (1-0.35) \times 0.267 + (0.12 \times 0.733) = 0.1001 = 10.01\%$$

b.   The after-tax WACC would increase to the extent of the loss of the tax deductibility of the interest on debt. Therefore, the after-tax WACC would equal the opportunity cost of capital, computed from the WACC formula without the tax-deductibility of interest:

$$\text{WACC} = r_D\frac{D}{V} + r_E\frac{E}{V} = (0.07 \times 0.267) + (0.12 \times 0.733) = 0.1067 = 10.67\%$$

22.   We make use of the basic relationship:

$$r_A = \left(r_D(1-T_C)\frac{D}{V} \right) + \left(r_E \times \frac{E}{V} \right)$$

Since overall beta (β_A) is not affected by capital structure or taxes, then:

$$r_A = r_f + \beta_A (r_m - r_f) = 0.06 + (1.5 \times 0.08) = 0.18$$

The following table shows the value of r_E for various values of D/E (and the corresponding values of D/V), derived from the above formula. The graph is on the next page.

D/E	D/V	r_A	r_D	r_E
0.00	0.00000	0.18	0.0600	0.1800
0.05	0.04762	0.18	0.0600	0.1871
0.10	0.09091	0.18	0.0600	0.1941
0.15	0.13043	0.18	0.0600	0.2012
0.20	0.16667	0.18	0.0600	0.2082
0.25	0.20000	0.18	0.0600	0.2153
0.30	0.23077	0.18	0.0610	0.2221
0.35	0.25926	0.18	0.0620	0.2289
0.40	0.28571	0.18	0.0630	0.2356
0.45	0.31034	0.18	0.0640	0.2423
0.50	0.33333	0.18	0.0650	0.2489
0.55	0.35484	0.18	0.0660	0.2554
0.60	0.37500	0.18	0.0670	0.2619
0.65	0.39394	0.18	0.0680	0.2683
0.70	0.41176	0.18	0.0690	0.2746
0.75	0.42857	0.18	0.0690	0.2814
0.80	0.44444	0.18	0.0700	0.2876
0.85	0.45946	0.18	0.0725	0.2929
0.90	0.47368	0.18	0.0750	0.2981
0.95	0.48718	0.18	0.0775	0.3031
1.00	0.50000	0.18	0.0800	0.3080

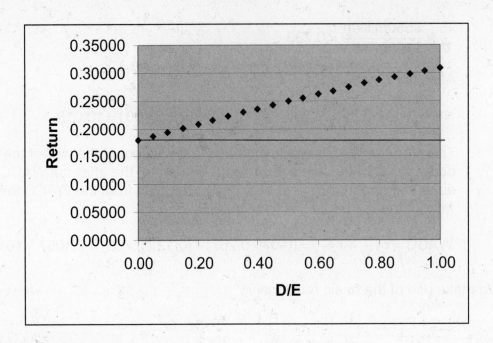

Challenge Questions

23. Assume the election is near so that we can safely ignore the time value of money.

Because one, and only one, of three events will occur, the guaranteed payoff from holding all three tickets is $10. Thus, the three tickets, taken together, could never sell for less than $10. This is true whether they are bundled into one composite security or unbundled into three separate securities.

However, unbundled they may sell for more than $10. This will occur if the separate tickets fill a need for some currently unsatisfied clientele. If this is indeed the case, then Proposition I fails. The sum of the parts is worth more than the whole.

24. Some shoppers may want only the chicken drumstick. They could buy a whole chicken, cut it up, and sell off the other parts in the supermarket parking lot. This is costly. It is far more efficient for the store to cut up the chicken and sell the pieces separately. But this also has some cost, hence the observation that supermarkets charge more for chickens after they have been cut.

The same considerations affect financial products, but:

a. The proportionate costs to companies of repackaging the cash flow stream are generally small.

b. Investors can also repackage cash flows cheaply for themselves. In fact, specialist financial institutions can often do so more cheaply than the companies can do it themselves.

25. Firms that are able to identify an 'unsatisfied' clientele and then design a financial service or instrument that satisfies the demands of this clientele can, in violation of MM's capital-structure irrelevance theory, enhance firm value. However, if this

is done successfully by one financial innovator, others will follow, eventually restoring the validity of the MM irrelevance theory.

If the financial innovation can be patented, the creator of the innovation can restrict the use of the innovation by other financial managers and thereby continue to use the innovation to create value. Consequently, MM's capital-structure irrelevance theory would potentially be violated during the life of the patent.

CHAPTER 19

How Much Should a Firm Borrow?

Answers to Practice Questions

12. a. $\text{PV(tax shield)} = \dfrac{T_c(r_D D)}{1 + r_D} = \dfrac{0.35(0.08 \times \$1,000)}{1.08} = \$25.93$

 b. $\text{PV(tax shield)} = \sum\limits_{t=1}^{5} \dfrac{0.35(0.08 \times \$1,000)}{(1.08)^t} = \$111.80$

 c. $\text{PV(tax shield)} = T_C D = \$350$

13. For $1 of debt income:

  Corporate tax = $0
  Personal tax = 0.35 × $1 = $0.350
    Total = $0.350

 For $1 of equity income, with all capital gains realized immediately:

  Corporate tax = 0.35 × $1 = $0.350
  Personal tax = 0.35 × 0.5 × [$1 − (0.35×$1)] + 0.15 × 0.5 × [$1 − (0.35×$1)] = $0.163
    Total = $0.513

 For $1 of equity income, with all capital gains deferred forever:

  Corporate tax = 0.35 × $1 = $0.350
  Personal tax = 0.35 × 0.5 × [$1 − (0.35×$1)] = $0.114
    Total = $0.464

14. Consider a firm that is levered, has perpetual expected cash flow X, and has an interest rate for debt of r_D. The personal and corporate tax rates are T_p and T_c, respectively. The cash flow to stockholders each year is:

 $(X - r_D D)(1 - T_c)(1 - T_p)$

 Therefore, the value of the stockholders' position is:

 $$V_L = \dfrac{(X)(1 - T_c)(1 - T_p)}{(r)(1 - T_p)} - \dfrac{(r_D)(D)(1 - T_c)(1 - T_p)}{(r_D)(1 - T_p)}$$

 $$V_L = \dfrac{(X)(1 - T_c)(1 - T_p)}{(r)(1 - T_p)} - [(D)(1 - T_c)]$$

where r is the opportunity cost of capital for an all-equity-financed firm. If the stockholders borrow D at the same rate r_D, and invest in the unlevered firm, their cash flow each year is:

$$[(X)(1-T_c)(1-T_p)] - [(r_D)(D)(1-T_p)]$$

The value of the stockholders' position is then:

$$V_U = \frac{(X)(1-T_c)(1-T_p)}{(r)(1-T_p)} - \frac{(r_D)(D)(1-T_p)}{(r_D)(1-T_p)}$$

$$V_U = \frac{(X)(1-T_c)(1-T_p)}{(r)(1-T_p)} - D$$

The difference in stockholder wealth, for investment in the same assets, is:

$$V_L - V_U = DT_c$$

This is the change in stockholder wealth predicted by MM.

If individuals could not deduct interest for personal tax purposes, then:

$$V_U = \frac{(X)(1-T_c)(1-T_p)}{(r)(1-T_p)} - \frac{(r_D)(D)}{(r_D)(1-T_p)}$$

Then:

$$V_L - V_U = \frac{(r_D)(D) - [(r_D)(D)(1-T_c)(1-T_p)]}{(r_D)(1-T_p)}$$

$$V_L - V_U = (D T_c) + \left(D \frac{T_p}{(1-T_p)} \right)$$

So the value of the shareholders' position in the levered firm is relatively greater when no personal interest deduction is allowed.

15. Long-term debt increases by: $10,000 − $6,126 = $3,874 million

The corporate tax rate is 35%, so firm value increases by:

0.35 × $3,874 = $1,355.9 million

The market value of the firm is now: $83,385.0 + $1,355.9 = $84,740.9 million

The market value balance sheet is:

Net working capital	$7,746.00	$10,000.00	Long-term debt
PV interest tax shield	3,679.90	8,500.00	Other long-term liabilities
Long-term assets	73,315.00	66,240.90	Equity
Total Assets	$84,740.90	$84,740.90	Total value

16. Internet exercise; answers will vary depending on the time period.

17. Assume the following facts for Circular File:

Book Values

Net working capital	$20	$50	Bonds outstanding
Fixed assets	80	50	Common stock
Total assets	$100	$100	Total value

Market Values

Net working capital	$20	$25	Bonds outstanding
Fixed assets	10	5	Common stock
Total assets	$30	$30	Total value

a. <u>Playing for Time</u>
Suppose Circular File foregoes replacement of $10 of capital equipment, so that the new balance sheet may appear as follows:

Market Values

Net working capital	$30	$29	Bonds outstanding
Fixed assets	8	9	Common stock
Total assets	$38	$38	Total value

Here the shareholder is better off but has obviously diminished the firm's competitive ability.

b. <u>Cash In and Run</u>
Suppose the firm pays a $5 dividend:

Market Values

Net working capital	$15	$23	Bonds outstanding
Fixed assets	10	2	Common stock
Total assets	$25	$25	Total value

Here the value of common stock should have fallen to zero, but the bondholders bear part of the burden.

c. <u>Bait and Switch</u>

Market Values

Net working capital	$30	$20	New Bonds outstanding
		20	Old Bonds outstanding
Fixed assets	20	10	Common stock
Total assets	$50	$50	Total value

18. Answers here will vary according to the companies chosen; however, the important considerations are given in the text, Section 19.3.

19. a. Stockholders win. Bond value falls since the value of assets securing the bond has fallen.

b. Bondholder wins if we assume the cash is left invested in Treasury bills. The bondholder is sure to get $26 plus interest. Stock value is zero because there is no chance that the firm value can rise above $50.

c. The bondholders lose. The firm adds assets worth $10 and debt worth $10. This would increase Circular's debt ratio, leaving the old bondholders more exposed. The old bondholders' loss is the stockholders' gain.

d. Both bondholders and stockholders win. They share the (net) increase in firm value. The bondholders' position is not eroded by the issue of a junior security. (We assume that the preferred does not lead to still more game playing and that the new investment does not make the firm's assets safer or riskier.)

e. Bondholders lose because they are at risk for a longer time. Stockholders win.

20. a. SOS stockholders could lose if they invest in the positive NPV project and then SOS becomes bankrupt. Under these conditions, the benefits of the project accrue to the bondholders.

b. If the new project is sufficiently risky, then, even though it has a negative NPV, it might increase stockholder wealth by more than the money invested. This is a result of the fact that, for a very risky investment, undertaken by a firm with a significant risk of default, stockholders benefit if a more favorable outcome is actually realized, while the cost of unfavorable outcomes is borne by bondholders.

c. Again, think of the extreme case: Suppose SOS pays out all of its assets as one lump-sum dividend. Stockholders get all of the assets, and the bondholders are left with nothing.

21. a. The bondholders benefit. The fine print limits actions that transfer wealth from the bondholders to the stockholders.

b. The stockholders benefit. In the absence of fine print, bondholders charge a higher rate of interest to ensure that they receive a fair deal. The firm would probably issue the bond with standard restrictions. It is likely that the restrictions would be less costly than the higher interest rate.

22. Other things equal, the announcement of a new stock issue to fund an investment project with an NPV of $40 million should increase equity value by $40 million (less issue costs). But, based on past evidence, management expects equity value to fall by $30 million. There may be several reasons for the discrepancy:

(i) Investors may have already discounted the proposed investment. (However, this alone would not explain a fall in equity value.)

(ii) Investors may not be aware of the project at all, but they may believe instead that cash is required because of, say, low levels of operating cash flow.

(iii) Investors may believe that the firm's decision to issue equity rather than debt signals management's belief that the stock is overvalued.

If the stock is indeed overvalued, the stock issue merely brings forward a stock price decline that will occur eventually anyway. Therefore, the fall in value is not an issue cost in the same sense as the underwriter's spread. If the stock is not overvalued, management needs to consider whether it could release some information to convince investors that its stock is correctly valued, or whether it could finance the project by an issue of debt.

23. a. Masulis' results are consistent with the view that debt is always preferable because of its tax advantage, but are not consistent with the 'tradeoff' theory, which holds that management strikes a balance between the tax advantage of debt and the costs of possible financial distress. In the tradeoff theory, exchange offers would be undertaken to move the firm's debt level toward the optimum. That ought to be good news, if anything, regardless of whether leverage is increased or decreased.

b. The results are consistent with the evidence regarding the announcement effects on security issues and repurchases.

c. One explanation is that the exchange offers signal management's assessment of the firm's prospects. Management would only be willing to take on more debt if they were quite confident about future cash flow, for example, and would want to decrease debt if they were concerned about the firm's ability to meet debt payments in the future.

24. a.

	Expected Payoff to Bank	Expected Payoff to Ms. Ketchup
Project 1	+10.0	+5
Project 2	$(0.4 \times 10) + (0.6 \times 0) = +4.0$	$(0.4 \times 14) + (0.6 \times 0) = +5.6$

Ms. Ketchup would undertake Project 2.

b. Break even will occur when Ms. Ketchup's expected payoff from Project 2 is equal to her expected payoff from Project 1. If X is Ms. Ketchup's payment on the loan, then her payoff from Project 2 is:

$0.4 (24 - X)$

Setting this expression equal to 5 (Ms. Ketchup's payoff from Project 1), and solving, we find that: $X = 11.5$

Therefore, Ms. Ketchup will borrow less than the present value of this payment.

25. Internet exercise; answers will vary.

26. Internet exercise; answers will vary.

Challenge Questions

27. The right measure in principle is the ratio derived from market-value balance sheets. Book balance sheets represent historical values for debt and equity which can be significantly different from market values. Any changes in capital structure are made at current market values.

    The trade-off theory proposes to explain market leverage. Increases or decreases in debt levels take place at market values. For example, a decision to reduce the likelihood of financial distress by retirement of debt means that existing debt is acquired at market value, and that the resulting decrease in interest tax shields is based on the market value of the retired debt. Similarly, a decision to increase interest tax shields by increasing debt requires that new debt be issued at current market prices.

    Similarly, the pecking-order theory is based on market values of debt and equity. Internal financing from reinvested earnings is equity financing based on current market values; the alternative to increased internal financing is a distribution of earnings to shareholders. Debt capacity is measured by the current market value of debt because the financial markets view the amount of existing debt as the payment required to pay off that debt.

28. Internet exercise; answers will vary.

CHAPTER 20

Financing and Valuation

Answers to Practice Questions

11. If the bank debt is treated as permanent financing, the capital structure proportions are:

Bank debt (r_D = 10 percent)	$280	9.4%
Long-term debt (r_D = 9 percent)	1800	60.4
Equity (r_E = 18 percent, 90 x 10 million shares)	900	30.2
	$2980	100.0%

$$\text{WACC*} = [0.10\times(1 - 0.35)\times0.094] + [0.09\times(1 - 0.35)\times0.604] + [0.18\times0.302]$$
$$= 0.096 = 9.6\%$$

12. Forecast after-tax incremental cash flows as explained in Section 7.1. Interest is not included; the forecasts assume an all-equity financed firm.

13. Calculate APV by subtracting $4 million from base-case NPV.

14. We make three adjustments to the balance sheet:

- Ignore deferred taxes; this is an accounting entry and represents neither a liability nor a source of funds
- 'Net out' accounts payable against current assets
- Use the market value of equity (7.46 million x $46)

Now the right-hand side of the balance sheet (in thousands) is:

Short-term debt	$75,600
Long-term debt	208,600
Shareholders' equity	343,160
Total	$627,360

The after-tax weighted-average cost of capital formula, with one element for each source of funding, is:

$$\text{WACC} = [r_{D\text{-}ST}\times(1 - T_c)\times(D\text{-}ST/V)]+[r_{D\text{-}LT}\times(1 - T_c)\times(D\text{-}LT/V)]+[r_E \times(E/V)]$$

$$\text{WACC} = [0.06\times(1 - 0.35)\times(75,600/627,360)]+[0.08\times(1 - 0.35)\times(208,600/627,360)]$$
$$+ [0.15\times(343,160/627,360)]$$
$$= 0.004700 + 0.017290 + 0.082049 = 0.1040 = 10.40\%$$

15. Assume that short-term debt is temporary. From Practice Question 14:

Long-term debt $208,600
Share holder equity 343,160
Total $551,760

Therefore:

$$D/V = \$208,600/\$551,760 = 0.378$$

$$E/V = \$343,160/\$551,760 = 0.622$$

Step 1:

$$r = r_D (D/V) + r_E (E/V) = (0.08 \times 0.378) + (0.15 \times 0.622) = 0.1235$$

Step 2:

$$r_E = r + (r - r_D)(D/E) = 0.1235 + (0.1235 - 0.08) \times 0.403 = 0.1410$$

Step 3:

$$WACC = [r_D \times (1 - T_C) \times (D/V)] + [r_E \times (E/V)]$$

$$= (0.08 \times 0.65 \times 0.287) + (0.1410 \times 0.713) = 0.1155 = 11.55\%$$

16. Base case NPV = $-\$1,000 + (\$600/1.12) + (\$700/1.12^2) = \$93.75$ or $93,750

Year	Debt Outstanding at Start Of Year	Interest	Interest Tax Shield	PV (Tax Shield)
1	300	24	7.20	6.67
2	150	12	3.60	3.09

APV = $93.75 + $6.67 + $3.09 = 103.5 or $103,500

17. a. Base-case NPV = $-\$1,000,000 + (\$95,000/0.10) = -\$50,000$

PV(tax shields) = $0.35 \times \$400,000 = \$140,000$

APV = $-\$50,000 + \$140,000 = \$90,000$

b. PV(tax shields, approximate) = $(0.35 \times 0.07 \times \$400,000)/0.10 = \$98,000$

APV = $-\$50,000 + \$98,000 = \$48,000$

The present value of the tax shield is higher when the debt is fixed and therefore the tax shield is certain. When borrowing a constant proportion of the market value of the project, the interest tax shields are as uncertain as the value of the project, and therefore must be discounted at the project's opportunity cost of capital.

18. The immediate source of funds (i.e., both the proportion borrowed and the expected return on the stocks sold) is irrelevant. The project would not be any more valuable if the university sold stocks offering a lower return. If borrowing

is a zero-NPV activity for a tax-exempt university, then base-case NPV equals APV, and the adjusted cost of capital r* equals the opportunity cost of capital with all-equity financing. Here, base-case NPV is negative; the university should not invest.

19. a. $$\text{Base-case NPV} = -\$10 + \sum_{t=1}^{10} \frac{\$1.75}{1.12^t} = -\$0.11 \text{ or } -\$110,000$$

APV = Base-case NPV + PV(tax shield)

PV(tax shield) is computed from the following table:

Year	Debt Outstanding at Start of Year	Interest	Interest Tax Shield	Present Value of Tax Shield
1	$5,000	$400	$140	$129.63
2	4,500	360	126	108.02
3	4,000	320	112	88.91
4	3,500	280	98	72.03
5	3,000	240	84	57.17
6	2,500	200	70	44.11
7	2,000	160	56	32.68
8	1,500	120	42	22.69
9	1,000	80	28	14.01
10	500	40	14	6.48
			Total	575.74

APV = –$110,000 + $575,740 = $465,740

b. APV = Base-case NPV + PV(tax shield) – equity issue costs

= –$110,000 + $575,740 – $400,000 = $65,740

20. Answers will vary.

21. Note the following:

- The costs of debt and equity are not 8.5% and 19%, respectively. These figures assume the issue costs are paid every year, not just at issue.

- The fact that Bunsen can finance the entire cost of the project with debt is irrelevant. The cost of capital does not depend on the immediate source of funds; what matters is the project's contribution to the firm's overall borrowing power.

- The project is expected to support debt in perpetuity. The fact that the first debt issue is for only 20 years is irrelevant.

Assume the project has the same business risk as the firm's other assets. Because it is a perpetuity, we can use the firm's weighted-average cost of capital. If we ignore issue costs:

$$WACC = [r_D \times (1 - T_C) \times (D/V)] + [r_E \times (E/V)]$$

$$WACC = [0.07 \times (1 - 0.35) \times 0.4] + [0.14 \times 0.6] = 0.1022 = 10.22\%$$

Using this discount rate:

$$NPV = -\$1,000,000 + \frac{\$130,000}{0.1022} = \$272,016$$

The issue costs are:

Stock issue: $0.050 \times \$1,000,000 = \$50,000$

Bond issue: $0.015 \times \$1,000,000 = \$15,000$

Debt is clearly less expensive. Project NPV net of issue costs is reduced to: ($272,016 – $15,000) = $257,016. However, if debt is used, the firm's debt ratio will be above the target ratio, and more equity will have to be raised later. If debt financing can be obtained using retaining earnings, then there are no other issue costs to consider. If stock will be issued to regain the target debt ratio, an additional issue cost is incurred.

A careful estimate of the issue costs attributable to this project would require a comparison of Bunsen's financial plan 'with' as compared to 'without' this project.

22.   Disagree. The Goldensacks calculations are based on the assumption that the cost of debt will remain constant, and that the cost of equity capital will not change even though the firm's financial structure has changed. The former assumption is appropriate while the latter is not.

23.   a.   Assume that the expected future Treasury-bill rate is equal to the 20-year Treasury bond rate (4.8%) less the average historical premium of Treasury bonds over Treasury bills over the period 1900–2005 (1.3%), so that the risk-free rate (r_f) is 3.5%. Also assume that the market risk premium ($r_m - r_f$) is 8%. Then, using the CAPM, we find r_E as follows:

$$r_E = r_f + \beta_A \times [r_m - r_f] = 3.5\% + (0.98 \times 8\%) = 11.34\%$$

Market value of equity (E) is equal to: $330.7 \times \$66.51 = \$21,994.9$ so that:

$V = \$2,019.8 + \$21,994.9 = \$24,014.7$

$D/V = \$2,019.8/\$24,014.7 = 0.084$

$E/V = \$21,994.9/\$24,014.7 = 0.916$

$WACC = (0.916 \times 11.34\%) + (0.084 \times 0.65 \times 6.3\%) = 10.73\%$

b.   Opportunity cost of capital = $r = r_D \times (D/V) + r_E \times (E/V)$

$$= 6.3\% \times 0.084 + 11.34\% \times 0.916 = 10.92\%$$

c.   Internet exercise; answers will vary.

24.

		Latest year	Forecast				
		0	1	2	3	4	5
1.	Sales	40,123.0	36,351.0	30,155.0	28,345.0	29,982.0	30,450.0
2.	Cost of Goods Sold	22,879.0	21,678.0	17,560.0	16,459.0	15,631.0	14,987.0
3.	Other Costs	8,025.0	6,797.0	5,078.0	4,678.0	4,987.0	5,134.0
4.	EBITDA (1 – 2 – 3)	9,219.0	7,876.0	7,517.0	7,208.0	9,364.0	10,329.0
5.	Depreciation and Amortization	5,678.0	5,890.0	5,670.0	5,908.0	6,107.0	5,908.0
6.	EBIT (Pretax profit) (4 – 5)	3,541.0	1,986.0	1,847.0	1,300.0	3,257.0	4,421.0
7.	Tax at 35%	1,239.4	695.1	646.5	455.0	1,140.0	1,547.4
8.	Profit after tax (6 – 7)	2,301.7	1,290.9	1,200.6	845.0	2,117.1	2,873.7
9.	Change in working capital	784.0	–54.0	–342.0	–245.0	127.0	235.0
10.	Investment (change in Gross PP&E)	6,547.0	7,345.0	5,398.0	5,470.0	6,420.0	6,598.0
11.	Free Cash Flow (8 + 5 – 9 – 10)	648.7	–110.1	1,814.6	1,528.0	1,677.1	1,948.7

PV Free cash flow, years 1–4	**3,501.6**	**Horizon value in year 4**
PV Horizon value	**15,480.0**	**24,358.1**
PV of company	**18,981.7**	

The total value of the equity is: $18,981.7 – $5,000 = $13,981.7

Value per share = $13,981.7/865 = $16.16

25.   The award is risk-free because it is owed by the U.S. government. The after-tax amount of the award is: 0.65 × $16 million = $10.40 million

The after-tax discount rate is: 0.65 × 0.055 = 0.03575 = 3.575%

The present value of the award is: $10.4 million/1.03575 = $10.04 million

26.   The after-tax cash flows are: 0.65 × $100,000 = $65,000 per year

The after-tax discount rate is: 0.65 × 0.09 = 0.0585 = 5.85%

The present value of the lease is equal to the present value of a five-year annuity of $65,000 per year plus the immediate $65,000 payment:

$65,000 × [annuity factor, 5.85%, 5 years] + $65,000 =

($65,000 × 4.2296) + $65,000 = $339,924

27.   a.   For a one-period project to have zero APV:

$$APV = C_0 + \frac{C_1}{1 + r_A} + \frac{(T_C \times r_D \times D)}{1 + r_D} = 0$$

Rearranging gives:

$$\frac{C_1}{-C_0} - 1 = r - (T_C \times r_D)\left(\frac{D}{-C_0}\right)\left(\frac{1 + r_A}{1 + r_D}\right)$$

For a one-period project, the left-hand side of this equation is the project IRR. Also, $(D/-C_0)$ is the project's debt capacity. Therefore, the minimum acceptable return is:

$$r^* = r_A - (T_C \times r_D \times L)\left(\frac{1 + r_A}{1 + r_D}\right)$$

    b. $r^* = 0.0984 - (0.35 \times 0.06 \times 0.20)\left(\dfrac{1.0984}{1.06}\right) = .09405$

28.   Fixed debt levels, without rebalancing, are not necessarily better for stockholders. Note that, when the debt is rebalanced, next year's interest tax shields are fixed and, thus, discounted at a lower rate. The following year's interest is not known with certainty for one year and, hence, is discounted for one year at the higher risky rate and for one year at the lower rate. This is much more realistic since it recognizes the uncertainty of future events.

29.   The table below is a modification of Table 20.1 based on the assumption that, after year 7:

- Sales remain constant (that is, growth = 0%);
- Costs remain at 76.0% of sales;
- Depreciation remains at 14.0% of net fixed assets;
- Net fixed assets remain constant at 93.8;
- Working capital remains at 13.0% of sales.

TABLE 20.1 Free cash flow projections and company value for Rio Corporation ($ millions)

		Latest year				Forecast				
		0	**1**	**2**	**3**	**4**	**5**	**6**	**7**	**8**
1.	Sales	83.6	89.5	95.8	102.5	106.6	110.8	115.2	118.7	118.7
2.	Cost of goods sold	63.1	66.2	71.3	76.3	79.9	83.1	87.0	90.2	90.2
3.	EBITDA (1 − 2)	20.5	23.3	24.4	26.1	26.6	27.7	28.2	28.5	28.5
4.	Depreciation	3.3	9.9	10.6	11.3	11.8	12.3	12.7	13.1	13.1
5.	Profit before tax (EBIT) (3 − 4)	17.2	13.4	13.8	14.8	14.9	15.4	15.5	15.4	15.4
6.	Tax	6.0	4.7	4.8	5.2	5.2	5.4	5.4	5.4	5.4
7.	Profit after tax (5 − 6)	11.2	8.7	9.0	9.6	9.7	10.0	10.1	10.0	10.0
8.	Investment in fixed assets	11.0	14.6	15.5	16.6	15.0	15.6	16.2	15.9	13.1
9.	Investment in working capital	1.0	0.5	0.8	0.9	0.5	0.6	0.6	0.4	0.0
10.	Free cash flow (7 + 4 − 8 − 9)	2.5	3.5	3.2	3.4	5.9	6.1	6.0	6.8	10.0
	PV Free cash flow, years 1–7	24.0								
	PV Horizon value	60.7					(Horizon value in year 7) 110.9				
	PV of company	84.7								
	Assumptions:									
	Sales growth (percent)	6.7	7.0	7.0	7.0	4.0	4.0	4.0	3.0	0.0
	Costs (percent of sales)	75.5	74.0	74.5	74.5	75.0	75.0	75.5	76.0	76.0
	Working capital (% of sales)	13.3	13.0	13.0	13.0	13.0	13.0	13.0	13.0	13.0
	Net fixed assets (% of sales)	79.2	79.0	79.0	79.0	79.0	79.0	79.0	79.0	79.0
	Depreciation (% net fixed assets)	5.0	14.0	14.0	14.0	14.0	14.0	14.0	14.0	14.0
	Tax rate, %	35.0								
	Cost of debt, % (r_D)	6.0								
	Cost of equity, % (r_E)	12.4								
	Debt ratio (D/V)	0.4								
	WACC, %	9.0								

Long-term growth forecast, %	0.0							

Fixed assets and working capital

Gross fixed assets	95.0	109.6	125.1	141.8	156.8	172.4	188.6	204.5	217.6
Less accumulated depreciation	29.0	38.9	49.5	60.8	72.6	84.9	97.6	110.7	123.9
Net fixed assets	66.0	70.7	75.6	80.9	84.2	87.5	91.0	93.8	93.8
Net working capital	11.1	11.6	12.4	13.3	13.9	14.4	15.0	15.4	15.4

CHAPTER 21

Understanding Options

Answers to Practice Questions

12. a. The put places a floor on value of investment, i.e., less risky than buying stock. The risk reduction comes at the cost of the option premium.

    b. Benefit from upside, but also lose on the downside.

    c. A naked option position is riskier than the underlying asset. Investor gains from increase in stock price, but loses entire investment if stock price is less than exercise price at expiration.

    d. Investor exchanges uncertain upside changes in stock price for the known up-front income from the option premium.

    e. Safe investment if the debt is risk free.

    f. From put-call parity, this is equivalent (for European options) to 'buy bond.' Therefore, this is a safe investment.

    g. Another naked, high-risk position with known up-front income but exposure to down movements in stock price.

13 While it is true that both the buyer of a call and the seller of a put hope the price will rise, the two positions are not identical. The buyer of a call will find her profit changing from zero and increasing as the stock price rises [see text Figure 21.1(a)], while the seller of a put will find his loss decreasing and then remaining at zero as the stock price rises [see text Figure 21.2(b)].

14. You would buy the American call for $75, exercise the call immediately in order to purchase a share of Pintail stock for $50, and then sell the share of Pintail stock for $200. The net gain is: $200 – ($75 + $50) = $75.

    If the call is a European call, you should buy the call, deposit in the bank an amount equal to the present value of the exercise price, and sell the stock short. This produces a current cash flow equal to: $200 – $75 – ($50/1 + r)

    At the maturity of the call, the action depends on whether the stock price is greater than or less than the exercise price. If the stock price is greater than $50, then you would exercise the call (using the cash from the bank deposit) and buy back the stock. If the stock price is less than $50, then you would let the call expire and buy back the stock. The cash flow at maturity is the greater of zero (if the stock price is greater than $50) or [$50 – stock price] (if the stock price is less than $50). Therefore, the cash flows are positive now and zero or positive one year from now.

15   [Note: In order to solve this problem, we assume r = 5%.]

Let P_3 = the value of the three month put, C_3 = the value of the three month call, S = the market value of a share of stock, and EX = the exercise price of the options. Then, from put-call parity:

$$C_3 + [EX/(1 + r)^{0.25}] = P_3 + S$$

Since both options have an exercise price of $60 and both are worth $10, then:

$$S = EX/(1 + r)^{0.25} = \$60/(1.05)^{0.25} = \$59.27$$

16.   From put-call parity:

$$C + [EX/(1 + r)^{(1/3)}] = P + S$$

$$P = -S + C + [EX/(1 + r)^{(1/3)}] = -39 + 2.85 + [40/(1.053^{(1/3)})] = \$3.17$$

17.   Internet exercise; answers will vary.

18.   The $100 million threshold can be viewed as an exercise price. Since she gains 20% of all profits in excess of this level, it is comparable to a call option. Whether this provides an adequate incentive depends on how achievable the $100 million threshold is and how Ms. Cable evaluates her prospects of generating income greater than this amount.

19.   a.   The payoffs at expiration for the two options are shown in the following position diagram:

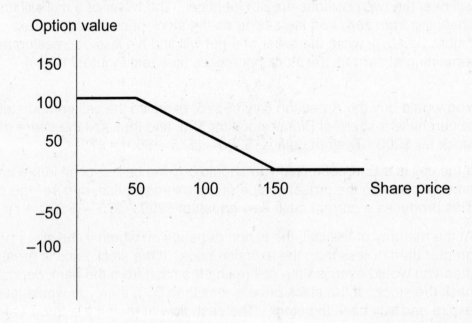

Taking into account the $100 that must be repaid at expiration, the net payoffs are:

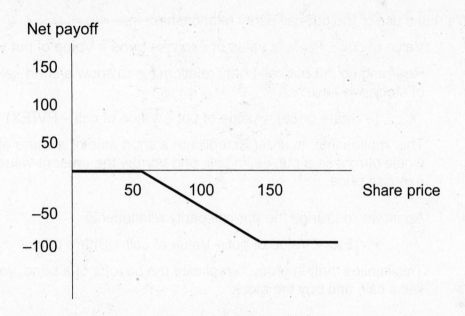

b.	Here we can use the put-call parity relationship:

Value of call + Present value of exercise price = Value of put + Share price

The value of Mr. Colleoni's position is:

Value of put (EX = 150) – Value of put (EX = 50) – PV (150 – 50)

Using the put-call parity relationship, we find that this is equal to:

Value of call (EX = 150) – Value of call (EX = 50)

Thus, one combination that gives Mr. Colleoni the same payoffs is:

- Buy a call with an exercise price of $150
- Sell a call with an exercise price of $50

Similarly, another combination with the same set of payoffs is:

- Buy a put with an exercise price of $150
- Buy a share of stock
- Borrow the present value of $150
- Sell a call with an exercise price of $50

20.	Statement (b) is correct. The appropriate diagrams are in Figure 21.6 in the text. The first row of diagrams in Figure 21.6 shows the payoffs for the strategy:

Buy a share of stock and buy a put.

The second row of Figure 21.6 shows the payoffs for the strategy:

Buy a call and lend an amount equal to the exercise price.

21. Answers here will vary depending on the options chosen, but the formulas will work very well; discrepancies should be on the order of 5 percent or so, at most.

22. We make use of the put-call parity relationship:

Value of call + Present value of exercise price = Value of put + Share price

a. Rearranging the put-call parity relationship to show a short sale of a share of stock, we have:

(– Share price) = Value of put – Value of call – PV(EX)

This implies that, in order to replicate a short sale of a share of stock, you would purchase a put, sell a call, and borrow the present value of the exercise price.

b. Again we rearrange the put-call parity relationship:

PV(EX) = Value of put – Value of call + Share price

This implies that, in order to replicate the payoffs of a bond, you buy a put, sell a call, and buy the stock.

23. a. Use the put-call parity relationship for European options:

Value of call + Present value of exercise price = Value of put + Share price

Solve for the value of the put:

Value of put = Value of call + PV(EX) – Share price

Thus, to replicate the payoffs for the put, you would buy a 26-week call with an exercise price of $100, invest the present value of the exercise price in a 26-week risk-free security, and sell the stock short.

b. Using the put-call parity relationship, the European put will sell for:

$8 + ($100/1.05) – $90 = $13.24

24. a.

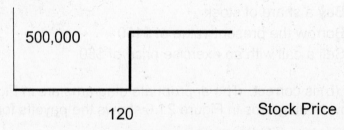

b. This incentive scheme is a combination of the following options:

- Buy 4,000,000 call options with an exercise price of $119.875.
- Sell 4,000,000 call options with an exercise price of $120.

25.   Straddle

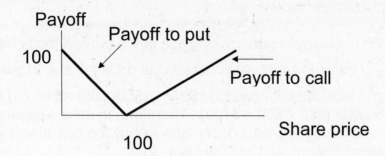

Butterfly

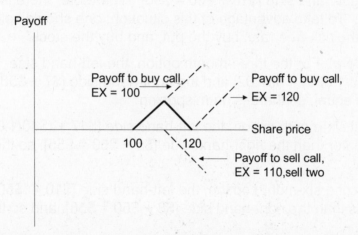

The buyer of the straddle profits if the stock price moves substantially in either direction; hence, the straddle is a bet on high variability. The buyer of the butterfly profits if the stock price doesn't move very much, and hence, this is a bet on low variability.

26.   Answers here will vary according to the stock and the specific options selected, but all should exhibit properties very close to those predicted by the theory described in the chapter.

27.   Imagine two stocks, each with a market price of $100. For each stock, you have an at-the-money call option with an exercise price of $100. Stock A's price now falls to $50 and Stock B's rises to $150. The value of your portfolio of call options is now:

	Value
Call on A	0
Call on B	50
Total	$50

Now compare this with the value of an at-the-money call to buy a portfolio with equal holdings of A and B. Since the average change in the prices of the two stocks is zero, the call expires worthless.

This is an example of a general rule: An option on a portfolio is less valuable than a portfolio of options on the individual stocks because, in the latter case, you can choose which options to exercise.

28. Consider each company in turn, making use of the put-call parity relationship:

Value of call + Present value of exercise price = Value of put + Share price

Drongo Corp. Here, the left-hand side [$52 + ($50/1.05) = $99.62] is less than the right-hand side [$20 + $80 = $100]. Therefore, there is a slight mispricing. To take advantage of this situation, one should buy the call, invest $47.62 at the risk-free rate, sell the put, and sell the stock short.

Ragwort, Inc. Here, the left-hand side [$15 + ($100/1.05) = $110.24) is greater than the right-hand side [$10 + $80 = $90]. Therefore, there is a significant mispricing. To take advantage of this situation, one should sell the call, borrow $95.24 at the risk-free rate, buy the put, and buy the stock.

Wombat Corp. For the three-month option, the left-hand side [$18 + ($40/1.025) = $57.02] and the right-hand side [$7 + $50 = $57] are essentially equal, so there is no mispricing.

For the first six-month option, the left-hand side [$17 + ($40/1.05) = $55.10] is slightly greater than the right-hand side [$5 + $50 = $55], so there is a slight mispricing.

For the second six-month option, the left-hand side [$10 + ($50/1.05) = $57.62] is slightly less than the right-hand side [$8 + $50 = $58], and so there is a slight mispricing.

29. One strategy might be to buy a straddle, that is, buy a call and a put with exercise price equal to the asset's current price. If the asset price does not change, both options become worthless. However, if the price falls, the put will be valuable and, if price rises, the call will be valuable. The larger the price movement in either direction, the greater the profit.

If investors have underestimated volatility, the option prices will be too low. Thus, an alternative strategy is to buy a call (or a put) and hedge against changes in the asset price by simultaneously selling (or, in the case of the put, buying) delta shares of stock.

Challenge Questions

30. a. Purchase a call with a given exercise price and sell a call with a higher exercise price; borrow the difference necessary. (This is known as a 'Bull Spread.')

    b. Sell a put and sell a call with the same exercise price. (This is known as a 'Short Straddle.')

c. Borrow money and use this money to buy a put and buy the stock.

d. Buy one call with a given exercise price, sell two calls with a higher exercise price, and buy one call with a still higher exercise price. (This is known as a 'Butterfly Spread.')

31. a. If the land is worth more than $110 million, Bond will exercise its call option. If the land is worth less than $110 million, the buyer will exercise its put option.

b. Bond has: (1) sold a share; (2) sold a put; and (3) purchased a call. Therefore:

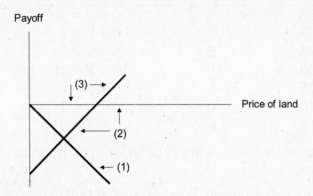

This is equivalent to:

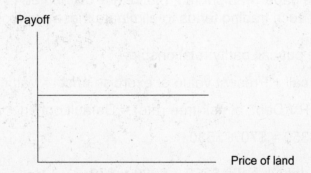

c. The interest rate can be deduced using the put-call parity relationship. We know that the call is worth $20, the exercise price is $110, and the combination [sell share and sell put option] is worth $110. Therefore:

Value of call + Present value of exercise price = Value of put + Share price

Value of call + PV(EX) = Value of put + Share price

$20 + [110/(1 + r)] = 110$

$r = 0.222 = 22.2\%$

d. From the answer to Part (a), we know that Bond will end up owning the land after the expiration of the options. Thus, in an economic sense, the land has not really been sold, and it seems misleading to declare a profit on a sale that did not really take place. In effect, Bond has borrowed money, not sold an asset.

32. One way to profit from Hogswill options is to purchase the call options with exercise prices of $90 and $110, respectively, and sell two call options with an exercise price of $100. The immediate benefit is a cash inflow of:

$$(2 \times \$11) - (\$5 + \$15) = \$2$$

Immediately prior to maturity, the value of this position and the net profit (at various possible stock prices) is:

Stock Price	Position Value	Net Profit
85	0	0 + 2 = 2
90	0	0 + 2 = 2
95	5	5 + 2 = 7
100	10	10 + 2 = 12
105	5	5 + 2 = 7
110	0	0 + 2 = 2
115	0	0 + 2 = 2

Thus, no matter what the final stock price, we can make a profit trading in these Hogswill options.

It is possible, but very unlikely, that you can identify such opportunities from data published in the newspaper. Someone else has most likely already noticed (even before the paper was printed, much less distributed to you) and traded on the information; such trading tends to eliminate these profit opportunities.

33. a. From the put-call parity relationship:

Value of call + Present value of exercise price = Value of put + Share price

Equity + PV(Debt, at risk-free rate) = Default option + Assets

$250 + $350 = $70 + $530

b. Value of default put = $350 – $280 = $70

Answers to Practice Questions

9.   a. $u = e^{0.24\sqrt{0.5}} = 1.185$; $d = 1/u = 0.844$

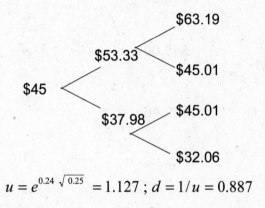

$u = e^{0.24\sqrt{0.25}} = 1.127$; $d = 1/u = 0.887$

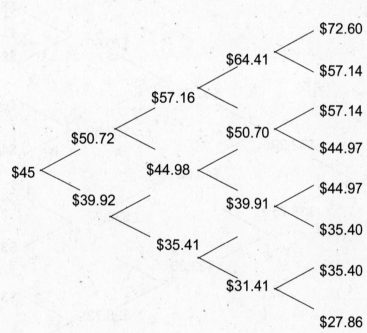

b. $u = e^{0.3\sqrt{0.5}} = 1.236$, $d = 1/u = 0.809$

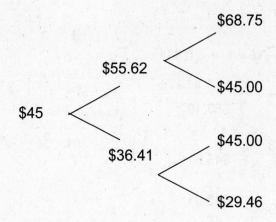

$u = e^{0.3\sqrt{0.25}} = 1.162$; $d = 1/u = 0.861$

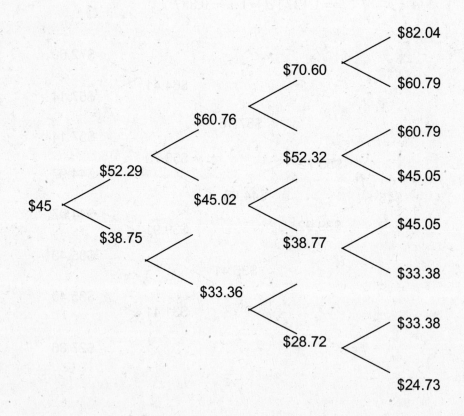

10.   a.   Let p equal the probability of a rise in the stock price. Then, if investors are risk-neutral:

$(p \times 0.15) + (1 - p) \times (-0.13) = 0.10$

$p = 0.821$

The possible stock prices next period are:

$$\$60 \times 1.15 = \$69.00$$

$$\$60 \times 0.87 = \$52.20$$

Let X equal the break-even exercise price. Then the following must be true:

$$X - 60 = [(p)(\$0) + (1 - p)(X - 52.20)]/1.10$$

That is, the value of the put if exercised immediately equals the value of the put if it is held to next period. Solving for X, we find that the break-even exercise price is $61.52.

b. If the interest rate is increased, the value of the put option decreases.

11. a. The future stock prices of Moria Mining are:

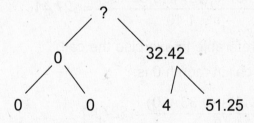

With dividend

Ex-dividend

Let p equal the probability of a rise in the stock price. Then, if investors are risk-neutral:

$$(p \times 0.25) + (1 - p) \times (-0.20) = 0.10$$

$$p = 0.67$$

Now, calculate the expected value of the call in month 6.

If stock price decreases to $80 in month 6, then the call is worthless. If stock price increases to $125, then, if it is exercised at that time, it has a value of ($125 – $80) = $45. If the call is not exercised, then its value is:

$$\frac{(0.67 \times \$51.25) + (0.33 \times \$4)}{1.10} = \$32.42$$

Therefore, it is preferable to exercise the call.

The value of the call in month 0 is:

$$\frac{(0.67 \times \$45) + (0.33 \times \$0)}{1.10} = \$27.41$$

b. The future stock prices of Moria Mining are:

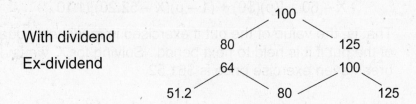

With dividend

Ex-dividend

Let p equal the probability of a rise in the price of the stock. Then, if investors are risk-neutral:

$(p \times 0.25) + (1 - p) \times (-0.20) = 0.10$

$p = 0.67$

Now, calculate the expected value of the call in month 6.

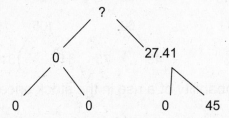

If stock price decreases to $80 in month 6, then the call is worthless. If stock price increases to $125, then, if it is exercised at that time, it has a value of ($125 – $80) = $45. If the call is not exercised, then its value is:

$$\frac{(0.67 \times \$45) + (0.33 \times \$0)}{1.10} = \$27.41$$

Therefore, it is preferable to exercise the call.

The value of the call in month 0 is:

$$\frac{(0.67 \times \$45) + (0.33 \times \$0)}{1.10} = \$27.41$$

12. a. The possible prices of Buffelhead stock and the associated call option values (shown in parentheses) are:

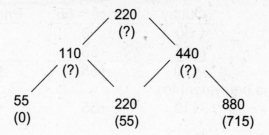

Let p equal the probability of a rise in the stock price. Then, if investors are risk-neutral:

$$p (1.00) + (1 - p) \times (-0.50) = 0.10$$

$$p = 0.4$$

If the stock price in month 6 is $110, then the option will not be exercised so that it will be worth:

$$[(0.4 \times \$55) + (0.6 \times \$0)]/1.10 = \$20$$

Similarly, if the stock price is $440 in month 6, then, if it is exercised, it will be worth ($440 − $165) = $275. If the option is not exercised, it will be worth:

$$[(0.4 \times \$715) + (0.6 \times \$55)]/1.10 = \$290$$

Therefore, the call option will not be exercised, so that its value today is:

$$[(0.4 \times \$290) + (0.6 \times \$20)]/1.10 = \$116.36$$

b. (i) If the price rises to $440:

$$\text{Delta} = \frac{715-55}{880-220} = 1.0$$

(ii) If the price falls to $110:

$$\text{Delta} = \frac{55-0}{220-55} = 0.33$$

c. The option delta is 1.0 when the call is certain to be exercised and is zero when it is certain not to be exercised. If the call is certain to be exercised, it is equivalent to buying the stock with a partly deferred payment. So a one-dollar change in the stock price must be matched by a one-dollar change in the option price. At the other extreme, when the call is certain not to be exercised, it is valueless, regardless of the change in the stock price.

d.   If the stock price is $110 at 6 months, the option delta is 0.33. Therefore, in order to replicate the stock, we buy three calls and lend, as follows:

	Initial Outlay	Stock Price = 55	Stock Price = 220
Buy 3 calls	–60	0	165
Lend PV(55)	–50	+55	+55
	–110	+55	+220

This strategy Is equivalent to:

Buy stock	–110	+55	+220

13.   a.   Yes, it is rational to consider the early exercise of an American put option.

    b.   The possible prices of Buffelhead stock and the associated American put option values (shown in parentheses) are:

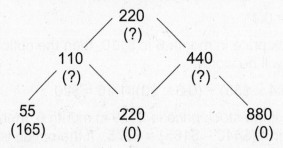

Let p equal the probability of a rise in the stock price. Then, if investors are risk-neutral:

p (1.00) + (1 – p) × (–0.50) = 0.10

p = 0.4

If the stock price in month 6 is $110, and if the American put option is not exercised, it will be worth:

[(0.4 × $0) + (0.6 × $165)]/1.10 = $90

On the other hand, if it is exercised after 6 months, it is worth $110. Thus, the investor should exercise the put early.

Similarly, if the stock price in month 6 is $440, and if the American put option is not exercised, it will be worth:

[(0.4 × $0) + (0.6 × $0)]/1.10 = $0

On the other hand, if it is exercised after 6 months, it will cost the investor $220. The investor should not exercise early.

Finally, the value today of the American put option is:

[(0.4 × $0) + (0.6 × $110)]/1.10 = $60

c. Unlike the American put in part (b), the European put can not be exercised prior to expiration. We noted in part (b) that, If the stock price in month 6 is $110, the American put would be exercised because its value if exercised (i.e., $110) is greater than its value if not exercised (i.e., $90). For the European put, however, the value at that point is $90 because the European put can not be exercised early. Therefore, the value of the European put is:

$$[(0.4 \times \$0) + (0.6 \times \$90)]/1.10 = \$49.09$$

14. a. The following tree shows stock prices, with option values in parentheses:

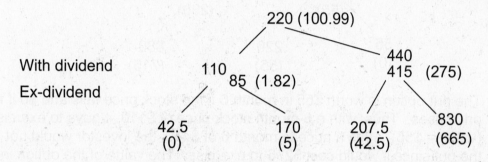

We calculate the option value as follows:

1. The option values in month 6, if the option is not exercised, are computed as follows:

$$\frac{(0.4 \times \$5) + (0.6 \times \$0)}{1.10} = \$1.82$$

$$\frac{(0.4 \times \$665) + (0.6 \times \$42.5)}{1.10} = \$265$$

If the stock price in month 6 is $110, then it would not pay to exercise the option. If the stock price in month 6 is $440, then the call is worth: ($440 – $165) = $275. Therefore, the option would be exercised at that time.

2. Working back to month 0, we find the option value as follows:

$$\text{Option value} = \frac{(0.4 \times \$275) + (0.6 \times \$1.82)}{1.10} = \$100.99$$

b. If the option were European, it would not be possible to exercise early. Therefore, if the price rises to $440 at month 6, the value of the option is $265, not $275 as is the case for the American option. Therefore, in this case, the value of the European option is less than the value of the American option. The value of the European option is computed as follows:

$$\text{Option value} = \frac{(0.4 \times \$265) + (0.6 \times \$1.82)}{1.10} = \$97.36$$

15. The following tree (see Practice Question 12) shows stock prices, with the values for the option in parentheses:

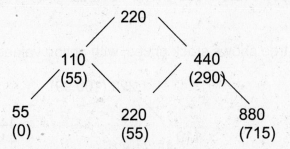

The put option is worth $55 in month 6 if the stock price falls and $0 if the stock price rises. Thus, with a 6-month stock price of $110, it pays to exercise the put (value = $55). With a price in month 6 of $440, the investor would not exercise the put since it would cost $275 to exercise. The value of the option in month 6, if it is not exercised, is determined as follows:

$$\frac{(0.4 \times \$715) + (0.6 \times \$55)}{1.10} = \$290$$

Therefore, the month 0 value of the option is:

$$\text{Option value} = \frac{(0.4 \times \$290) + (0.6 \times \$55)}{1.10} = \$135.45$$

16. a. The following tree shows stock prices (with put option values in parentheses):

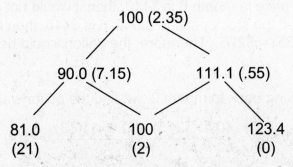

Let p equal the probability that the stock price will rise. Then, for a risk-neutral investor:

$$(p \times 0.111) + (1 - p) \times (-0.10) = 0.05$$

$$p = 0.71$$

If the stock price in month 6 is C$111.1, then the value of the European put is:

$$\frac{(0.71 \times C\$0) + (0.29 \times C\$2)}{1.05} = C\$0.55$$

If the stock price in month 6 is C$90.0, then the value of the put is:

$$\frac{(0.71 \times C\$2) + (0.29 \times C\$21)}{1.05} = C\$7.15$$

Since this is a European put, it can not be exercised at month 6.

The value of the put at month 0 is:

$$\frac{(0.71 \times C\$0.55) + (0.29 \times C\$7.15)}{1.05} = C\$2.35$$

b. Since the American put can be exercised at month 6, then, if the stock price is C$90.0, the put is worth (C$102 – C$90) = C$12 if exercised, compared to C$7.15 if not exercised. Thus, the value of the American put in month 0 is:

$$\frac{(0.71 \times C\$0.55) + (0.29 \times C\$12)}{1.05} = C\$3.69$$

17. a. P = 200   EX = 180 σ = 0.223   t = 1.0 r_f = 0.21

$d_1 = \log[P/PV(EX)]/\sigma\sqrt{t} + \sigma\sqrt{t}/2$

$\quad = \log[200/(180/1.21)]/(0.223 \times \sqrt{1.0}) + (0.223 \times \sqrt{1.0})/2 = 1.4388$

$d_2 = d_1 - \sigma\sqrt{t} = 1.4388 - (0.223 \times \sqrt{1.0}) = 1.2158$

$N(d_1) = N(1.4388) = 0.9249$

$N(d_2) = N(1.2158) = 0.8880$

Call value = $[N(d_1) \times P] - [N(d_2) \times PV(EX)]$

$\quad\quad\quad = [0.9249 \times 200] - [0.8880 \times (180/1.21)] = \$52.88$

b.

$1 + \text{upside change} = u = e^{\sigma\sqrt{h}} = e^{0.223\sqrt{1.0}} = 1.2498$

$1 + \text{downside change} = d = 1/u = 1/1.2498 = 0.8001$

Let p equal the probability that the stock price will rise. Then, for a risk-neutral investor:

$\quad\quad (p \times 0.25) + (1 - p) \times (-0.20) = 0.21$

$\quad\quad p = 0.91$

In one year, the stock price will be either $250 or $160, and the option values will be $70 or $0, respectively. Therefore, the value of the option is:

$$\frac{(0.91 \times 70) + (0.09 \times 0)}{1.21} = \$52.64$$

c.

$$1 + \text{upside change} = u = e^{\sigma\sqrt{h}} = e^{0.223\sqrt{0.5}} = 1.1708$$
$$1 + \text{downside change} = d = 1/u = 1/1.1708 = 0.8541$$

Let p equal the probability that the stock price will rise. Then, for a risk-neutral investor:

$$(p \times 0.171) + (1 - p) \times (-0.146) = 0.10$$
$$p = 0.776$$

The following tree gives stock prices, with option values in parentheses:

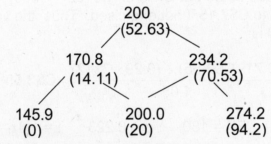

```
                        200
                      (52.63)
            170.8              234.2
           (14.11)            (70.53)
     145.9         200.0             274.2
      (0)          (20)              (94.2)
```

Option values are calculated as follows:

1. $\dfrac{(0.776 \times \$20) + (0.224 \times \$0)}{1.10} = \$14.11$

2. $\dfrac{(0.224 \times \$20) + (0.776 \times \$94.2)}{1.10} = \$70.53$

3. $\dfrac{(0.224 \times \$14.11) + (0.776 \times \$70.53)}{1.10} = \$52.63$

d. (i) $$\text{Option delta} = \frac{\text{spread of possible option prices}}{\text{spread of possible stock prices}}$$

$$\text{Option delta} = \frac{70.53 - 14.11}{234.2 - 170.8} = 0.89$$

To replicate a call, buy 0.89 shares and borrow:

$$[(0.89 \times \$170.8) - \$14.11]/1.10 = \$125.37$$

(ii) $\qquad$ Option delta $= \dfrac{94.2 - 20}{274.2 - 200} = 1.00$

To replicate a call, buy one share and borrow:

[(1.0 × $274.2) – $94.2]/1.10 = $163.64

(iii) $\qquad$ Option delta $= \dfrac{20 - 0}{200 - 145.9} = 0.37$

To replicate a call, buy 0.37 shares and borrow:

[(0.37 × $200) – $20]/1.10 = $49.09

18. To hold time to expiration constant, we will look at a simple one-period binomial problem with different starting stock prices. Here are the possible stock prices:

Now consider the effect on option delta:

Option Deltas		Current Stock Price	
		100	110
In-the-money	(EX = 60)	140/150 = 0.93	160/165 = 0.97
At-the-money	(EX = 100)	100/150 = 0.67	120/165 = 0.73
Out-of-the-money	(EX = 140)	60/150 = 0.40	80/165 = 0.48

Note that, for a given difference in stock price, out-of-the-money options result in a larger change in the option delta. If you want to minimize the number of times you rebalance an option hedge, use in-the-money options.

19. a. The call option. (You would delay the exercise of the put until after the dividend has been paid and the stock price has dropped.)

b. The put option. (You never exercise a call if the stock price is below exercise price.)

c. The put when the interest rate is high. (You can invest the exercise price.)

20. a. When you exercise a call, you purchase the stock for the exercise price. Naturally, you want to maximize what you receive for this price, and so you would exercise on the with-dividend date in order to capture the dividend.

b. When you exercise a put, your gain is the difference between the price of the stock and the amount you receive upon exercise, i.e., the exercise price.

Therefore, in order to maximize your profit, you want to minimize the price of the stock and so you would exercise on the ex-dividend date.

21. Internet exercise; answers will vary.

22. a. The value of the alternative share = (V/N) where V is the total value of equity (common stock plus warrants) and N is the number of shares outstanding. For Electric Bassoon:

$$\frac{V}{N} = \frac{20{,}000 + 5{,}000}{2{,}000} = \$12.50$$

When valuing the warrant, we use the standard deviation of this alternative 'share.' This can be obtained from the following relationship:

The proportion of the firm financed by equity (calculated before the issue of the warrant) *times* the standard deviation of stock returns (calculated before the issue of the warrant)

is equal to

the proportion of the firm financed by equity (calculated after the issue of the warrant) *times* the standard deviation of the alternative share.

b. The value of the warrant is equal to the value of [1/(1 + q)] call options on the alternative share, where q is the number of warrants issued per share outstanding. For Electric Bassoon:

q = 1,000/2,000 = 0.5

Therefore:

1/(1 + q) = 1/1.5 = 0.67

The value of the warrant is: (0.67 × $6) = $4
At the current price of $5 the warrants are overvalued.

23. P = 8.30   EX = 12.45 σ = 0.87   t = 5.0 r_f = 0.028

$d_1 = \log[P/PV(EX)]/\sigma\sqrt{t} + \sigma\sqrt{t}/2$

$\quad = \log[8.30/(12.45/1.028)]/(0.87 \times \sqrt{5.0}) + (0.87 \times \sqrt{5.0})/2 = 0.8352$

$d_2 = d_1 - \sigma\sqrt{t} = 0.8352 - (0.87 \times \sqrt{5.0}) = -1.1101$

$N(d_1) = N(0.8352) = 0.7982$

$N(d_2) = N(-1.1101) = 0.1335$

Call value = $[N(d_1) \times P] - [N(d_2) \times PV(EX)]$

$\quad = [0.7982 \times 8.30] - [0.1335 \times (8.30/1.028^5)] = \$5.18$

24. Individual exercise; answers will vary.

25.   For the one-period binomial model, assume that the exercise price of the options (EX) is between u and d. Then, the spread of possible option prices is:

For the call: [(u – EX) – 0]

For the put: [(d – EX) – 0]

The option deltas are:

Option delta(call) = [(u – EX) – 0]/(u – d) = (u – EX)/(u – d)

Option delta(put) = [(d – EX) – 0]/(u – d) = (d – EX)/(u – d)

Therefore:

[Option delta(call) – 1] = [(u – EX)/(u – d)] – 1

= [(u – EX)]/(u – d)] – [(u – d)/(u – d)]

= [(u – EX) – (u – d)]/(u – d)

= [d – EX]/(u – d) = Option delta(put)

26.   If the exercise price of a call is zero, then the option is equivalent to the stock, so that, in order to replicate the stock, you would buy one call option. Therefore, if the exercise price is zero, the option delta is one. If the exercise price of a call is indefinitely large, then the option value remains low even if there is a large percentage change in the price of the stock. Therefore, the dollar change in the value of the option will be much smaller than the dollar change in the price of the stock, so that the option delta is close to zero. Between these two extreme cases, the option delta varies between zero and one.

27.   Both of these announcements may convey information about company prospects, and thereby affect the price of the stock. But, when the dividend is paid, stock price decreases by an amount approximately equal to the amount of the dividend. This price decrease reduces the value of the option. On the other hand, a stock repurchase at the market price does not affect the price of the stock. Therefore, you should hope that the board will decide to announce a stock repurchase program.

28.   a.   As the life of the call option increases, the present value of the exercise price becomes infinitesimal. Thus the only difference between the call option and the stock is that the option holder misses out on any dividends. If dividends are negligible, the value of the option approaches its upper bound, i.e., the stock price.

b.   While it is true that the value of an option approaches the upper bound as maturity increases and dividend payments on the stock decrease, a stock that never pays dividends is valueless.

CHAPTER 23

Real Options

Answers to Practice Questions

9. a. A five-year American call option on oil. The initial exercise price is C$70 a barrel, but the exercise price rises by 5% per year.

    b. An American put option to abandon the restaurant at an exercise price of $5 million. The restaurant's current value is ($700,000/r). The annual standard deviation of the changes in the value of the restaurant as a going concern is 15%.

    c. A put option, as in (b), except that the exercise price should be interpreted as $5 million in real estate value plus the present value of the future fixed costs avoided by closing down the restaurant. Thus, the exercise price is: $5,000,000 + ($300,000/0.10) = $8,000,000. Note: The underlying asset is now PV(revenue – variable cost), with annual standard deviation of 10.5%.

    d. A complex option that allows the company to abandon temporarily (an American put) and (if the put is exercised) to subsequently restart (an American call).

    e. An in-the-money American option to choose between two assets; that is, the developer can defer exercise and then determine whether it is more profitable to build a hotel or an apartment building. By waiting, however, the developer loses the cash flows from immediate development.

    f. A call option that allows Air France to fix the delivery date and price.

10. a. $P = 467 \qquad EX = 800 \qquad \sigma = 0.35 \qquad t = 3.0 \qquad r_f = 0.10$

    $$d_1 = \log[P/PV(EX)]/\sigma\sqrt{t} + \sigma\sqrt{t}/2$$

    $$= \log[467/(800/1.10^3)]/(0.35 \times \sqrt{3.0}) + (0.35 \times \sqrt{3.0})/2 = -0.1132$$

    $$d_2 = d_1 - \sigma\sqrt{t} = -0.1132 - (0.35 \times \sqrt{3.0}) = -0.7194$$

    $N(d_1) = N(-0.1132) = 0.4550$

    $N(d_2) = N(-0.7194) = 0.2360$

    Call value $= [N(d_1) \times P] - [N(d_2) \times PV(EX)]$

    $$= [0.4550 \times 467] - [0.2360 \times (800/1.10^3)] = \$70.64$$

b. $\quad$ P = 500 $\qquad$ EX = 900 $\qquad$ σ = 0.35 $\qquad$ t = 3.0 $\qquad$ r_f = 0.10

$$d_1 = \log[P/PV(EX)]/\sigma\sqrt{t} + \sigma\sqrt{t}/2$$

$$= \log[500/(900/1.10^3)]/(0.35 \times \sqrt{3.0}) + (0.35 \times \sqrt{3.0})/2 = -0.1948$$

$$d_2 = d_1 - \sigma\sqrt{t} = -0.1948 - (0.35 \times \sqrt{3.0}) = -0.8010$$

$N(d_1) = N(-0.1948) = 0.4228$

$N(d_2) = N(-0.8010) = 0.2116$

Call value = $[N(d_1) \times P] - [N(d_2) \times PV(EX)]$

$$= [0.4228 \times 500] - [0.2116 \times (900/1.10^3)] = \$68.33$$

c. $\quad$ P = 467 $\qquad$ EX = 900 $\qquad$ σ = 0.20 $\qquad$ t = 3.0 $\qquad$ r_f = 0.10

$$d_1 = \log[P/PV(EX)]/\sigma\sqrt{t} + \sigma\sqrt{t}/2$$

$$= \log[467/(900/1.10^3)]/(0.20 \times \sqrt{3.0}) + (0.20 \times \sqrt{3.0})/2 = -0.8953$$

$$d_2 = d_1 - \sigma\sqrt{t} = -0.8953 - (0.20 \times \sqrt{3.0}) = -1.2417$$

$N(d_1) = N(-0.8953) = 0.1853$

$N(d_2) = N(-1.2417) = 0.1072$

Call value = $[N(d_1) \times P] - [N(d_2) \times PV(EX)]$

$$= [0.1853 \times 467] - [0.1072 \times (900/1.10^3)] = \$14.07$$

11. $\quad$ P = 1.7 $\qquad$ EX = 2 $\qquad$ σ = 0.15 $\qquad$ t = 1.0 $\qquad$ r_f = 0.12

$$d_1 = \log[P/PV(EX)]/\sigma\sqrt{t} + \sigma\sqrt{t}/2$$

$$= \log[1.7/(2/1.12^1)]/(0.15 \times \sqrt{1.0}) + (0.15 \times \sqrt{1.0})/2 = -0.2529$$

$$d_2 = d_1 - \sigma\sqrt{t} = -0.2529 - (0.15 \times \sqrt{1.0}) = -0.4029$$

$N(d_1) = N(-0.2529) = 0.4002$

$N(d_2) = N(-0.4029) = 0.3435$

Call value = $[N(d_1) \times P] - [N(d_2) \times PV(EX)]$

$$= [0.4002 \times 1.7] - [0.3435 \times (2/1.12^1)] = \$0.0669 \text{ million or } \$66,900$$

12. $\quad$ The asset value from Practice Question 11 is now reduced by the present value of the rents:

PV(rents) = 0.15/1.12 = 0.134

Therefore, the asset value is now (1.7 − 0.134) = 1.566

$\quad$ P = 1.566 $\qquad$ EX = 2 $\qquad$ σ = 0.15 $\qquad$ t = 1.0 r_f = 0.12

$$d_1 = \log[P/PV(EX)]/\sigma\sqrt{t} + \sigma\sqrt{t}/2$$
$$= \log[1.566/(2/1.12^1)]/(0.15 \times \sqrt{1.0}) + (0.15 \times \sqrt{1.0})/2 = -0.8003$$
$$d_2 = d_1 - \sigma\sqrt{t} = -0.8003 - (0.15 \times \sqrt{1.0}) = -0.9503$$

$$N(d_1) = N(-0.8003) = 0.2118$$

$$N(d_2) = N(-0.9503) = 0.1710$$

Call value = $[N(d_1) \times P] - [N(d_2) \times PV(EX)]$

$= [0.2118 \times 1.566] - [0.1710 \times (2/1.12^1)] = \$0.0263$ million or \$26,300

13.　a.　The values in the binomial tree below are the ex-dividend values, with the option values shown in parentheses.

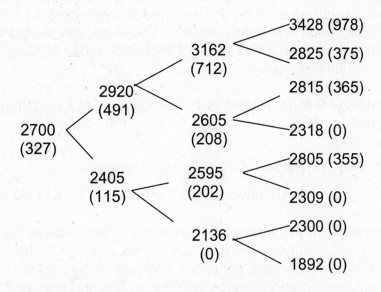

　　b.　The option values in the binomial tree above are computed using the risk neutral method. Let p equal the probability of a rise in asset value. Then, if investors are risk-neutral:

　　　　$p (0.10) + (1 - p) \times (-0.0909) = 0.02$

　　　　$p = 0.581$

If, for example, asset value at month 6 is \$3,162 (this is the value after the \$50 cash flow is paid to the current owners), then the option value will be:

　　　　$[(0.419 \times 375) + (0.581 \times 978)]/1.02 = \$711$

If the option is exercised at month 6 when asset value is $3,212 then the option value is: $3,212 – $2,500 = $712
Therefore, the option value is $712.

At each asset value in month 3 and in month 6, the option value if the option is not exercised is greater than or equal to the option value if the option is exercised. (The one minor exception here is the calculation above where we show that the value is $712 if the option is exercised and $711 if it is not exercised. Due to rounding, this difference does not affect any of our results and conclusions.) Therefore, under the condition specified in part (b), you should not exercise the option now because its value if not exercised ($327) is greater than its value if exercised ($200).

c. If you exercise the option early, it is worth the with-dividend value less $2,500. For example, if you exercise in month 3 when the with-dividend value is $2,970, the option would be worth: ($2,970 – $2,500) = $470. Since the option is worth $491 if not exercised, you are better off keeping the option open. At each point before month 9, the option is worth more unexercised than exercised. (As noted above in part (b) there is one minor exception to this conclusion.) Therefore, you should wait rather than exercise today. The value of the option today is $327, as shown in the binomial tree above.

14. a. Technology B is equivalent to Technology A less a certain payment of $0.5 million. Since PV(A) = $11.5 million then, ignoring abandonment value:

$$PV(B) = PV(A) - PV(\text{certain } \$0.5 \text{ million})$$

$$= \$11.5 \text{ million} - (\$0.5 \text{ million}/1.07) = \$11.03 \text{ million}$$

b. Assume that, if you abandon Technology B, you receive the $10 million salvage value but no operating cash flows. Then, if demand is sluggish, you should exercise the put option and receive $10 million. If demand is buoyant, you should continue with the project and receive $18 million. So, in year 1, the put would be worth: ($10 million – $8 million) = $2 million if demand is sluggish and $0 if demand is buoyant.

We can value the put using the risk-neutral method. If demand is buoyant, then the gain in value is: ($18 million/$11.03 million) –1 = 63.2%
If demand is sluggish, the loss is: ($8 million/$11.03 million) – 1 = –27.5%
Let p equal the probability of a rise in asset value. Then, if investors are risk-neutral:

$$p (0.632) + (1 - p) \times (-0.275) = 0.07$$

$$p = 0.38$$

Therefore, the value of the option to abandon is:

$$[(0.62 \times 0) + (0.38 \times 2)]/1.07 = \$0.71 \text{ million}$$

15. a.

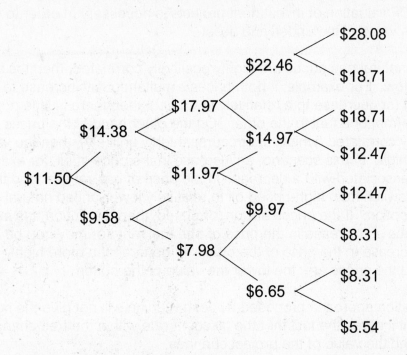

b. The only case in which one would want to abandon at the end of the year is if project value is $5.54 (i.e., if value declines in each of the four quarters). In this case, the value of the abandonment option would be: ($7 − $5.54) = $1.46

Let p equal the probability of a rise in asset value. Then, using the quarterly risk-free rate, we find that, if investors are risk-neutral:

$$p (0.25) + (1 - p) \times (-0.167) = 0.017$$

$$p = 0.441$$

The risk-neutral probability of a fall in value in each of the four quarters is:

$$(1 - 0.441)^4 = 0.0976$$

The expected risk-neutral value of the abandonment option is:

$$0.0976 \times 1.46 = 0.1425$$

The present value of the abandonment option is:

$$(0.0976 \times 1.46)/1.07 = 0.1332 \text{ or } \$133,200$$

16. a. You can't use any one discount rate for the option payoffs. The risk of an option changes as asset price changes and time passes.

b. The risky asset may be worth less as a consequence of its riskiness, but the option on the risky asset is more valuable because the option owner can capitalize from up moves while not losing due to down moves.

c.   The value of an option depends on the value of the underlying asset. DCF valuation of investment projects is necessary in order to determine the value of the underlying asset.

17.   If oil and natural gas prices are highly positively correlated, then the value of the option is low. For example, if both prices simultaneously increase to a relatively high level (or decrease to a relatively low level), then there is little or no benefit in switching from one fuel to the other. On the other hand, if the prices are negatively correlated (which is, or course, highly unlikely), then the value of the option is high. In this scenario, an increase in the price of oil, for example, will likely be associated with a decrease in the price of natural gas, and therefore the option to switch from high-priced oil to relatively lower-priced natural gas is a valuable option. If the prices are uncorrelated, then the option has moderate value, since an increase in the price of one fuel may (or may not) be associated with a decrease in the price of the other. In general, the more highly positively correlated the prices are, the lower the value of the option.

18.   The valuation approach proposed by Josh Kidding will not give the right answer because it ignores the fact that the discount rate within the tree changes as time passes and the value of the project changes.

19.   Excel problem; approaches will vary. However, answers should demonstrate the relationships identified in Table 21.2.

20.   The value of an option to acquire an asset (i.e., a call option) decreases with the difference between the risk-free rate of interest (r_f) and the weighted average cost of capital (WACC) of the asset. That is, as (WACC – r_f) increases, the value of the call option decreases. Suppose that the increase in (WACC – r_f) results from an increase in WACC, or a decrease in r_f, or both. Each of these changes decreases the value of a call. An increase in WACC reduces the present value of the underlying asset, which reduces the value of the call. Also, a decrease in r_f reduces the value of the call. An increase in (WACC – r_f) can also result from changes in both WACC and r_f in the same direction but by different amounts (e.g., both rates increase, but the percentage point increase in WACC is greater than the percentage point increase in r_f). While an increase in r_f increases the value of the call, this increase would typically be much smaller than the decrease in the value of the call resulting from an even larger percentage point increase in WACC. The impact of an increase r_f would arise from the effect of discounting over the life of the option, typically a relatively short period of time. An increase in WACC could have a substantial impact (due to the effect of discounting cash flows over long periods of time) on the present value of the underlying asset if cash flows occur several years in to the future.

21. You don't take delivery of the new plant until month 36. Think of the situation one month before completion. You have a call option to get the plant by paying the final month's construction costs to the contractors. One month before that, you have an option on the option to buy the plant. The exercise price of this second call option is the construction cost in the next to last month. And so on.

    Alternatively, you can think of the firm as agreeing to construction and putting the present value of the construction cost in an escrow account. Each month, the firm has the option to abandon the project and receive the unspent balance in the escrow account. Thus, in month 1, you have a put option on the project with an exercise price equal to the amount in the escrow account. If you do not exercise the put in month 1, you get another option to abandon it in month 2. The exercise price of this option is the amount in the escrow account in month 2. And so on.

22. a. An increase in PVGO increases the stock's risk. Since PVGO is a portfolio of expansion options, it has higher risk than the risk of the assets currently in place.

    b. The cost of capital derived from the CAPM is not the correct hurdle rate for investments to expand the firm's plant and equipment, or to introduce new products. The expected return will reflect the expected return on the real options as well as the assets in place. Consequently, the rate will be too high.

CHAPTER 24

Credit Risk and the Value of Corporate Debt

Answers to Practice Questions

9.   The value of Company A's zero-coupon bond depends only on the ten-year spot rate. In order to value Company B's ten-year coupon bond, each coupon interest payment must be discounted at the appropriate spot rate. This is not complicated if the term structure is flat so that all spot rates are the same. However, it can cause difficulties when long-term rates are very different from short-term rates.

10.   If Company X has successfully matched the terms of its assets and liabilities, the payment of $150 may be reasonably assured while the $50 is considerably smaller and not due until the distant future. Company Y has a relatively large amount due in an intermediate time frame. Thus, the risk exposure of Company Y to future events may be greater than that for Company X.

11.   Some common problems are:

   a.   Dishonest responses (usually not a significant problem).

   b.   The company never learns what would have happened to rejected applicants, nor can it revise the coefficients to allow for changing customer behavior.

   c.   The credit scoring system can only be used to separate (fairly obvious) sheep from goats.

   d.   Mechanical application may lead to social and legal problems (e.g., red-lining)

   e.   The coefficient estimation data are, of necessity, from a sample of actual loans; in other words, the estimation process ignores data from loan applications that have been rejected. This can lead to biases in the credit scoring system.

   f.   If a company overestimates the accuracy of the credit scoring system, it will reject too many applicants. It might do better to ignore credit scores altogether and offer credit to everyone.

12.   Internet exercise; answers will vary.

13.   Market-based risk models use comparisons between a firm's debt level and the market value of the firm's assets in order to assess the likelihood of default on the firm's debt. The probability of default is a function of the relationship between the amount of debt and the value of the firm's assets. Such models require estimates of growth in the value of the firm's assets, variability of asset values and the face value and maturity of the firm's debt. The value and the variability of the firm's assets are both difficult to estimate. Furthermore, a firm with a complex capital structure that includes several classes of debt can not be equated to a single value to compare to the value of the firm's assets.

14.	The spread between the promised yield and the risk-free rate is the insurance premium. In the case of Backwoods Chemical, the promised yield is:

$$(\$1,050/\$895) - 1 = 0.173184$$

The spread between the promised yield and the risk-free rate is:

$$0.173185 - 0.05 = 0.123184$$

The insurance premium (paid in year 1) is: $0.123184 \times \$895 = \$110.25$

Therefore, since the maturity payment is now guaranteed, the return in year 1 becomes: $\$1,050 - \$110.25 = \$939.75$

The guaranteed rate of return is: $(\$939.75/\$895) - 1 = 0.0500 = 5.00\%$

Challenge Questions

15.	We can consider the value of equity to be the value of a call on the firm's assets, with an exercise price equal to the payment due to the bondholders. For Backwoods, the exercise price is $1,090. Also:

$$P = 1200 \qquad \sigma = 0.45 \qquad t = 1.0 \qquad r_f = 0.09$$

$$d_1 = \log[P/PV(EX)]/\sigma\sqrt{t} + \sigma\sqrt{t}/2$$

$$= \log[1200/(1090/1.09^1)]/(0.45 \times \sqrt{1.0}) + (0.45 \times \sqrt{1.0})/2 = 0.6302$$

$$d_2 = d_1 - \sigma\sqrt{t} = 0.6302 - (0.45 \times \sqrt{1.0}) = 0.1802$$

$$N(d_1) = N(0.6302) = 0.7357$$

$$N(d_2) = N(0.1802) = 0.5714$$

Call value $= [N(d_1) \times P] - [N(d_2) \times PV(EX)]$

$$= [0.7357 \times 1200] - [0.5714 \times 1000)] = \$311.36$$

Thus, the value of equity is $311. With an asset market value of $1,200, the market value of debt is: $1,200 - $311 = $889

16.	For 100% leverage, we use the following assumptions:

- V = market value of assets = $100
- r_f = 0% so that D = face value of debt
  = face value discounted at the risk free interest rate = $100
- For Black-Scholes model: stock price = value of assets = $100
  and exercise price = face value of debt = $100
- Standard deviation of asset value = 40%

In the following table, we compute bond value as follows:

present value of promised payments to bond holders – value of put

Time to maturity of bond	Value of put	Value of bond	Bond yield
1	15.852	84.15	18.84%
2	22.270	77.73	13.42%
3	27.097	72.90	11.11%
4	31.084	68.92	9.75%
5	34.528	65.47	8.84%
6	37.579	62.42	8.17%
7	40.330	59.67	7.66%
8	42.839	57.16	7.24%
9	45.149	54.85	6.90%
10	47.291	52.71	6.61%
11	49.288	50.71	6.37%
12	51.158	48.84	6.15%
13	52.916	47.08	5.97%
14	54.574	45.43	5.80%
15	56.142	43.86	5.65%
16	57.629	42.37	5.51%
17	59.041	40.96	5.39%
18	60.386	39.61	5.28%
19	61.667	38.33	5.18%
20	62.891	37.11	5.08%
21	64.060	35.94	4.99%
22	65.180	34.82	4.91%
23	66.253	33.75	4.84%
24	67.281	32.72	4.77%
25	68.269	31.73	4.70%

For 60% leverage, we use the following assumptions:

- V = market value of assets = $100
- r_f = 0% so that D = face value of debt
  = face value discounted at the risk free interest rate = $60
- For Black-Scholes model: stock price = value of assets = $100 and exercise price = face value of debt = $60
- Standard deviation of asset value = 40%

The following table shows results for 60% leverage:

Time to maturity of bond	Value of put	Value of bond	Bond yield
1	1.461	58.54	2.50%
2	4.270	55.73	3.76%
3	6.952	53.05	4.19%
4	9.393	50.61	4.35%
5	11.616	48.38	4.40%
6	13.652	46.35	4.40%
7	15.531	44.47	4.37%
8	17.274	42.73	4.34%
9	18.899	41.10	4.29%
10	20.422	39.58	4.25%
11	21.853	38.15	4.20%
12	23.202	36.80	4.16%
13	24.478	35.52	4.11%
14	25.687	34.31	4.07%
15	26.835	33.17	4.03%
16	27.927	32.07	3.99%
17	28.969	31.03	3.95%
18	29.963	30.04	3.92%
19	30.912	29.09	3.88%
20	31.821	28.18	3.85%
21	32.692	27.31	3.82%
22	33.527	26.47	3.79%
23	34.328	25.67	3.76%
24	35.098	24.90	3.73%
25	35.838	24.16	3.71%

Graphs for 60% and 100% leverage are shown on the next page.

Leverage = 60%

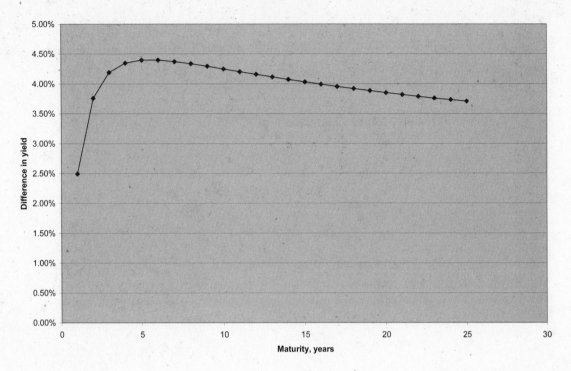

Leverage = 100%

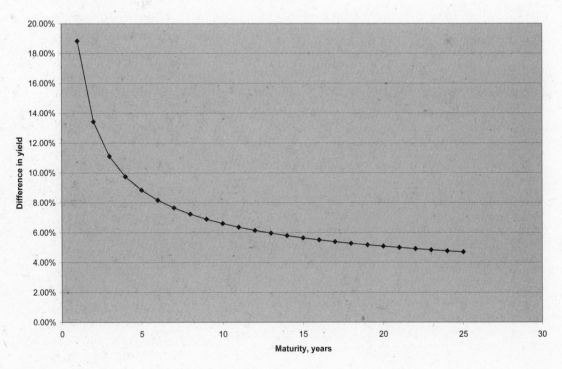

CHAPTER 25

The Many Different Kinds of Debt

Answers to Practice Questions

10. If the bond is issued at face value and investors demand a yield of 8.25%, then, immediately after the issue, the price will be $1,000. As time passes, the price will gradually rise to reflect accrued interest. For example, just before the first (semi-annual) coupon payment, the price will be $1,041.25, and then, upon payment of the coupon ($41.25), the price will drop to $1,000. This pattern will be repeated throughout the life of the bond as long as investors continue to demand a return of 8.25%.

11. Answers here will vary, depending on the company chosen. Some key areas that should be examined are: coupon rate, maturity, security, sinking fund provision, and call provision.

12. Floating-rate bonds provide bondholders with protection against inflation and rising interest rates, but this protection is not complete. In practice, the extent of the protection depends on the frequency of the rate adjustments and the benchmark rate. (Not only can the yield curve shift, but yield spreads can shift as well.)

    Similarly, puttable bonds provide the bondholders with protection against an increase in default risk, but this protection is not absolute. If the company's problems suddenly become public knowledge, the value of the company may fall so quickly that bondholders might still suffer losses even if they put their bonds immediately.

13. First mortgage bondholders will receive the $200 million proceeds from the sale of the fixed assets. The remaining $50 million of mortgage bonds then rank alongside the unsecured senior debentures. The remaining $100 million in assets will be divided between the mortgage bondholders and the senior debenture holders. Thus, the mortgage bondholders are paid in full, the senior debenture holders receive $50 million and the subordinated debenture holders receive nothing.

14. If the assets are sold and distributed according to strict precedence, the following distribution will result. In Subsidiary A, the $320 million of debentures will be paid off and ($500 million – $320 million) = $180 million will be remitted to the parent. In Subsidiary B, the $180 million of senior debentures will be paid off and ($220 million – $180 million) = $40 million of the $60 million subordinated debentures will be paid. In the holding company, the real estate will be sold and ($180 million + $80 million) = $260 million will be paid in partial satisfaction of the $400 million senior collateral trust bonds.

15. a. Typically, a variable-rate mortgage has a lower interest rate than a comparable fixed-rate mortgage. Thus, you can buy a bigger house for the same mortgage payment if you use a variable-rate mortgage. The second consideration is risk. With a variable-rate mortgage, the borrower assumes the interest rate risk (although in practice this is mitigated somewhat by the use of caps), whereas, with a fixed-rate mortgage, the lending institution assumes the risk.

   b. If borrowers have an option to prepay on a fixed-rate mortgage, they are likely to do so when interest rates are low. Of course, this is not the time that lenders want to be repaid because they do not want to reinvest at the lower rates. On the other hand, the option to prepay has little value if rates are floating, so floating rate mortgages reduce the reinvestment risk for holders of mortgage pass-through certificates.

16. A sharp increase in interest rates reduces the price of an outstanding bond relative to the price of a newly issued bond. For a given call price, this implies that the value to the firm of the call provision is greater for the newly issued bond. Other things equal, the yield of the more recently issued bonds should be greater, reflecting the higher probability of call. Notice, however, that the outstanding bond will probably have a lower call price and perhaps a shorter period of call protection; these may be offsetting factors.

17. If the company acts rationally, it will call a bond as soon as the bond price reaches the call price. For a zero-coupon bond, this will never happen because the price will always be below the face value. For the coupon bond, there is some probability that the bond will be called. To put this somewhat differently, the company's option to call is meaningless for the zero-coupon bond, but has some value for the coupon bond. Therefore, the price of the coupon bond (all else equal) will be less than the price of the zero, and, hence, the yield on the coupon bond will be higher.

18. a. Using Figure 25.2 in the text, we can see that, if interest rates rise, the change in the price of the noncallable bond will be greater than the change in price of the callable bond.

   b. On that date, it will be in one party's interest to exercise its option, and the bonds will be repaid.

19. See figure below.

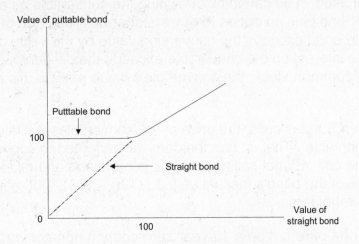

20. Alpha Corp.'s net tangible asset limit is 200 percent of senior debt. Therefore, with net tangible assets of $250 million, Alpha's total debt cannot exceed $125 million. Alpha can issue an additional $25 million in senior debt.

21. a. There are two primary reasons for limitations on the sale of company assets. First, coupon and sinking fund payments provide a regular check on the company's solvency. If the firm does not have the cash, the bondholders would like the shareholders to put up new money or default. But this check has little value if the firm can sell assets to pay the coupon or sinking fund contribution. Second, the sale of assets in order to reinvest in more risky ventures harms the bondholders.

 b. The payment of dividends to shareholders reduces assets that can be used to pay off debt. In the extreme case, a dividend that is equal to the value of the assets leaves bondholders with nothing.

 c. If the existing debt is junior, then the original debtholders lose by having the new debt rank ahead of theirs. If the existing debt is senior, then the issuance of additional senior debt means that the same amount of equity supports a greater amount of debt; i.e., the firm's leverage has increased, and the firm faces a greater probability of default. This harms the original debtholders.

22. Project finance makes sense if the project is physically isolated from the parent, offers the lender tangible security and involves risks that are better shared between the parent and others. The best example is in the financing of major foreign projects, where political risk can often be minimized by involving international lenders.

23. a. With a $1,000 face value for the bonds, a bondholder can convert one bond into: $1,000/$25 = 40 shares
   The conversion value is: 40 × $30 = $1,200

b. A convertible sells at the conversion value only if the convertible is certain to be exercised. You can think of owning the convertible as equivalent to owning a bond plus an option to buy the shares. The price of the convertible bond exceeds the conversion value by the value of this call. Also, if the interest on the convertible exceeds the dividends on forty shares of common stock, the convertible's value reflects this additional income.

c. Yes. When Surplus calls, the price of the convertibles will fall to the conversion value. That is, bondholders will be forced to convert in order to escape the call. By not calling, Surplus is handing bondholders a 'free gift' worth 25% of the bond's face value [i.e., $(130 - 105)/100$], at the expense of the shareholders.

24. a. If the fair rate of return on a 10-year zero-coupon non-convertible bond is 8%, then the price would be:

$$\$1,000/1.08^{10} = \$463.19$$

The conversion value is: $10 \times \$50 = \$500$
By converting, you would gain: $\$500 - \$463.19 = \$36.81$
That is, you could convert, sell the ten shares for $500, and then buy a comparable straight bond for $463.19. Otherwise, if you do not convert, and the bond is no longer convertible in the future, you will own a non-convertible Piglet bond worth $463.19

b. Investors are paying $(\$550.00 - \$463.19) = \$86.81$ for the option to buy ten shares.

c. In one year, bond value = $\$1,000/1.08^9 = \$500.25$
(i.e., the value of a comparable non-convertible bond)

Then the value of the convertible bond is: $\$500.25 + \$86.81 = \$587.06$

25. a. Assume a face value of $1,000. The conversion price is:

$$\$1,000/27 = \$37.04$$

b. The conversion value is: $27 \times \$47 = \$1,269$

c. Yes, you should convert because the value of the shares ($1,269) is greater than the maturity value of the bond.

26. a. The yield to maturity on the bond is computed as follows:

$$\$1,000 = \$532.15 \times (1 + r)^{15}$$
$$1,000/532.15 = 1.8792 = (1 + r)^{15}$$
$$1.8792^{(1/15)} = 1.0430 = (1 + r)$$
$$r = 0.0430 = 4.30\%$$

b. The value of the non-convertible bond would be:

$$\$1{,}000/(1.10)^{15} = \$239.39$$

The conversion option was worth:

$$\$532.15 - \$239.39 = \$292.76$$

c. Conversion value of the bonds at time of issue was:

$$8.76 \times \$50 = \$442.38$$

d. The initial conversion price was:

$$\$532.15/8.76 = \$60.75$$

e. Call price in 2005 is:

$$\$603.71 \times 1.0430^6 = \$777.20$$

Therefore, the conversion price is:

$$\$777.20/8.76 = \$88.72$$

The increase in the conversion price reflects the accreted value of the bond since it has a zero coupon.

f. If investors act rationally, they should put the bond back to Marriott as soon as the market price falls to the put exercise price.

g. Call price in 2005 is:

$$\$603.71 \times 1.0430^7 = \$810.62$$

Marriott should call the bonds if the price is greater than $810.62

Challenge Questions

27. The existing bonds provide $30,000 per year for 10 years and a payment of $1,000,000 in the tenth year. Assuming that all bondholders are exempt from income taxes, the market value of the bonds is:

$$PV = \frac{\$30{,}000}{1.10} + \frac{\$30{,}000}{1.10^2} + \cdots + \frac{\$30{,}000}{1.10^{10}} + \frac{\$1{,}000{,}000}{1.10^{10}} = \$569{,}880$$

Thus, the debt could be repurchased with a payment of $569,880 today.

From the standpoint of the company, the cash outflows associated with the bonds are $1,000,000 in the tenth year, and $30,000 per year, less annual tax savings of $(0.35 \times \$30{,}000) = \$10{,}500$. Therefore, the net cash outflow is $(\$30{,}000 - \$10{,}500) = \$19{,}500$ per year. To calculate the amount of new 10% debt supported by these cash flows, discount the after-tax cash flows at the after-tax interest rate (6.5%):

$$PV = \frac{\$19,500}{1.065} + \frac{\$19,500}{1.065^2} + \cdots + \frac{\$19,500}{1.065^{10}} + \frac{\$1,000,000}{1.065^{10}} = \$672,908$$

In other words, the value of these bonds to the firm is $672,908 and the market value of the bonds is $569,880. The firm could repurchase the bonds for $569,880 and then issue $672,908 of new 10% debt that would require cash outflows with a present value equal to that of the original debt. The firm could also, of course, immediately pocket the difference ($103,028).

Now suppose that bondholders are subject to personal income taxes. High-income investors (i.e., those in high income tax brackets) will favor low-coupon bonds and will bid up the prices of those bonds. If the low coupon bonds are worth more to the high-income investor than they are to Dorlcote, then Dorlcote should not repurchase the bonds. (Note that, if Dorlcote issued the 3% bonds at face value and then repurchases the bonds for $569,880, then the company will be liable for taxes on the gain.)

28. The advantages of setting up a separately financed company for Hubco stem primarily from the attempt to align the interests of various parties with the successful operation of the plant. For example, the construction firm was also a shareholder in order to ensure that the plant would run according to specifications. By making it a separate entity, Hubco could also enter into contraction agreements without the need to gain approval from a parent company. Similarly, if Hubco failed, then no assets beyond the projects' could be attached. Independence also allowed Hubco to design contracts with suppliers, customers, and funding sources to meet specific needs and/or concerns.

29. a. In the case of the safe project, the payoff always exceeds $7 million, so that the lender will always receive the promised payment. Ms. Blavatsky has a 40% chance of receiving ($12.5 million – $7 million) = $5.5 million and a 60% chance of receiving ($8 million – $7 million) = $1 million. Thus, for the lender, the expected payoff is:

    (0.4 × $7 million) + (0.6 × $7 million) = $7 million

    For Ms. Blavatsky, the expected payoff is:

    (0.4 × $5.5 million) + (0.6 × $1 million) = $2.8 million

    b. In the case of the risky project, there is a 40% chance of a $20 million payoff, in which case the lender will receive $7 million and Ms. Blavatsky $13 million. There is also a 60% chance of a $5 million payoff, in which case the lender will receive $5 million and Ms. Blavatsky nothing.

    For the lender, the expected payoff is:

    (0.4 × $7 million) + (0.6 × $5 million) = $5.8 million

    For Ms. Blavatsky, the expected payoff is:

    (0.4 × $13 million) + (0.6 × $0 million) = $5.2 million

Thus, the lender will want Ms. Blavatsky to choose the safe project while Ms. Blavatsky will prefer the risky project.

Suppose now that the debt is convertible into 50% of the value of the firm. For the safe project, there is a 40% chance the lender will be faced with a choice of $7 million or 50% of the $12.5 million, which is $6.25 million; the lender will choose the former. There is also a 60% chance the lender will face a choice of $7 million or 50% of $8 million, which is $4 million; the lender will choose $7 million. Thus, the expected payoff to the lender from the safe project is:

$$(0.4 \times \$7 \text{ million}) + (0.6 \times \$7 \text{ million}) = \$7 \text{ million}$$

For the risky project, there is a 40% chance the lender will be faced with a choice of $7 million or 50% of $20 million, which is $10 million; the lender will choose the latter. There is also a 60% chance the lender will face a choice of $5 million or 50% of $5 million, which is $2.5 million; the lender will choose $5 million. Thus, the expected payoff to the lender from the risky project is:

$$(0.4 \times \$10 \text{ million}) + (0.6 \times \$5 \text{ million}) = \$7 \text{ million}$$

Therefore, the lender receives the same expected payoff (i.e., $7 million) from each of the two projects.

30. The existing shareholders will be harmed by the issue of convertible bonds. The conversion provision will be worth more than the convertible holders pay for it. The new convertible holders will gain less than new shareholders would gain, however. This can be seen by considering the convertible as the stock plus a put option. In general, if the stock is truly underpriced, the existing shareholders are better off issuing the safest possible asset; this prevents the new holders of the asset from sharing the rewards of an increase in stock value when an increase in new information becomes known.

The one exception to this result may occur when common stock is undervalued because investors overestimate the firm's risk. Remember that options written on risky assets are more valuable than options written on safe ones. Thus, in this case, investors may overvalue the conversion option, which may make the convertible issue more attractive than a stock issue.

CHAPTER 26

Leasing

Answers to Practice Questions

8. The present value of the costs and the present value of the lease payments are shown in the following table:

	t = 0	t = 1	t = 2	t = 3	t = 4	t = 5	t = 6
Initial Cost	−3000.00						
Depreciation		600.00	960.00	576.00	345.60	345.60	172.80
Depreciation tax shield		210.00	336.00	201.60	120.96	120.96	60.48
After-tax admin. costs	−260.00	−260.00	−260.00	−260.00	−260.00	−260.00	
Total	−3260.00	−50.00	76.00	−58.40	−139.04	−139.04	60.48
PV(at 9%) = −$3,439.80							
Break-even rent	1082.29	1082.29	1082.29	1082.29	1082.29	1082.29	
Tax	−378.80	−378.80	−378.80	−378.80	−378.80	−378.80	
Break-even rent after tax	703.49	703.49	703.49	703.49	703.49	703.49	
PV(at 9%) = −$3,439.80							
Cash Flow	−2556.51	653.49	779.49	645.09	564.45	564.45	60.48

The break-even lease rate (after tax) is the payment for a six-year annuity due whose present value is $3,439.80:

$$PV = C \times \left[\frac{1}{r} - \frac{1}{r \times (1+r)^6} \right] \times (1+r)$$

$$\$3,439.80 = C \times \left[\frac{1}{0.09} - \frac{1}{0.09 \times (1.09)^6} \right] \times 1.09 \Rightarrow C = \$703.49$$

The pre-tax lease rate is: $703.49/0.65 = $1,082.29

9. Administrative costs drop to $200 per year, so that the after-tax administrative costs are $130 per year and the present value of the costs is now: $2,804.15 Moreover, the lease payments are a fixed commitment of the blue-chip company. The six lease payments are discounted at the after-tax rate at which Acme would lend money, which is computed as follows: 0.06 × (1 − 0.35) = 0.039 = 3.9%

The break-even lease rate is computed as follows:

$$PV = C \times \left[\frac{1}{r} - \frac{1}{r \times (1+r)^6} \right] \times (1+r)$$

$$\$2,804.15 = C \times \left[\frac{1}{0.09} - \frac{1}{0.09 \times (1.09)^6} \right] \times 1.09 \Rightarrow C = \$513.17$$

The pre-tax lease rate is: $513.17/0.65 = $789.49

10. a. If the expected rate of inflation is 5% per year, then administrative costs increase by 5% per year. We further assume that the lease payments grow at the rate of inflation (i.e., the payments are indexed to inflation). However, the depreciation tax shield amounts do not change because depreciation is based on the initial cost of the desk. The appropriate nominal discount rate is now: $(1.05 \times 1.09) - 1 = 0.1445 = 14.45\%$

These changes yield the following, indicating that the initial lease payment has increased from $1,082 to about $1,113:

	t = 0	t = 1	t = 2	t = 3	t = 4	t = 5	t = 6
Initial Cost	−3000.00						
Depreciation		600.00	960.00	576.00	345.60	345.60	
							172.80
Depreciation tax shield		210.00	336.00	201.60	120.96	120.96	60.48
After-tax admin. costs	−260.00	−273.00	−286.65	−300.98	−316.03	−331.83	
Total	−3260.00	−63.00	49.35	−99.38	−195.07	−210.87	60.48
PV(at 14.45%) = −$3,537.83							
Break-even rent	1113.13	1168.79	1227.23	1288.59	1353.02	1420.67	
Tax	−389.60	−409.08	−429.53	−451.01	−473.56	−497.23	
Break-even rent after tax	723.53	759.71	797.70	837.58	879.46	923.43	
PV(at 14.45%) = −$3,537.83							
Cash Flow	−2536.47	696.71	847.05	738.20	684.39	712.56	60.48

Here, we solve for the break-even lease payments by first solving for the after-tax payment that provides a present value, discounted at 9%, equal to the present value of the costs, keeping in mind that the annuity begins immediately. We use the 9% discount rate in order to find the real value of the payments (i.e., $723.53). Then each of the subsequent payments reflects the 5% inflation rate. Solve for the break-even rent as follows:

Break-even rent = $723.53/(1 − 0.35) = $1,113.13

b. With a reduction in real lease rates of 10% each year, the nominal lease amount will decrease by 5.5% each year. That is, the nominal lease rate is multiplied by a factor of $(1.05 \times 0.9) = 0.945$ each year. Thus, we have:

	t = 0	t = 1	t = 2	t = 3	t = 4	t = 5	t = 6
Initial Cost	−3000.00						
Depreciation		600.00	960.00	576.00	345.60	345.60	172.80
Depreciation. tax shield		210.00	336.00	201.60	120.96	120.96	60.48
After-tax admin. costs	−260.00	−273.00	−286.65	−300.98	−316.03	−331.83	
Total	−3260.00	−63.00	49.35	−99.38	−195.07	−210.87	60.48
PV(at 14.45%) = −$3,537.83							
Break-even rent	1388.82	1312.44	1240.25	1172.04	1107.58	1046.66	
Tax	−486.09	−459.35	−434.09	−410.21	−387.65	−366.33	
Break-even rent after tax	902.73	853.08	806.16	761.83	719.92	680.33	
PV(at 14.45%) = −$3,537.77							
Cash Flow	−2357.27	790.08	855.51	662.44	524.85	469.46	60.48

Here, when we solve for the first after-tax payment, use a discount rate of:

$$(1.09/0.9) - 1 = 0.2111 = 21.11\%$$

11. If the cost of new limos decreases by 5% per year, then the lease payments also decrease by 5% per year. In terms of Table 26.1, the only change is in the break-even rent.

	t = 0	t = 1	t = 2	t = 3	t = 4	t = 5	t = 6
Total	−82.80	−2.55	0.60	−2.76	−4.78	−4.78	−6.29
Break-even rent	29.97	28.47	27.04	25.69	24.41	23.19	22.03
Tax	−10.49	−9.96	−9.47	−8.99	−8.54	−8.12	−7.71
Break-even rent after tax	19.48	18.51	17.58	16.70	15.87	15.07	14.32
Cash flow	−63.32	15.99	18.18	13.94	11.09	10.29	8.03

NPV (at 7%) = 0.00

Here, when we solve for the first after-tax payment, use a discount rate of:

$$(1.07/0.95) - 1 = 0.1263 = 12.63\%$$

12. a. The lease cash flows for years 1, 2 and 3 are discounted at:

$$0.10 \times (1 - 0.35) = 0.065 = 6.5\%$$

The value of the equivalent loan is the present value of the cash flows for years 1, 2 and 3: $59,307.30

b. The value of the lease is: $62,000 − $59,307.30 = $2,692.70

c. National Waferonics should not invest. The lease's value of +$2,692.70 does not offset the machine's negative NPV. On the other hand, the company would be happy to sign the same lease on a more attractive asset.

13. a.

	t = 0	t = 1	t = 2	t = 3	t = 4	t = 5	t = 6	t = 7
Cost of new bus	100.00							
Lost depreciation tax shield		−4.00	−6.40	−3.84	−2.30	−2.30	−1.15	0.00
Lease payment	−16.90	−16.90	−16.90	−16.90	−16.90	−16.90	−16.90	−16.90
Tax shield of lease payment	3.38	3.38	3.38	3.38	3.38	3.38	3.38	3.38
Cash flow of lease	86.48	−17.52	−19.92	−17.36	−15.82	−15.82	−14.67	−13.52

NPV (at 8.0%) = −$140

b. Assume the straight-line depreciation is figured on the same basis as the ACRS depreciation, namely 5 years, beginning halfway through the first year.

	t = 0	t = 1	t = 2	t = 3	t = 4	t = 5	t = 6	t = 7
Cost of new bus	100.00							
Lost depreciation tax shield		−3.50	−7.00	−7.00	−7.00	−7.00	−3.50	0.00
Lease payment	−16.90	−16.90	−16.90	−16.90	−16.90	−16.90	−16.90	−16.90
Tax shield of lease payment	5.92	5.92	5.92	5.92	5.92	5.92	5.92	5.92
Cash flow of lease	89.02	−14.49	−17.99	−17.99	−17.99	−17.99	−14.49	−10.99

NPV (at 6.5%) = $566

14. The net present value of the lessor's cash flows consists of the cost of the bus ($100), the present value of the depreciation tax shield ($29.469) and the present value of the after-tax lease payments:

$$-100 + 29.469 + (1 - 0.35) \times P \times \left(1 + \frac{1}{1.065} + \frac{1}{1.065^2} + \cdots + \frac{1}{1.065^7} \right)$$

To find the minimum rental, set NPV = 0 and solve for P:

4.21494P = 70.531

P = 16.73 or $16,730

Greymare should take the lease as long as the NPV of the lease is greater than or equal to zero. The net present value of the cash flows is the cost of the bus saved ($100) less the present value of the lease payments:

$$100 - P \times \left(1 + \frac{1}{1.10} + \frac{1}{1.10^2} + \cdots + \frac{1}{1.10^7} \right)$$

(Note that, because Greymare pays no taxes, the appropriate discount rate is 10 percent.)

Setting this expression equal to zero and solving for P, we find:

P = 17.04 or $17,040

This is the maximum amount that Greymare could pay. Thus, the lease payment will be between $16,730 and $17,040.

15. The original cash flows are as given in the text. In general, the net present value of the lessor's cash flows consists of the cost of the bus, the present value of the depreciation tax shield, and the present value of the after-tax lease payments. To find the minimum rental P, we set the net present value to zero and solve for P. We can then use this value for P to calculate the value of the lease to the lessee.

a. A lessor tax rate of 50%. Cash flows for the lessor are:

$$-100 + (0.50 \times 100) \times \left(\frac{0.2000}{1.05} + \frac{0.3200}{1.05^2} + \frac{0.1920}{1.05^3} + \frac{0.1152}{1.05^4} + \frac{0.1152}{1.05^5} + \frac{0.0576}{1.05^6} \right)$$

$$+ (1 - 0.50) \times P \times \left(1 + \frac{1}{1.05} + \frac{1}{1.05^2} + \cdots + \frac{1}{1.05^7} \right) = -100 + 43.730 + P(3.3932) = 0$$

P = 16.58 or $16,580

For Greymare, the net present value of the cash flows is the cost of the bus saved (100) less the present value of the lease payments:

$$100 - P \times \left(1 + \frac{1}{1.10} + \frac{1}{1.10^2} + \cdots + \frac{1}{1.10^7} \right) = 100 - (16.58 \times 5.8684) = 2.70 \text{ or } \$2,700$$

b.   Immediate 100% depreciation. Cash flows for the lessor are:

$$-100 + (0.35 \times 100) + (1 - 0.35) \times P \times \left(1 + \frac{1}{1.065} + \frac{1}{1.065^2} + \cdots + \frac{1}{1.065^7} \right) =$$

$$-100 + 35 + (P \times 4.2149) = 0$$

P = 15.42 or $15,420

For Greymare, the net present value of the cash flows is:

$$100 - P \times \left(1 + \frac{1}{1.10} + \frac{1}{1.10^2} + \cdots + \frac{1}{1.10^7} \right) = 100 - (15.42 \times 5.8684) = 9.51 \text{ or } \$9,510$$

c.   3-year lease with 4 annual rentals. Cash flows for the lessor are:

$$-100 + (0.35 \times 100) \times \left(\frac{0.2000}{1.065} + \frac{0.3200}{1.065^2} + \frac{0.1920}{1.065^3} + \frac{0.1152}{1.065^4} + \frac{0.1152}{1.065^5} + \frac{0.0576}{1.065^6} \right)$$

$$+ (1 - 0.35) \times P \times \left(1 + \frac{1}{1.065} + \frac{1}{1.065^2} + \frac{1}{1.065^3} \right) = -100 + 29.469 + P(2.3715) = 0$$

P = 29.74 or $29,740

For Greymare, the net present value of the cash flows is:

$$100 - P \times \left(1 + \frac{1}{1.10} + \frac{1}{1.10^2} + \frac{1}{1.10^3} \right) = 100 - (29.74 \times 3.4869) = -3.70 \text{ or } -\$3,700$$

d.   An interest rate of 20%. Cash flows for the lessor are:

$$-100 + (0.35 \times 100) \times \left(\frac{0.2000}{1.13} + \frac{0.3200}{1.13^2} + \frac{0.1920}{1.13^3} + \frac{0.1152}{1.13^4} + \frac{0.1152}{1.13^5} + \frac{0.0576}{1.13^6} \right)$$

$$+ (1 - 0.35) \times P \times \left(1 + \frac{1}{1.13} + \frac{1}{1.13^2} + \cdots + \frac{1}{1.13^7} \right) = -100 + 25.253 + P(3.5247) = 0$$

P = 21.21 or $21,210

For Greymare, the net present value of the cash flows is:

$$100 - P \times \left(1 + \frac{1}{1.20} + \frac{1}{1.20^2} + \cdots + \frac{1}{1.10^7}\right) = 100 - (21.21 \times 4.6046) = 2.34 \text{ or } \$2,340$$

16. If Greymare pays no taxes, its lease cash flows consist of an inflow of $100 at $t = 0$ and yearly outflows of $16.9 at $t = 0$ through $t = 7$. If the interest rate is zero, the NPV of the lease is the sum of these cash flows, or –$35.2 (–$35,200).

17. Under the conditions outlined in the text, the value to the lessor is $700 and the value to the lessee is $820. The key to structuring the lease is to realize that the lessee and the lessor are discounting at different interest rates: 10% for the lessee and 6.5% for the lessor. Thus, if we decrease the early lease payments and increase the later lease payments in such a way as to leave the lessor's NPV unchanged, the lessee, by virtue of the higher discount rate, will be better off. One such set of lease payments is shown in the following table:

	$t = 0$	$t = 1$	$t = 2$	$t = 3$	$t = 4$	$t = 5$	$t = 6$	$t = 7$
Cost of new bus	−100.00							
Depreciation tax shield		7.00	11.20	6.72	4.03	4.03	2.02	0.00
Lease payment	13.00	14.00	17.00	17.00	17.00	20.00	20.00	20.00
Tax on lease payment	−4.55	−4.90	−5.95	−5.95	−5.95	−7.00	−7.00	−7.00
Cash flow of lease	−91.55	16.10	22.25	17.77	15.08	17.03	15.02	13.00

Lessor NPV (at 6.5%) = 0.707 ($707)
Lessee NPV (at 10%) = 1.868 ($1,868)

The value to the lessor is $707 and the value to the lessee (still assuming it pays no tax) is $1,868.

18. a. Because Nodhead pays no taxes:

$$NPV = +250 - \sum_{t=0}^{5} \frac{62}{1.08^t} = -59.5 \text{ or } -\$59,500$$

   b. The cash flows to Compulease are as follows (assume 5-year ACRS beginning at $t = 0$):

	$t = 0$	$t = 1$	$t = 2$	$t = 3$	$t = 4$	$t = 5$	$t = 6$
Cost of computer	−250.00						
Depreciation		50.00	80.00	48.00	28.80	28.80	14.40
Depreciation tax shield		17.50	28.00	16.80	10.08	10.08	5.04
Lease payment	62.00	62.00	62.00	62.00	62.00	62.00	
Tax on lease payment	−21.70	−21.70	−21.70	−21.70	−21.70	−21.70	
Net Cash Flow	−209.70	57.80	68.30	57.10	50.38	50.38	5.04

   The after-tax interest rate is: $(1 - 0.35) \times 0.08 = 0.052 = 5.2\%$

   The NPV of the cash flows for Compulease is: 40.0 or $40,000.

   c. The overall gain from leasing is: $40,000 − $59,600 = −$19,600

26-6

19. The Safety Razor Company should take the lease as long as the NPV of the financing is greater than or equal to zero. If P is the annual lease payment, then the net present value of the lease to the company is:

$$NPV = 100 - P \times \left(1 + \frac{1}{1.10} + \cdots + \frac{1}{1.10^7}\right)$$

Setting NPV equal to zero and solving for P, we find the company's maximum lease payment is 17.04 or $17,040.

The NPV to the lessor has three components:

- Cost of machinery = −100

- PV of after-tax lease payments, discounted at the after-tax interest rate of: $[(1 - 0.35) \times 0.10] = .065 = 6.5\%$:

$$P \times (1 - 0.35) \times \left(1 + \frac{1}{1.065} + \cdots + \frac{1}{1.065^7}\right) = P \times 4.2149$$

- PV of the depreciation tax shield, discounted at the after-tax rate of 6.50% (we assume depreciation expense begins at t = 1):

$$(0.35 \times 100)\left(\frac{.1429}{1.065} + \frac{.2449}{1.065^2} + \frac{.1749}{1.065^3} + \frac{.1249}{1.065^4} + \frac{.0893}{1.065^5} + \frac{.0892}{1.065^6} + \frac{.0893}{1.065^7} + \frac{.0445}{1.065^8}\right) = 28.092$$

To find the minimum rental the lessor would accept, we sum these three components, set this total NPV equal to zero, then solve for P:

$$-100 + (P \times 4.2149) + 28.092 = 0$$

Thus, P is equal to 17.06 or $17,060, which is the minimum lease payment the lessor will accept.

20. Under certain circumstances, an equipment lessor is in a better protected position, compared to a secured lender, when a firm falls into bankruptcy. If the bankruptcy court concludes that the leased asset is essential to the operation of the firm's business, the court is said to 'affirm' the lease, which means that the firm continues its utilization of the asset and continues to pay the lease payments to the lessor. Meanwhile, the secured lender generally does not receive payments until the bankruptcy process is resolved. If, however, the court rules that the lease is rejected (i.e., that the leased asset is not essential to the firm's operations), the lessor is entitled to recovery of the asset. Further, when the lease is rejected, the lessor is also entitled to recover the difference between the present value of the remaining payments and the market value of the asset, but in this regard, the lessor is treated as an unsecured creditor by the court.

21 The value of the lease to the lessee is calculated as in Section 26.4. The lessee computes the cash flow of the lease for each year of the lease. These cash flows take in to consideration the lost depreciation tax shield (i.e., the tax shield the lessee would gain if the asset were purchased), the lease payment

and the tax shield of the lease payment. Then, the lease cash flows are discounted at the after-tax interest rate the firm would pay on an equivalent loan.

The APV of the lease to the lessor equals the NPV of the lease cash flows plus the present value of the sale price of the aircraft at the end of the lease. We find the value of the lease cash flows by first calculating the cash flows to the lessor after payment of interest and principal on the non-recourse debt and then discounting these flows at the after-tax borrowing rate.

Challenge Questions

22.   Consider first the choice between buying and a five-year financial lease. Ignoring salvage value, the incremental cash flows from leasing are shown in the following table:

	t = 0	t = 1	t = 2	t = 3	t = 4	t = 5
Buy: 0.80 probability that contract will be renewed for 5 years						
Initial cost of plane	500.00					
Depreciation tax shield		−35.00	−35.00	−35.00	−35.00	−35.00
Lease payment	−75.00	−75.00	−75.00	−75.00	−75.00	
Lease payment tax shield	26.25	26.25	26.25	26.25	26.25	
Total cash flow	451.25	−83.75	−83.75	−83.75	−83.75	−35.00
Buy: 0.20 probability that contract will not be renewed						
Initial cost of plane	500.00					
Depreciation tax shield		−35.00				
Lease payment	−75.00					
Lease payment tax shield	26.25					
Total cash flow	451.25	−35.00				
Expected cash flow	451.25	−74.00	−67.00	−67.00	−67.00	−28.00
PV(at 5.85%)	451.25	−69.91	−59.80	−56.49	−53.37	−21.07
Total PV(at 5.85%) = $190.60						

We have discounted these cash flows at the firm's after-tax borrowing rate:

$$0.65 \times 0.09 = 0.0585 = 5.85\%$$

The table above shows an apparent net advantage to leasing of $190.61. However, if Magna buys the plane, it receives the salvage value. There is an 80% probability that the plane will be kept for five years and then sold for $300 (less taxes) and there is a 20% probability that the plane will be sold for $400 in one year. Discounting the expected cash flows at the company cost of capital (these are risky flows) gives:

$$0.80 \times \left(\frac{300 \times (1 - 0.35)}{1.14^5} \right) + 0.20 \times \left(\frac{400}{1.14^1} \right) = \$151.20$$

The net gain to a financial lease is: $190.60 − $151.20 = $39.40

(Note that the above calculations assume that, if the contract is not renewed, Magna can, with certainty, charge the same rent on the plane that it is paying, and thereby zero-out all subsequent lease payments. This is an optimistic assumption.)

The after-tax cost of the operating lease for the first year is:

$$0.65 \times \$118 = \$76.70$$

Assume that a five-year old plane is as productive as a new plane, and that plane prices increase at the inflation rate (i.e., 4% per year). Then the expected payment on an operating lease will also increase by 4% per year. Since there is an 80% probability that the plane will be leased for five years, and a 20% probability that it will be leased for only one year, the expected cash flows for the operating lease are as shown in the table below:

	t = 0	t = 1	t = 2	t = 3	t = 4	t = 5
Lease: 0.80 probability that contract will be renewed for 5 years						
After-tax lease payment	−76.70	−79.77	−82.96	−86.28	−89.73	0.00
Lease: 0.20 probability that contract will not be renewed						
After-tax lease payment	−76.70					
Expected cash flow	−76.70	−63.82	−66.37	−69.02	−71.78	0.00
PV(at 14%)	−76.70	−55.97	−51.07	−46.59	−42.50	0.00

Total PV(at 14%) = $−272.84

These cash flows are risky and depend on the demand for light aircraft. Therefore, we discount these cash flows at the company cost of capital (i.e., 14%). The present value of these payments is greater than the present value of the safe lease payments from the financial lease, so it appears that the financial lease is the lower cost alternative. Notice, however, our assumption about future operating lease costs. If old planes are less productive than new ones, the lessor would not be able to increase lease charges by 4% per year.

23. The spreadsheet below shows cash flows to the equity investor for the leveraged lease. The entire lease payment goes to debt service until the loan is paid off (in year 7). The equity investor's initial outlay is followed by cash inflows from tax shields on depreciation and interest. Cash flows then subsequently turn negative as depreciation and interest payments decrease. There are positive cash flows in years 7 and 8 when the debt is paid off and when the $10,000 salvage value is realized. Despite the fact that there are three sign changes in the cash flows, there is only one IRR: 156.5%. The NPV to equity is positive at all discount rates between zero and 156.5%.

					Year				
	0	1	2	3	4	5	6	7	8
Cash flows									
Cost of new bus (salvage value year 8)	−100.00								10.00
Lease payment	16.90	16.90	16.90	16.90	16.90	16.90	16.90	16.90	
Debt payment	16.90	16.90	16.90	16.90	16.90	16.90	16.90	0.84	
Interest paid	8.80	7.91	6.92	5.82	4.60	3.25	1.75	0.08	
Depreciation	0.00	20.00	32.00	19.20	11.50	11.50	5.80	0.00	
Taxable income to equity	8.10	−11.01	−22.02	−8.12	0.80	2.15	9.35	16.82	
Income taxes (@35%)	2.84	−3.85	−7.71	−2.84	0.28	0.75	3.27	5.89	3.50
Cash flow to equity	−2.84	3.85	7.71	2.84	−0.28	−0.75	−3.27	10.18	6.50
Debt service									
Lease payment	16.90	16.90	16.90	16.90	16.90	16.90	16.90	16.90	
Debt (initially 80% of cost)	80.00	71.90	62.91	52.93	41.85	29.55	15.91	0.76	
Interest rate	11.0%	11.0%	11.0%	11.0%	11.0%	11.0%	11.0%	11.0%	
Interest paid	8.80	7.91	6.92	5.82	4.60	3.25	1.75	0.08	
Principal repaid	8.10	8.99	9.98	11.08	12.30	13.65	15.15	0.76	
Remaining principal balance	71.90	62.91	52.93	41.85	29.55	15.91	0.76	0.00	

It is difficult to determine the 'cost of equity' in this situation. The lessor is better off using APV in order to value the investment. For the lessor, the NPV of the lease, as calculated in Section 26.4 of the text, is +$700. We then add the PV of the after-tax salvage value, discounted at a risk-adjusted rate. If we use the 12% discount rate suggested in Section 26.4, the PV of the (after-tax) $6,500 salvage value in year 8, discounted at 12%, is $2,625. Therefore, total APV is $3,325. Next, add or subtract the NPV of the non-recourse loan. If the loan is at fair terms, then APV remains at +$3,325. If the loan generates some net economic advantage, then APV is greater than +$3,325.

CHAPTER 27

Managing Risk

Answers to Practice Questions

13.   Insurance companies have the experience to assess routine risks and to advise companies on how to reduce the frequency of losses. Insurance company experience and the very competitive nature of the insurance industry result in correct pricing of routine risks. However, BP, for example, has concluded that insurance industry pricing of coverage for large potential losses is not efficient because of the industry's lack of experience with such losses. Consequently, BP has chosen to self insure against these large potential losses. Effectively, this means that BP uses the stock market, rather than insurance companies, as its vehicle for insuring against large losses. In other words, large losses result in reductions in the value of BP's stock. The stock market can be an efficient risk-absorber for these large but diversifiable risks.

Insurance company expertise can be beneficial to large businesses because the insurance company's experience allows the insurance company to correctly price insurance coverage for routine risks and to provide advice on how to minimize the risk of loss. In addition, the insurance company is able to pool risks and thereby minimize the cost of insurance. Rarely does it pay for a company to insure against all risks, however. Typically, large companies self-insure against small potential losses.

14.   If payments are reduced when claims against one issuer exceed a specified amount, the issuer is co-insured above some level, and some degree of on-going viability is ensured in the event of a catastrophe. The disadvantage is that, knowing this, the insurance company may over-commit in this area in order to gain additional premiums. If the payments are reduced based on claims against the entire industry, an on-going and viable insurance market may be assured but some firms may under-commit and yet still enjoy the benefits of lower payments. Basis risk will be highest in the first case due to the larger firm specific risk.

15.   The list of commodity futures contracts is long, and includes:

- Gold   Buyers include jewelers.
            Sellers include gold-mining companies.
- Sugar   Buyers include bakers.
            Sellers include sugar-cane farmers.
- Aluminum   Buyers include aircraft manufacturers.
            Sellers include bauxite miners.

16. a. If the spot price falls to $1,100 per ounce in three months' time, Phoenix Motors has a loss on the futures contract equal to:

$$10,000 \times (\$1,250 - \$1,100) = \$1,500,000$$

Phoenix Motors has locked in the cost of purchasing 10,000 ounces of platinum at $1,250 per ounce, or: $10,000 \times \$1,250 = \$12,500,000$

Phoenix can now buy 10,000 ounces in the spot market for $1,100 per ounce: $10,000 \times \$1,100 = \$11,000,000$

The cost in the spot market plus the loss in the futures markets gives a total cost of $12,500,000.

b. If the spot price increases to $1,400, then Phoenix has a gain in the futures market that offsets the increased cost in the spot market. The gain in the futures market is:

$$10,000 \times (\$1,400 - \$1,250) = \$1,500,000$$

The cost in the spot market is: $10,000 \times \$1,400 = \$14,000,000$
The total cost is still $12,500,000.

17. $F_t = S_0 (1 + r_f - y)^t = 44,530(1 + 0.127 - 0.04)^{1/4} = 45,468.44$

The futures are not fairly priced.

18. [Note that the yields given in the problem statement are annualized.]

If we purchase a 9-month Treasury bill futures contract today, we are agreeing to spend a certain amount of money nine months from now for a 3-month Treasury bill. So, the valuation of this futures contract involves three steps:

- First, find the expected yield of a 3-month Treasury bill 9 months from now (y_f).

- Second, find the corresponding price of the 3-month Treasury bill 9 months from now (P_f). (Note: P_f is the answer to this Practice Question, so step 3 is not a required step for this solution.)

- Third, find the corresponding spot price today.

The yield of a 3-month Treasury bill nine months from today is found as follows (where r denotes a spot rate and the subscripts refer to the time to maturity, in months):

$$(1 + r_9)^{3/4} \times (1 + y_f)^{1/4} = (1 + r_{12})^1$$
$$(1 + 0.07)^{3/4} \times (1 + y_f)^{1/4} = (1 + 0.08)^1$$

Solving, we find that: $y_f = 0.1106 = 11.06\%$ (annualized rate)

It follows that the price (per dollar) of a 3-month Treasury bill nine months from now will be:

$$P_f = \frac{\$1}{(1.1106)^{1/4}} = \$0.9741$$

The corresponding spot price today is:

$$P = \frac{\$0.9741}{(1.07)^{3/4}} = \$0.9259$$

19.   To check whether futures are correctly priced, we use the following basic relationships for commodities and for financial futures, respectively:

$$F_t = S_0 (1 + r_f + \text{storage costs} - \text{convenience yield})^t$$

$$F_t = S_0 (1 + r_f - y)^t$$

This gives the following:

		Actual Futures Price	Value of Future
a.	Magnoosium	$2728.50	$2728.50
b.	Quiche	0.514	0.585
c.	Nevada Hydro	78.39	78.39
d.	Pulgas	6,900.00	7,126.18
e.	Establishment Industries stock	97.54	97.54
f.	Wine	14,200.00	13,125.00*

* Assumes surplus storage cannot be rented out. Otherwise, futures are overpriced as long as the opportunity cost of storage is less than: $14,200 – $13,125 = $1,075

For Establishment Industries stock, compute the total future value of the two dividend payments, as of six months from now, and then compute y in the above formula by dividing this total future value by the current stock price.

Note that for the currency futures in part (d), the futures and spot currency quotes are indirect quotes (i.e., pulgas per dollar) rather than direct quotes (i.e., dollars per pulga). If I buy pulgas today, I pay ($1/9300) per pulga in the spot market and earn interest of $[(1.95^{0.5}) - 1] = 0.3964 = 39.64\%$ for six months. If I buy pulgas in the futures market, I pay ($1/6900) per pulga and I earn 7% interest on my dollars. Thus, the futures price of one pulga should be:

1.3964/(9300 × 1.07) = 0.00014033 = 1/7126.18

Therefore, a futures buyer should demand 7126.18 pulgas for $1.

Where the futures are overpriced [i.e., (f) above], it pays to borrow, buy the goods on the spot market, and sell the future. Where they are underpriced [i.e., (b) and (d)], it pays to buy the future, sell the commodity on the spot market, and invest the receipts in a six-month account.

20.   We make use of the basic relationship between the value of futures and the spot price:

$$F_t = S_0 (1 + r_f)^t$$

This gives the following values:

	Contract Length (Months)			
	3	9	15	21
$(1 + r_f)^t$	1.01084	1.03869	1.06097	1.09017
r_f	4.41%	5.19%	4.85%	5.06%

21. a. The NPV of a swap at initiation is zero, assuming the swap is fairly priced.

b. If the long-term rate rises, the value of a five-year note with a coupon rate of 4.5% would decline to 957.30:

$$\frac{45}{(1.055)^1}+\frac{45}{(1.055)^2}+\frac{45}{(1.055)^3}+\frac{45}{(1.055)^4}+\frac{1045}{(1.055)^5}=957.30$$

With hindsight, it is clear that A would have been better off keeping the fixed-rate debt. A loses as a result of the increase in rates, and the dealer gains.

c. A now has a liability equal to: $1,000 - 957.30 = 42.70$
The dealer has a corresponding asset.

22. a. Duration $= \frac{1}{V}\{[PV(C_1)]\times1]+[PV(C_2)]\times2]+[PV(C_3)]\times3]\}$

For Security A:

$$V_A = \frac{40}{(1.08)^1}+\frac{40}{(1.08)^2}+\frac{40}{(1.08)^3}=103.08$$

$$Duration_A = \frac{1}{103.08}\left\{\left[\frac{40}{(1.08)^1}\times1\right]+\left[\frac{40}{(1.08)^2}\times2\right]+\left[\frac{40}{(1.08)^3}\times3\right]\right\}=1.95 \text{ years}$$

For Security B:

$$V_B = \frac{120}{(1.08)^1}=111.11$$

$$Duration_B = \frac{1}{111.11}\left[\frac{120}{(1.08)^1}\times1\right]=1.00 \text{ year}$$

For Security C:

$$V_C = \frac{10}{(1.08)^1}+\frac{10}{(1.08)^2}+\frac{110}{(1.08)^3}=105.15$$

$$Duration_C = \frac{1}{105.15}\left\{\left[\frac{10}{(1.08)^1}\times1\right]+\left[\frac{10}{(1.08)^2}\times2\right]+\left[\frac{110}{(1.08)^3}\times3\right]\right\}=2.74 \text{ years}$$

b. $\text{Duration}_A = [(X) (\text{Duration}_B)] + [(1 - X) (\text{Duration}_C)]$

$1.95 = 1.0X + [(1 - X) (2.74)] \Rightarrow X = 0.454$ and $(1 - X) = 0.546$

Therefore, the following position would immunize the investment: a short position of $4,540,000 in Security B and a short position of $5,460,000 in Security C.

c. $\text{Duration}_B = [(X) (\text{Duration}_A)] + [(1 - X) (\text{Duration}_C)]$

$1.0 = 1.95X + [(1 - X) (2.74)] \Rightarrow X = 2.203$ and $(1 - X) = -1.203$

Therefore, the following position would immunize the investment: a short position of $22,030,000 in Security A and a long position of $12,030,000 in Security C.

23. Suppose you own an asset A and wish to hedge against changes in the value of this asset by selling another asset B. In order to minimize your risk, you should sell delta units of B; delta measures the sensitivity of A's value to changes in the value of B.

In practice, delta can be measured by using regression analysis, where the value of A is the dependent variable and the value of B is the independent variable. Delta is the regression coefficient of B. Sometimes considerable judgement must be used. For example, it may be that the hedge you wish to establish has no historical data that can be used in a regression analysis.

24.

Gold Price Per Ounce	(a) Unhedged Revenue	(b) Futures-Hedged Revenue	(c) Options-Hedged Revenue
$600	$600,000	$660,000	$605,000
$630	$630,000	$660,000	$605,000
$680	$680,000	$660,000	$635,000

25. Standard & Poor's index futures are contracts to buy or sell a mythical share, which is worth $500 times the value of the index. For example, if the index is currently at 400, each 'share' is worth: $500 \times 400 = \$200,000$

Legs' portfolio is equivalent to five such 'shares.'

If Legs sells five index futures contracts, then, in six months, he will receive:

$5 \times \$500 \times \text{price of futures}$

If the relationship between the futures price and the spot price is used, this is equivalent to receiving:

$5 \times 500 \times (\text{spot price of index}) \times (1 + r_f)^{1/2} = \$1,000,000 \times (1 + r_f)^{1/2}$

This is exactly what he would receive in six months if he sold his portfolio now and put the money in a six-month deposit. Of course, when he sells the futures,

Legs also agrees to hand over the value of a portfolio of five index 'shares.' So, at the end of six months, he can sell his portfolio and use the proceeds to settle his futures obligation. Thus, by hedging his portfolio, Legs can 'cash in' without selling his portfolio today.

26. a. $0.75 \times \$100,000 = \$75,000$

  b. $\delta = 0.75$

  c. You could sell $(1.2 \times \$100,000) = \$120,000$ of gold (or gold futures) to hedge your position. However, since the R^2 is less (0.5 versus 0.6 for Stock B), you would be less well hedged.

27. a. For the lease:

Year	C_t	PV(C_t) at 10%	Proportion of Total Value	Proportion of Total Value Times Year
1	2	1.8182	0.1068	0.1068
2	2	1.6529	0.0971	0.1941
3	2	1.5026	0.0882	0.2647
4	2	1.3660	0.0802	0.3209
5	2	1.2418	0.0729	0.3647
6	2	1.1289	0.0663	0.3978
7	2	1.0263	0.0603	0.4219
8	2	0.9330	0.0548	0.4384
9	2	0.8482	0.0498	0.4483
10	2	0.7711	0.0453	0.4529
11	2	0.7010	0.0412	0.4529
12	2	0.6373	0.0374	0.4491
13	2	0.5793	0.0340	0.4423
14	2	0.5267	0.0309	0.4330
15	2	0.4788	0.0281	0.4218
16	2	0.4353	0.0256	0.4090
17	2	0.3957	0.0232	0.3951
18	2	0.3597	0.0211	0.3803
19	2	0.3270	0.0192	0.3649
20	2	0.2973	0.0175	0.3492
		V = 17.0271	Duration =	7.5081

For the debt:

Year	C_t	PV(C_t) at 10%	Proportion of Total Value	Proportion of Total Value Times Year
1	1.7	1.5455	0.0909	0.0909
2	1.7	1.4050	0.0826	0.1653
3	1.7	1.2772	0.0751	0.2254
4	1.7	1.1611	0.0683	0.2732
5	1.7	1.0556	0.0621	0.3105
6	1.7	0.9596	0.0564	0.3387
7	1.7	0.8724	0.0513	0.3592
8	1.7	0.7931	0.0467	0.3732
9	1.7	0.7210	0.0424	0.3817
10	1.7	0.6554	0.0386	0.3855
11	1.7	0.5958	0.0350	0.3855
12	18.7	5.9584	0.3505	4.2059
	V =	17.0000	Duration =	7.4951

b.   See the table below. Potterton is no longer fully hedged. The value of the liability ($28.845 million) is now less than the value of the asset ($29.755 million). A one percent change in interest rates affects the value of the asset more than the value of the liability.

	Lease		Debt	
Yield	Value	Change	Value	Change
2.5%	31.178	4.784%	30.079	4.276%
3.0%	29.755		28.845	
3.5%	28.425	−4.470%	27.678	−4.047

28. Assume the current price of oil is $70 per barrel, the futures price is $80, and the option exercise price is $80.

Oil Price Per Barrel	Futures-Hedged Expense	Options-Hedged Expense
$70	$80	$70
$80	$80	$80
$90	$80	$80

The advantages of using futures are that risk is eliminated and that the hedge, once in place, can be safely ignored. The disadvantage, compared to hedging with options, is that options allow for the possibility of a gain. Hedging with options has a cost (i.e., the cost of the option).

29. a.   To calculate the six-month futures price, we use the following basic relationships for commodities and for financial futures, respectively:

$$F_t = S_0 (1 + r_f + \text{storage costs} - \text{convenience yield})^t$$

$$F_t = S_0 (1 + r_f - y)^t$$

Thus, the six-month futures prices are:

Magnoosium:	$2,800 \times (1.03 - 0.02) =$	$2,828 per ton
Oat Bran:	$0.44 \times (1.03 - 0.03) =$	$0.44 per bushel
Biotech:	$140.2 \times 1.03 =$	$144.41
Allen Wrench:	$58.00 \times [1.03 - (1.20/58.00)] =$	$58.54
5-Year T-Note:	$108.93 \times [1.03 - (4.00/108.93)] =$	$108.20
Ruple:	*	3.017 ruples/$

*Note that, for the currency futures (i.e., the Westonian ruple), the spot currency quote is an indirect quote (i.e., ruples per dollar) rather than a direct quote (i.e., dollars per ruple). If I buy ruples today in the spot market, I pay ($1/3.1) per ruple in the spot market and earn interest of $[(1.12^{0.5}) - 1] = 0.0583 = 5.83\%$ for six months. If I buy ruples in the futures market, I pay ($1/X) per ruple (where X is the indirect futures quote) and I earn 6% interest on my dollars.

Thus, the futures price of one ruple should be:

$$1.0583/(3.1 \times 1.03) = 0.33144 = 1/3.017$$

Therefore, a futures buyer should demand 3.017 ruples for $1.

b. The magnoosium producer would sell 1,000 tons of six-month magnoosium futures.

c. Because magnoosium prices have fallen, the magnoosium producer will receive payment from the exchange. It is not necessary for the producer to undertake additional futures market trades to restore its hedge position.

d. No, the futures price depends on the spot price, the risk-free rate of interest, and the convenience yield.

e. The futures price will fall to $48.24 (same calculation as above, with a spot price of $48):

$$48.00 \times [1.03 - (1.20/48.00)] = \$48.24$$

f. First, we recalculate the current spot price of the 5-year Treasury note. The spot price given ($108.93) is based on semi-annual interest payments of $40 each (annual coupon rate is 8%) and a flat term structure of 6% per year. Assuming that 6% is the compounded rate, the six-month rate is:

$$(1 + 0.06)^{1/2} - 1 = 0.02956 = 2.956\%$$

Incorporating similar assumptions with the new term structure specified in the problem, the new spot price of the 5-year Treasury note will be $118.16. Thus, the futures price of the 5-year T-note will be:

$$118.16 \times [1.02 - (4.00/118.16)] = \$116.52$$

The dealer who shorted 100 notes at the (previous) futures price has lost money.

g. The importer could buy a three-month option to exchange dollars for ruples, or the importer could buy a futures contract, agreeing to exchange dollars for ruples in three months' time.

30. Both a total return swap on a bond and a credit default swap provide risk protection for bond holder. However, each swap protects the owner of the bond against the occurrence of a different event. The total return swap protects the bond holder against a decline in the market value of the bond while the credit default swap provides insurance against a default by the issuer of the bond. In a credit default swap, the owner of the bond pays an insurance premium (i.e., the spread) in exchange for an insurance policy against a default by the issuer of the bond; in the event of a default, the bond holder receives a payment from the seller of the swap (i.e., the seller of the insurance) equal to the difference between the face value and the market value of the bond. Therefore, in a credit default swap, the owner of the bond is assured of receiving the face value of the bond. In a total return swap, the owner of the bond (i.e., the total return payer) pays the total return on the bond to the total return receiver. The total return receiver pays an agreed upon payment (often based on LIBOR) to the total return payer. If the market value of the bond decreases, then the owner of the bond pays an amount equal to the interest on the bond less the capital loss. However, if the total return is negative, then it represents an additional payment from the total return receiver to the owner of the bond, thus providing the bond owner protection against a decline in the market value of the bond.

31. Think of Legs Diamond's problem (see Practice Question 13). If futures are underpriced, he will still be hedged by selling futures and borrowing, but he will make a known loss (the amount of the underpricing). If, for example, he hedges by selling seven-month futures, he not only needs to know that they are fairly priced now but also that they will be fairly priced when he buys them back in six months. If there is uncertainty about the fairness of the repurchase price, he will not be fully hedged.

Speculators like mis-priced futures. For example, if six-month futures are overpriced, speculators can make arbitrage profits by selling futures, borrowing and buying the spot asset. This arbitrage is known as 'cash-and-carry.'

32. We find the appropriate delta by using regression analysis, with the change in the value of Swiss Roll as the dependent variable and the change in the value of Frankfurter Sausage as the independent variable. The result is that the regression coefficient, which is the delta, is 0.5. In other words, the short position in Frankfurter Sausage should be half as large as that in Swiss Roll, or $50 million.

Challenge Questions

33. a. Phillips is not necessarily stupid. The company simply wants to eliminate interest rate risk.

b. The initial terms of the swap (ignoring transactions costs and the dealer's profit) will be such that the net present value of the transaction is zero. Phillips will borrow $20 million for five years at a fixed rate of 9% and simultaneously lend $20 million at a floating rate two percentage points above the three-month Treasury bill rate which is currently a rate of 7%.

c. Under the terms of the swap agreement, Phillips is obligated to pay $0.45 million per quarter ($20 million at 2.25% per quarter) and, in turn, receives $0.40 million per quarter ($20 million at 2% per quarter). That is, Phillips has a net swap payment of $0.05 million per quarter.

d. Long-term rates have decreased, so the present value of Phillips' long-term borrowing has increased. Thus, in order to cancel the swap, Phillips will have to pay the dealer. The amount paid is the difference between the present values of the two positions:

- The present value of the borrowed money is the present value of $0.45 million per quarter for 16 quarters, plus $20 million at quarter 16, evaluated at 2% per quarter (8% annual rate, or two percentage points over the long-term Treasury rate). This present value is $20.68 million.
- The present value of the lent money is the present value of $0.40 million per quarter for 16 quarters, plus $20 million at quarter 16, evaluated at 2% per quarter. This present value is $20 million, as we would expect. Because the rate floats, the present value does not change.

Thus, the amount that must be paid to cancel the swap is $0.68 million.

CHAPTER 28

Managing International Risk

Answers to Practice Questions

10. Answers will vary, depending on when the problem is assigned.

11. a. The dollar is selling at a forward premium on the rand.

    b. $4 \times \left(\dfrac{7.0942}{7.1620} - 1 \right) = -0.0379 = -3.79\%$

    c. Using the expectations theory of exchange rates, the forecast is:

    $1 = 7.1620 rand

    d. 100,000 rand = $(100,000/7.1620) = $13,962.58

12. We can utilize the interest rate parity theory:

    $$\frac{1 + r_{rand}}{1 + r_{\$}} = \frac{f_{rand/\$}}{s_{rand/\$}}$$

    $$\frac{1 + r_{rand}}{1.053} = \frac{7.1620}{7.0942} \Rightarrow r_{rand} = 0.0631 = 6.31\%$$

    If the three-month rand interest rate were substantially higher than 6.31%, then you could make an immediate arbitrage profit by buying rands, investing in a three-month rand deposit, and selling the proceeds forward.

13. Answers will vary depending on when the problem is assigned. However, we can say that if a bank has quoted a rate substantially different from the market rate, an arbitrage opportunity exists.

14. If international capital markets are competitive, the real cost of funds in Japan must be the same as the real cost of funds elsewhere. That is, the low Japanese yen interest rate is likely to reflect the relatively low expected rate of inflation in Japan and the expected appreciation of the Japanese yen. Note that the parity relationships imply that the difference in interest rates is equal to the expected change in the spot exchange rate. If the funds are to be used outside Japan, then Ms. Stone should consider whether to hedge against changes in the exchange rate, and how much this hedging will cost.

15.	Suppose, for example, that the real value of the euro declines relative to the dollar. Competition may not allow Lufthansa to raise trans-Atlantic fares in dollar terms. Thus, if dollar revenues are fixed, Lufthansa will earn fewer euros. This will be offset by the fact that Lufthansa's costs may be partly set in dollars, such as the cost of fuel and new aircraft. However, wages are fixed in euros. So the net effect will be a fall in euro profits from its trans-Atlantic business.

However, this is not the whole story. For example, revenues may not be wholly in dollars. Also, if trans-Atlantic fares are unchanged in dollars, there may be extra traffic from German passengers who now find that the euro cost of travel has fallen. In addition, Lufthansa may be exposed to changes in the nominal exchange rate. For example, it may have bills for fuel that are awaiting payment. In this case, it would lose from a rise in the dollar.

Note that Lufthansa is partly exposed to a commodity price risk (the price of fuel may rise in dollars) and partly to an exchange rate risk (the rise in fuel prices may not be offset by a fall in the value of the dollar). In some cases, the company can, to a great extent, fix the dollar cash flows, such as by buying oil futures. However, it still needs at least a rough-and-ready estimate of the hedge ratios, i.e., the percentage change in company value for each 1% change in the exchange rate. Lufthansa can then hedge in either the exchange markets (forwards, futures, or options) or the loan markets.

16.	Suppose a firm has a known foreign currency income (e.g., a foreign currency receivable). Even if the law of one price holds, the firm is at risk if the overseas inflation rate is unexpectedly high and the value of the currency declines correspondingly. The firm can hedge this risk by selling the foreign currency forward or by borrowing foreign currency and selling it spot. Note, however, that this is a relative inflation risk, rather than a currency risk; e.g., if you were less certain about your domestic inflation rate, you might prefer to keep the funds in the foreign currency.

If the firm owns a foreign real asset (like Outland Steel's inventory), your worry is that changes in the exchange rate may not affect relative price changes. In other words, you are exposed to changes in the real exchange rate. You cannot so easily hedge against these changes unless, say, you can sell commodity futures to fix income in the foreign currency and then sell the currency forward.

17.	The dealer estimates the following relationship in order to calculate the hedge ratio (delta):

Expected change in company value = a + ($\delta \times$ Change in value of yen)

For the Ford dealer:

Expected change in company value = a + ($5 \times$ Change in value of yen)

Thus, to fully hedge exchange rate risk, the dealer should sell yen forward in an amount equal to five times the current company value.

18. The future cash flows from the two strategies are as follows:

Sell Euro Forward	Euro Appreciates to $1.40/euro	Euro Depreciates to $1.30/euro
i. Do not receive order (must buy euros at future spot rate to settle contract)	1,000,000(1.3620) – 1,000,000(1.40) = –$38,000	1,000,000(1.3620) – 1,000,000(1.30) = $62,000
ii. Receive order (deliver) (inflow of 1,000,000 euros to settle contract)	1,000,000(1.3620) = $1,362,000	1,000,000(1.3620) = $1,362,000

Buy 6-Month Put Option	Euro Appreciates to $1.40/euro	Euro Depreciates to $1.30/euro
i. Do not receive order (if euro depreciates, buy euros at future spot rate and exercise put)	$0	1,000,000(1.3620) – 1,000,000(1.30) = $62,000
ii. Receive order (sell euros received at the higher of the spot or put exercise price)	1,000,000(1.40) = $1,400,000	1,000,000(1.3620) = $1,362,000

Note that, if the firm is uncertain about receiving the order, it cannot completely remove the uncertainty about the exchange rate. However, the put option does place a downside limit on the cash flow although the company must pay the option premium to obtain this protection.

19. a. Pesos invested = 1,000 × 500 pesos = 500,000 pesos

Dollars invested = 500,000/10.9815 = 45,531.12

b. $\text{Total return in pesos} = \dfrac{(550 - 500) \times (1000)}{500 \times 1000} = 0.10 = 10.0\%$

Dollars received = (550 × 1000)/12.0 = 45,833.33

$\text{Total return in dollars} = \dfrac{45,833.33 - 45,531.12}{45,531.12} = 0.0066 = 0.66\%$

c. There has been a return on the investment of 10% but a loss on the exchange rate.

20. To determine whether arbitrage opportunities exist, we use the interest rate theory. For example, we check to see whether the following relationship between the U.S. and Costaguana holds:

$$\frac{1 + r_{pulgas}}{1 + r_{\$}} = \frac{f_{pulgas/\$}}{s_{pulgas/\$}}$$

For the different currencies, we have:

	Ratio of Interest Rates	Ratio of Forward Rate to Spot Rate
Costaguana	1.194175	1.194200
Westonia	1.019417	1.019231
Gloccamorra	1.048544	1.064327
Anglosaxophonia	1.010680	0.991304

For Anglosaxophonia and Gloccamorra, there are arbitrage opportunities because interest rate parity does not hold. For example, one could borrow $1,019 at 3% today, convert $1,000 to 2,300 wasps, and invest at 4.1%. This yields 2,394.3 wasps in one year. With a forward contract to sell these for dollars, one receives (2,394.3/2.28) = $1,050 dollars in one year. This is just sufficient to repay the $1,019 loan: $1,019 × 1.03 = $1,049.57
The $19 difference between the amount borrowed ($1,019) and the amount converted to wasps ($1,000) is risk-free profit today.

21. A major point in finance is that risk is undesirable particularly when it can be reduced or eliminated. This is the purpose of hedging. At the time the hedge was initiated, the hedger's opinion was that sterling was priced correctly (otherwise the hedge would not have been placed) and that any deviations from the expected value were unacceptable.

22. $$NPV_G = -78 + \frac{12.877}{1.10} + \frac{19.134}{(1.10)^2} + \frac{18.953}{(1.10)^3} + \frac{25.033}{(1.10)^4} + \frac{24.797}{(1.10)^5} + \frac{24.563}{(1.10)^6} = \$10.12$$

$$NPV_S = -80 + \frac{13.462}{1.10} + \frac{20.386}{(1.10)^2} + \frac{20.582}{(1.10)^3} + \frac{24.244}{(1.10)^4} + \frac{24.477}{(1.10)^5} + \frac{24.712}{(1.10)^6} = \$10.26$$

Sample calculations:

$$(1.3 \times 10) \times \left(\frac{1.05}{1.06}\right) = 12.877$$

$$\left(\frac{20}{1.5}\right) \times \left(\frac{1.05}{1.04}\right) = 13.462$$

Since both projects have a positive NPV, both should be accepted. If the firm must choose, then the Swiss plant is the better choice. Note that the NPV calculation is in dollars and implicitly assumes currency hedging.

Challenge Questions

23. a. Revenues are in dollars, expenses are in Swiss francs: SwissAir stock price will decline.

b.   Both revenues and expenses are in a wide range of currencies, none of which is tied directly to the Swiss franc: Nestle stock price will be unaffected.

c.   Non-Swiss franc monetary positions are hedged, expenses are in Swiss francs: UBS stock price will be unaffected or may increase, depending on the nature of the hedge.

24.   Alpha has revenues in euros and expenses in dollars. If the value of the euro falls, its profit will decrease. In the short run, Alpha could hedge this exchange risk by entering into a forward contract to sell euros for dollars.

Omega has revenues in dollars and expenses in euros. If the value of the euro falls, its profit will increase. In the short run, Omega could hedge this exchange risk by entering into a forward contract to sell dollars for euros.

CHAPTER 29

Financial Analysis and Planning

Answers to Practice Questions

15.   Internet exercise; answers will vary.

16.   Internet exercise; answers will vary.

17.   Internet exercise; answers will vary.

18.   a.   The following are examples of items that may not be shown on the company's books: intangible assets, off-balance sheet debt, pension assets and liabilities (if the pension plan has a surplus), derivatives positions.

       b.   The value of intangible assets generally does not show up on the company's balance sheet. This affects accounting rates of return because book assets are too low. It can also make debt ratios seem high, again because assets are undervalued. Research and development expenditures are generally recorded as expenses rather than assets, thereby understating income and understating assets. Patents and trademarks, which can be extremely valuable assets, are not recorded as assets unless they are acquired from another company.

19.   The answer, as in all questions pertaining to financial ratios, is, "It depends on what you want to use the measure for." For most purposes, a financial manager is concerned with the market value of the assets supporting the debt, but, since intangible assets may be worthless in the event of financial distress, the use of book values may be an acceptable proxy. You may need to look at the market value of debt, e.g., when calculating the weighted average cost of capital. However, if you are concerned with, say, probability of default, you are interested in what a firm has promised to pay, not necessarily in what investors think that promise is worth.

Looking at the face value of debt may be misleading when comparing firms with debt having different maturities. After all, a certain payment of $1,000 ten years from now is worth less than a certain payment of $1,000 next year. Therefore, if the information is available, it may be helpful to discount face value at the risk-free rate, i.e., calculate the present value of the exercise price on the option to default. (Merton refers to this measure as the quasi-debt ratio.)

You should not exclude items just because they are off-balance-sheet, but you need to recognize that there may be other offsetting off-balance-sheet items, e.g., the pension fund.

How you treat preferred stock depends upon what you are trying to measure. Preferred stock is largely a fixed charge that accentuates the risk of the common stock. On the other hand, as far as lenders are concerned, preferred stock is a junior claim on firm assets.

Deferred tax reserves arise because companies typically use accelerated depreciation for tax calculations while they use straight-line depreciation for financial reporting. In the event that the company's investment slows down or ceases, this tax would become payable, but, for most companies, deferred tax reserves are a permanent feature.

Minority interests arise because the company consolidates all the assets of its subsidiaries even though some subsidiaries may be less than 100% owned. Minority interests reflect the portion of the equity of these subsidiaries that is not owned by the company's shareholders. For most purposes, it makes sense to exclude deferred tax and minority interests from measures of leverage.

20.   a.   Liquidity ratios:

1.   Net working capital to total assets =

$$\frac{(900 + 300) - (460 + 300)}{1450 + 300} = 0.251 \text{ (decrease)}$$

2.   Current ratio $= \dfrac{900 + 300}{460 + 300} = 1.58$ (decrease)

3.   Quick ratio $= \dfrac{110 + 300 + 440}{460 + 300} = 1.12$ (decrease)

4.   Cash ratio $= \dfrac{110 + 300}{460 + 300} = 0.539$ (increase)

5.   Interval measure $= \dfrac{110 + 300 + 440}{1980 \div 365} = 156.7$ days (increase)

b.   Leverage ratios:

1.   The Debt Ratio and the Debt-Equity Ratio would be unchanged at 0.45 and 0.83, respectively. These calculations involve only long-term debt, leases and equity, none of which is affected by a short-term loan that increases cash. However, the Debt Ratio (including short-term debt) changes from 0.50 to 0.61, as shown below:

$$\frac{100 + 450}{100 + 450 + 540} = 0.50$$

$$\frac{100 + 450 + 300}{100 + 450 + 540 + 300} = 0.61$$

2. Times interest earned would decrease because approximately the same amount would be added to the numerator (interest earned on the marketable securities) and the denominator (interest expense associated with the short-term loan).

21. The effect on the current ratio of the following transactions:

    a. Inventory is sold $\Rightarrow$ no effect

    b. The firm takes out a bank loan to pay its suppliers $\Rightarrow$ no effect

    c. A customer pays its overdue bills $\Rightarrow$ no effect

    d. The firm uses cash to purchase additional inventories $\Rightarrow$ no effect

22. After the merger, sales will be $100, assets will be $70, and profit will be $14. The financial ratios for the firms are:

	Federal Stores	Sara Togas	Merged Firm
Sales-to-Assets	2.00	1.00	1.43
Profit Margin	0.10	0.20	0.14
ROA	0.20	0.20	0.20

Note that the calculation of profit is straightforward in one sense, but in another it is somewhat complicated. Before the merger, Federal's cost of goods includes the $20 it purchases from Sara, and Sara's cost of goods sold is: ($20 – $4) = $16 After the merger, therefore, the cost of goods sold will be: ($90 – $20 + $16) = $86 With sales of $100, profit will be $14.

23. The dividend per share is $2 and the dividend yield is 4%, so the stock price per share is $50. A market-to-book ratio of 1.5 indicates that the book value per share is 2/3 of the market price, or $33.33. The number of outstanding shares is 10 million, so that the book value of equity is $333.3 million.

24. Total liabilities + Equity = 115 $\Rightarrow$ Total assets = 115

    Total current liabilities = 30 + 25 = 55

    Current ratio = 1.4 $\Rightarrow$ Total current assets = 1.4 $\times$ 55 = 77

    Cash ratio = 0.2 $\Rightarrow$ Cash = 0.2 $\times$ 55 = 11

    Quick ratio = 1.0 $\Rightarrow$ Cash + Accounts receivable = current liabilities = 55 $\Rightarrow$
       Accounts receivable = 44

    Total current assets = 77 = Cash + Accounts receivable + Inventory $\Rightarrow$
       Inventory = 22

    Total assets = Total current assets + Fixed assets = 115 $\Rightarrow$ Fixed assets = 38

    Long-term debt + Equity = 115 – 55 = 60

    Debt ratio = 0.4 = Long-term debt/(Long-term debt + Equity) $\Rightarrow$
       Long-term debt = 24

    Equity = 60 – 24 = 36

Average inventory = (22 + 26)/2 = 24

Inventory turnover = 5.0 = (Cost of goods sold/Average inventory) $\Rightarrow$
Cost of goods sold = 120

Average receivables = (34 + 44)/2 = 39

Receivables' collection period = 71.2 = Average receivables/(Sales/365) $\Rightarrow$
Sales = 200

EBIT = 200 − 120 − 10 − 20 = 50

Times-interest-earned = 11.2 = (EBIT + Depreciation)/Interest $\Rightarrow$ Interest = 6.25

Earnings before tax = 50 − 6.25 = 43.75

Average total assets = (105 + 115)/2 = 110

Return on total assets = 0.18 = (EBIT − Tax)/Average total assets $\Rightarrow$ Tax = 30.2

Average equity = (30 + 36)/2 = 33

Return on equity = 0.41 = Earnings available for common stock/average equity $\Rightarrow$
Earnings available for common stockholders = 13.53

The result is:

Fixed assets	$38	Sales	200.0
Cash	11	Cost of goods sold	120.0
Accounts receivable	44	Selling, general, and	
Inventory	22	Administrative	10.0
Total current assets	77	Depreciation	20.0
TOTAL	$115	EBIT	50.0
Equity	$36	Interest	6.27
Long-term debt	24	Earnings before tax	43.75
Notes payable	30	Tax	30.20
Accounts payable	25	Available for common	13.55
Total current liabilities	55		
TOTAL	$115		

25. Two obvious choices are:

a. Total industry income over total industry market value:

Company	A	B	C	D	E	Total
Net income	10	0.5	6.67	−1.0	6.67	22.84
Market value	300	20	100	40	100	560

Price/earnings = 560/22.84 = 24.5

b. Average of the individual companies' P/Es:

Company	A	B	C	D	E
EPS	3.33	0.125	3.34	−0.20	0.67
Share price	100	5	50	8	10
P/E	30	40	15	−40	15

Average P/E = 12.0

Clearly, the method of calculation has a substantial impact on the result. The first method is generally preferable. Here, the second method gives too much weight to Company D, which is a small company and has a negative P/E that is large in absolute value.

26. Rapid inflation distorts virtually every item on a firm's balance sheet and income statement. For example, inflation affects the value of inventory (and, hence, cost of goods sold), the value of plant and equipment, the value of debt (both long-term and short-term); and so on. Given these distortions, the relevance of the numbers recorded is greatly diminished.

    The presence of debt introduces more distortions. As mentioned above, the value of debt is affected, but so is the rate demanded by bondholders, who include the effects of inflation in their lending decisions.

27. All of the financial ratios are likely to be helpful, although to varying degrees. Presumably, those ratios that relate directly to the variability of earnings and the behavior of the stock price have the strongest associations with market risk; likely candidates include the debt-equity ratio and the P/E ratio. Other accounting measures of risk might be devised by taking five-year averages of these ratios.

28. Answers will vary depending on companies and industries chosen.

29. Bottom-up models may be excessively detailed and can prevent managers from seeing the forest for the trees. However, if the firm has diverse operations or large, discrete investments, it may be essential to forecast separately for individual divisions or projects. Thus, we would expect conglomerates or companies with individually large projects (e.g., Boeing) to use a bottom-up approach.

    It is easier to express and implement corporate strategy with a top-down model. We expect to find such models used for homogeneous businesses, especially where growth is rapid, markets are changing, and intangible assets are important. Of course, the danger is that such models lose contact with plant-by-plant, product-by-product developments that are the activities that actually generate profits and growth.

    It is generally easier to evaluate performance if the detail of a bottom-up model is available.

30. The ability to meet or beat the targets embodied in a financial plan is obviously a reassuring signal of management talent and motivation. Moreover, the financial plan focuses attention on the specific targets that top management deems most important. There are, however, several dangers.

    a. Financial plans are usually accounting-based, and thus, are subject to the biases inherent in book profitability measures.

    b. Managers may sacrifice the firm's best long-term interests in order to meet the plan's short- or medium-run targets.

c.　Manager A may make all the right decisions, but fail to meet the plan because of events beyond his control. Manager B may make the wrong decisions, but be rescued by good luck. In other words, it may be difficult to separate performance and ability from results.

31.　A financial model describes a series of relationships among financial variables. Given these required relationships, it might not be possible to find a solution unless one variable is unconstrained. This allows all stated relationships to be met by setting the unconstrained variable, called the "balancing item," at the level required so that the Balance Sheet and the Sources and Uses Statement are reconciled.

If dividends were made the balancing item, then an equation relating borrowing to some other variable would be required.

32.　From Table 29.9, we see that, in 2006, total uses of funds equals $312. Since total sources of funds equals $153.4, the firm requires $158.6 of external capital (assuming dividends of $59.0). If no dividends are paid, the firm's external financing required is: $158.6 − $59.0 = $99.6

33.　a.

Pro Forma Income Statement	2005	2006	2007
Revenues	2,200.0	2,860.0	3,718.0
Costs (90% of revenues)	1,980.0	2,574.0	3,346.2
Depreciation (10% of fixed assets at start of year)	53.3	55.0	71.5
EBIT	166.7	231.0	300.3
Interest (10% of long-term debt at start of year)	42.5	45.0	70.2
Tax (40% of pretax profit)	49.7	74.4	92.0
Net Income	74.5	111.6	138.1
Operating cash flow	127.8	166.6	209.6

Pro Forma Sources & Uses of Funds	2005	2006	2007
Sources			
Net Income	74.5	111.6	138.1
Depreciation	53.3	55.0	71.5
Operating cash flow	127.8	166.6	209.6
Issues of long-term debt	25.0	252.4	330.9
Issues of equity	0.0	0.0	0.00
Total sources	152.8	419.0	540.5
Uses			
Increase in net working capital	38.5	132.0	171.6
Investment in fixed assets	70.5	220.0	286.0
Dividends	43.8	67.0	82.9
Total uses	152.8	419.0	540.5
External capital required	25.0	252.4	330.9

Pro Forma Balance Sheet	2005	2006	2007
Net working capital (20% of revenues)	440.0	572.0	743.6
Net fixed assets (25% of revenues)	550.0	715.0	929.5
Total net assets	990.0	1,287.0	1,673.1
Long-term debt	450.0	702.4	1,033.3
Equity	540.0	584.6	639.8
Total long-term liabilities and equity	990.0	1287.0	1,673.1

b. For the year 2006, the firm's debt ratio is: $702.4/$1,287.0 = 0.546
and the interest coverage ratio is: ($231 + $55)/$45 = 6.356
For the year 2007, the firm's debt ratio is: $1,033.3/$1,673.1 = 0.618
and the interest coverage ratio is: ($300.3 + $71.5)/$70.2 = 5.296

c. It would be difficult to finance continuing growth at this rate by borrowing
alone. The debt ratio is already very high, and is continuing to increase.

34. a. & b.

Pro Forma Income Statement	2007	2008
Revenue	1,785.0	2,100.0
Fixed costs	53.0	53.0
Variable costs (80% of revenue)	1,428.0	1,680.0
Depreciation	80.0	100.0
EBIT	224.0	267.0
Interest (at 11.8%)	24.0	28.3
Taxes (at 40%)	80.0	95.5
Net Income	120.0	143.2
Operating cash flow	200.0	243.2

Pro Forma Sources & Uses of Funds	2007	2008
Sources		
Net Income	120.0	143.2
Depreciation	80.0	100.0
Operating cash flow	200.0	243.2
Issues of long-term debt	36.0	30.0
Issues of equity	104.0	72.3
Total sources	340.0	345.5
Uses		
Increase in net working capital	60.0	50.0
Investment in fixed assets	200.0	200.0
Dividends	80.0	95.5
Total uses	340.0	345.5
External capital required	140.0	102.3

Pro Forma Balance Sheet	2007	2008
Net working capital	400.0	450.0
Net fixed assets	800.0	900.0

Total net assets	1,200.0	1,350.0
Long-term debt	240.0	270.0
Equity	960.0	1,080.0
Total long-term liabilities and equity	1,200.0	1,350.0

35. a. With a growth rate of 15%, total assets will increase to $3,450, implying required funding of $450. With a growth rate of 15% and using a tax rate of ($200/$700) = 28.57%, Eagle's Income Statement for 2009 will be:

Sales	$1,092.5
Costs	287.5
EBIT	805.0
Taxes	230.0
Net Income	$575.0

Dividends will be: $0.6 \times \$575 = \$345$
Retained earnings will be: $0.4 \times \$575 = \$230$
Thus, the needed external funds will be: $\$450 - \$230 = \$220$

b. Debt must be the balancing item, and will increase by $220 to a total value of $1,220.

c. With no new shares of stock, and debt increased by $100, the only other source of the additional $120 is retained earnings, which must increase to $350. Dividends will thus be reduced to $225.

36. a. Internal growth rate = retained earnings/net assets

Internal growth rate = $230/$3000 = 0.077 = 7.7%

b. Sustainable growth rate $=$ Plowback ratio $\times$ Return on equity $= \dfrac{RE}{NI} \times \dfrac{NI}{Equity}$

Sustainable growth rate $=0.4 \times \dfrac{575}{2000} = 0.115 = 11.5\%$

37. a.

Internal growth rate $=\dfrac{\text{retained earnings}}{\text{net assets}} =$ Plowback ratio $\times$ ROE $\times \dfrac{Equity}{\text{Net assets}}$

Internal growth rate $=\dfrac{0.20 \times 1,000,000 \times 0.40}{1,000,000} = 0.40 \times 0.20 \times 1.0 = 0.08 = 8.0\%$

b. The need for external financing is equal to the increase in assets less the retained earnings:

$(0.30 \times 1,000,000) - (0.20 \times 1,000,000 \times 0.40) = \$220,000$

c. With no dividends, the plowback ratio becomes 1.0 and:

$$\text{Internal growth rate} = \frac{0.20 \times 1,000,000 \times 1.0}{1,000,000} = 0.20 = 20.0\%$$

d. Retained earnings will now be $200,000 and the need for external funds is reduced to $100,000. Clearly, the more generous the dividend policy (i.e., the higher the payout ratio), the greater the need for external financing.

Challenge Questions

38. Because both current assets and current liabilities are, by definition, short-term accounts, 'netting' them out against each other and then calculating the ratio in terms of total capitalization is preferable when evaluating the safety of long-term debt. Having done this, the bank loan would not be included in debt.

Whether or not the other accounts (i.e., deferred taxes, R&R reserve, and the unfunded pension liability) are included in the calculation would depend on the time horizon of interest. All of these accounts represent long-term obligations of the firm. If the goal is to evaluate the safety of Geomorph's debt, the key question is: What is the maturity of this debt relative to the obligations represented by these accounts? If the debt has a shorter maturity, then they should not be included because the debt is, in effect, a senior obligation. If the debt has a longer maturity, then they should be included. [It may be of interest to note here that some companies have recently issued debt with a maturity of 100 years.]

39. Internet exercise; answers will vary.

CHAPTER 30

Working Capital Management

Answers to Practice Questions

15. a. There is a 2% discount if the bill is paid within 30 days of the invoice date; otherwise, the full amount is due within 60 days.

     b. There is a 2% discount if payment is made within 5 days of the end of the month; otherwise, the full amount is due within 30 days of the invoice date.

     c. Cash on delivery. Payment is due in full amount of the invoice upon delivery of goods.

16. a. Paying in 60 days (as opposed to 30) is like paying interest of $2 on a $98 loan for 30 days. Therefore, the equivalent annual rate of interest, with compounding, is:

$$\left(\frac{100}{98}\right)^{(365/30)} - 1 = 0.2786 = 27.86\%$$

     b. For a purchase made at the end of the month, these terms allow the buyer to take the discount for payments made within five days, or to pay the full amount within thirty days. For these purchases, the interest rate is computed as follows:

$$\left(\frac{100}{98}\right)^{(365/25)} - 1 = 0.3431 = 34.31\%$$

     All sales are treated as if they were made at the end of the month; therefore, the above calculation is correct for all sales.

17. When the company sells its goods cash on delivery, for each $100 of sales, costs are $95 and profit is $5. Assume now that customers take the cash discount offered under the new terms. Sales will increase to $104, but after rebating the cash discount, the firm receives: $0.98 \times \$104 = \$101.92$
     Since customers pay with a ten-day delay, the present value of these sales is:

$$\frac{\$101.92}{1.06^{(10/365)}} = \$101.757$$

     Since costs remain unchanged at $95, profit becomes:

     $101.757 − $95 = $6.757

If customers pay on day 30 and sales increase to $104, then the present value of these sales is:

$$\frac{\$104}{1.06^{(30/365)}} = \$103.503$$

Profit becomes: $103.503 – $ 95 = $8.503

In either case, granting credit increases profits.

18. The more stringent policy should be adopted because profit will increase. For every $100 of current sales:

	Current Policy	More Stringent Policy
Sales	$100.0	$95.0
Less: Bad Debts*	6.0	3.8
Less: Cost of Goods**	80.0	76.0
Profit	$14.0	$15.2

* 6% of sales under current policy; 4% under proposed policy
** 80% of sales

19. Consider the NPV (per $100 of sales) for selling to each of the four groups:

Classification	NPV per $100 Sales
1	$-85 + \dfrac{100\times(1-0)}{1.15^{45/365}} = \$13.29$
2	$-85 + \dfrac{100\times(1-0.02)}{1.15^{42/365}} = \$11.44$
3	$-85 + \dfrac{100\times(1-0.10)}{1.15^{40/365}} = \$3.63$
4	$-85 + \dfrac{100\times(1-0.20)}{1.15^{80/365}} = -\$7.41$

If customers can be classified without cost, then Velcro should sell only to Groups 1, 2 and 3. The exception would be if non-defaulting Group 4 accounts subsequently became regular and reliable customers (i.e., members of Group 1, 2 or 3). In that case, extending credit to new Group 4 customers might be profitable, depending on the probability of repeat business.

20. By making a credit check, Velcro Saddles avoids a $7.41 loss per $100 sale 25% of the time. Thus, the expected benefit (loss avoided) from a credit check is:

0.25 × $7.41 = $1.85 per $100 of sales, or 1.85%

A credit check is not justified if the value of the sale is less than x, where:

$$0.0185\,x = \$95$$
$$x = \$5{,}135$$

21. Original terms:

$$\text{NPV per }\$100\text{ sales} = -\$80 + \frac{\$100}{1.12^{75/365}} = \$17.70$$

Changed terms: Assume the average purchase is at mid-month and that the months have 30 days.

$$\text{NPV per }\$100\text{ sales} = -\$80 + \frac{0.60 \times \$98}{1.12^{30/365}} + \frac{0.40 \times \$100}{1.12^{80/365}} = \$17.27$$

22. For every $100 of prior sales, the firm now has sales of $102. Thus, the cost of goods sold increases by 2%, as do sales, both cash discount and net:

NPV per $100 of initial sales = 1.02 × $17.27 = $17.62

23. Internet exercise; answers will vary.

24. a. Knob collects $180 million per year, or (assuming 360 days per year) $0.5 million per day. If the float is reduced by three days, then Knob gains by increasing average balances by $1.5 million.

    b. The line of credit can be reduced by $1.5 million, for savings per year of:

    $1,500,000 × 0.12 = $180,000

    c. The cost of the old system is $40,000 plus the opportunity cost of the extra float required ($180,000), or $220,000 per year. The cost of the new system is $100,000. Therefore, Knob will save $120,000 per year by switching to the new system.

25. a. The total cost of the $0.40 per check fee is: 300 × $0.40 = $120 per day

    The total cost of the $800,000 compensating balance is:

    0.09 × $800,000 = $72,000 per year

    $72,000/365 = $197 per day

    The $0.40 per check charge is less expensive than the compensating balance.

    b. The lock-box system costs $120 per day, or $43,800 per year. In order to generate this $43,800 in interest, the firm would require additional cash of: $43,800/0.09 = $486,667

Therefore, this is the amount of cash the lock-box system must generate. The cash flow is: $300 × 1,500 = $450,000 per day.

The lock-box system must speed up average collection time by:

$$486,667/\$450,000 = 1.08 \text{ days}$$

26. The cost of a wire transfer is $10, and the cash is available the same day. The cost of a check is $0.80 plus the loss of interest for three days, or:

$$\$0.80 + [0.12 \times (3/365) \times (\text{amount transferred})]$$

Setting this equal to $10 and solving, we find the minimum amount transferred is $9,328.

27. a. The lock-box will collect an average of ($300,000/30) = $10,000 per day. The money will be available three days earlier so this will increase the cash available to JAC by $30,000. Thus, JAC will be better off accepting the compensating balance offer. The cost is $20,000, but the benefit is $30,000.

    b. Let x equal the average check size for break-even. Then, the number of checks written per month is (300,000/x) and the monthly cost of the lock-box is:

    $$(300,000/x)\,(0.10)$$

    The alternative is the compensating balance of $20,000. The monthly cost is the lost interest, which is equal to:

    $$(20,000)\,(0.06/12)$$

    These costs are equal if x = $300. Thus, if the average check size is greater than $300, paying per check is less costly; if the average check size is less than $300, the compensating balance arrangement is less costly.

    c. In part (a), we compare available dollar balances: the amount made available to JAC compared to the amount required for the compensating balance. In part (b), one cost is compared to another. The interest foregone by holding the compensating balance is compared to the cost of processing checks, and so here we need to know the interest rate.

28. Price of three-month Treasury bill = 100 − [(3/12) × 10] = 97.50

    Yield = $(100/97.50)^4 − 1 = 0.1066 = 10.66\%$

    Price of six-month Treasury bill = 100 − [(6/12) × 10] = 95.00

    Yield = $(100/95.00)^2 − 1 = 0.1080 = 10.80\%$

    Therefore, the six-month Treasury bill offers the higher yield.

29. The annually compounded yield of 5.18% is equivalent to a two-month yield of:

$$1.0518^{(2/12)} - 1 = 0.008453 = 0.8453\%$$

The price (P) must satisfy the following:

$$(100/P) - 1 = 0.008453$$

Therefore: P = $99.1618

The return for the month is:

$$(\$99.1618/\$98.75) - 1 = 0.004170$$

The annually compounded yield is:

$$1.004170^{12} - 1 = 0.0512 = 5.12\%$$

30. Price of the one-month bill is: $100 - [(1/12) \times 5] = 99.5833$

Return over one month is: $(\$100/\$99.5833) - 1 = 0.004184 = 0.4184\%$

Yield (on a simple interest basis) is: $0.004184 \times 12 = 0.05021 = 5.021\%$

Realized return over two months is: $(\$99.5833/\$98.75) - 1 = 0.0084 = 0.84\%$

31. Answers here will vary depending on when the problem is assigned.

32. Let X = the investor's marginal tax rate. Then, the investor's after-tax return is the same for taxable and tax-exempt securities, so that:

$$0.0352 (1 - X) = 0.0244$$

Solving, we find that X = 0.3068 = 30.68%, so that the investor's marginal tax rate is 30.68%.

Numerous other factors might affect an investor's choice between the two types of securities, including the securities' respective maturities, default risk, coupon rates, and options (such as call options, put options, convertibility).

33. If the IRS did not prohibit such activity, then corporate borrowers would borrow at an effective after-tax rate equal to [(1 − tax rate) × (rate on corporate debt)], in order to invest in tax-exempt securities if this after-tax borrowing rate is less than the yield on tax-exempts. This would provide an opportunity for risk-free profits.

34. For the individual paying 35% tax on income, the expected after-tax yields are:

a. On municipal note: 7.0%
b. On Treasury bill: $0.10 \times (1 - 0.35) = 0.065 = 6.5\%$
c. On floating-rate preferred: $0.075 \times (1 - 0.35) = 0.04875 = 4.875\%$

For a corporation paying 35% tax on income, the expected after-tax yields are:

a. On municipal note: 7.0%
b. On Treasury bill: $0.10 \times (1 - 0.35) = 0.065 = 6.50\%$

c. On floating-rate preferred (a corporate investor excludes from taxable income 70% of dividends paid by another corporation):

Tax $= 0.075 \times (1 - 0.70) \times 0.35 = 0.007875$

After-tax return $= 0.075 - 0.007875 = 0.067125 = 6.7125\%$

Two important factors to consider, other than the after tax yields, are the credit risk of the issuer and the effect of interest rate changes on long-term securities.

Challenge Questions

35. [Note: in the following solution, we have assumed an interest rate of 10%.]
At a purchase price of $10, the sales of 30,000 umbrellas will generate $300,000 in sales and $47,000 in profit. It follows that the cost of goods sold is:

($300,000 − $47,000)/30,000 = $8.43 per umbrella

Assume that, if Plumpton pays, it does so on the due date. Then, at a 10% interest rate, the net present value of profit per umbrella is:

NPV per umbrella = PV(Sales price) − Cost of goods

NPV per umbrella $= [\$10/(1.10)^{(60/365)}] - \$8.43 = \$1.41$

(If Plumpton pays 30 days slow, i.e., in 90 days, then the NPV falls to $1.34)

Thus, the sales have a positive NPV if the probability of collection exceeds 86%. However, if Reliant thinks this sale may lead to more profitable sales in Nevada, then it may go ahead even if the probability of collection is less than 86%.

Relevant credit information includes a fair Dun and Bradstreet rating, but some indication of current trouble (i.e., other suppliers report Plumpton paying 30 days slow) and indications of future trouble (a pending re-negotiation of a term loan). Financial ratios can be calculated and compared with those for the industry.

Debt ratio	=	0.15
Net working capital / total assets	=	0.39
Current ratio	=	2.2
Quick ratio	=	0.40
Sales / total assets	=	3.0
Net profit margin	=	0.020 = 2.0%
Inventory turnover	=	2.9
Return on total assets	=	0.059 = 5.9%
Return on equity	=	0.054 = 5.4%

Some things the credit manager should consider are:

i. What does the stock market seem to be saying about Plumpton?
ii. How critical is the term loan renewal? Can we get more information about this from the bank or delay the credit decision until after renewal?
iii. Is there any way to make the debt more secure, e.g., use a promissory note, time draft, or conditional sale?

iv. Should Reliant seek to reduce risk, e.g., by a lower initial order or credit insurance? How painful would default be to Reliant?

v. What alternatives are available? Are there better ways to enter the Nevada market? What is the competition?

36. a. For every $100 in current sales, Galenic has $5.0 profit, ignoring bad debts. This implies the cost of goods sold is $95.0. If the bad debt ratio is 1%, then per $100 sales the bad debts will be $1 and actual profit will be $4.0, a net profit margin of 4%.

b. Sales will fall to 91.6% of their previous level (9,160/10,000), or to $91.6 per $100 of original sales. With a cost of goods sold ratio of 95%, CGS will be $87.0. Bad debts will be: $(0.007 \times \$91.6) = \$0.64$
Therefore, the profit under the new scoring system, per $100 of original sales, will be $4.0. Profit will be unaffected.

c. There are many reasons why the predicted and actual default rates may differ. For example, the credit scoring system is based on historical data and does not allow for changing customer behavior. Also, the estimation process ignores data from loan applications that have been rejected, which may lead to biases in the credit scoring system. If a company overestimates the accuracy of the credit scoring system, it will reject too many applications.

d. If one of the variables is whether the customer has an account with Galenic, the credit scoring system is likely to be biased because it will ignore the potential profit from new customers who might generate repeat orders.

CHAPTER 31

Short-term Financial Planning

Answers to Practice Questions

8. Unless otherwise stated in the problem, assume all expenses are for cash.

	February	March	April
Sources of cash			
Collections on cash sales	$100	$110	$90
Collections on accounts receivable	90	100	110
Total sources of cash	190	210	200
Uses of cash			
Payments of accounts payable	30	40	30
Cash purchases of materials	70	80	60
Other expenses	30	30	30
Capital expenditures	100	0	0
Taxes, interest, and dividends	10	10	10
Total uses of cash	240	160	130
Net cash inflow	–50	50	70
Cash at start of period	100	50	100
+ Net cash inflow	–50	50	70
= Cash at end of period	50	100	170
+ Minimum operating cash balance	100	100	100
= Cumulative short-term financing required	$50	$0	$0

9. *30-Day Delay*: This quarter it will pay 1/3 of last quarter's purchases and 2/3 of this quarter's.

   60-Day Delay: This quarter it will pay 2/3 of last quarter's purchases and 1/3 of this quarter's.

10. a. *Rise in interest rates:* Interest payments on bank loan and interest on marketable securities.

    b. *Interest for late payments:* Stretching payables; net new borrowing.

    c. *Underpayment of taxes:* Cash required for operations.

    (Bear in mind, however, that if any of these events were unforeseen, they would not appear in the financial plan, which is constructed well in advance of the beginning of the first quarter.)

11. Sources and Uses of Cash:
     Sources
          Sold marketable securities   2
          Increased bank loans   1
          Increased accounts payable   5
          Cash from operations:
               Net income   6
               Depreciation   2
     Total sources   16

     Uses
          Increased inventories   6
          Increased accounts receivable   3
          Invested in fixed assets   6
          Dividend   1
     Total uses   16

          Increase in cash balance   0

Sources and Uses of Funds:
     Sources
          Cash from operations
               Net income   6
               Depreciation   2
     Total sources   8

     Uses
          Invested in fixed assets   6
          Dividend   1
     Total uses   7

          Increase in net working capital   1

12. The new plan is shown below:

	First Quarter	Second Quarter	Third Quarter	Fourth Quarter
New borrowing:				
1. Bank loan	41.50	8.50	0.00	0.00
2. Stretching payables	0.00	7.64	0.00	0.00
3. Total	41.50	16.14	0.00	0.00
Repayments:				
4. Bank loan	0.00	0.00	16.63	33.37
5. Stretching payables	0.00	0.00	7.64	0.00
6. Total	0.00	0.00	24.27	33.37
7. Net new borrowing	41.50	16.14	−24.27	−33.37
8. Plus securities sold	5.00	0.00	0.00	0.00
9. Less securities bought	0.00	0.00	0.00	0.70
10. Total cash raised	46.50	16.14	−24.27	−34.07
Interest payments:				
11. Bank loan	0.00	1.04	1.25	0.83
12. Stretching payables	0.00	0.00	0.38	0.00
13. Interest on securities sold	0.00	0.10	0.10	0.10
14. Net interest paid	0.00	1.14	1.73	0.93
15. Cash required for operations	46.50	15.00	−26.00	−35.00
16. Total cash required	46.50	16.14	−24.27	−34.07

13.   a.

	First Quarter	Second Quarter	Third Quarter	Fourth Quarter
Sources of cash:				
Collections on accounts receivable	85.0	80.3	108.5	128.0
Other	0.0	0.0	12.5	0.0
Total sources	85.0	80.3	121.0	128.0
Uses of cash:				
Payments on accounts payable	65.0	60.0	55.0	50.0
Labor, administrative, other	30.0	30.0	30.0	30.0
Capital expenditures	2.5	1.3	5.5	8.0
Lease	1.5	1.5	1.5	1.5
Taxes, interest, and dividends	4.0	4.0	4.5	5.0
Total uses	103.0	96.8	96.5	94.5
Sources - uses	−18.0	−16.5	24.5	33.5
Calculation of short-term financing requirement				
1. Cash at start of period	5.0	−13.0	−29.5	−5.0
2. Change in cash balance	−18.0	−16.5	24.5	33.5
3. Cash at end of period	−13.0	−29.5	−5.0	28.5
4. Minimum operating cash balance	5.0	5.0	5.0	5.0
Cumulative short-term financing required	18.0	34.5	10.0	−23.5

13. b.

	First Quarter	Second Quarter	Third Quarter	Fourth Quarter
New borrowing:				
1. Bank loan	13.00	16.93	0.00	0.00
2. Stretching payables	0.00	0.00	0.00	0.00
3. Total	13.00	16.93	0.00	0.00
Repayments:				
4. Bank loan	0.00	0.00	23.65	6.28
5. Stretching payables	0.00	0.00	0.00	0.00
6. Total	0.00	0.00	23.65	6.28
7. Net new borrowing	13.00	16.93	−23.65	−6.28
8. Plus securities sold	5.00	0.00	0.00	0.00
9. Less securities bought	0.00	0.00	0.00	26.96
10. Total cash raised	18.00	16.93	−23.65	−33.24
Interest payments:				
11. Bank loan	0.00	0.33	0.75	0.16
12. Stretching payables	0.00	0.00	0.00	0.00
13. Interest on securities sold	0.00	0.10	0.10	0.10
14. Net interest paid	0.00	0.43	0.85	0.26
15. Cash required for operations	18.00	16.50	−24.50	−33.50
16. Total cash required	18.00	16.93	−23.65	−33.24

14. Newspaper or internet exercise; answers will vary depending on time period.

15. The following assets are most likely to be good collateral:

   a ⇒ a tanker load of fuel in transit from the Middle East

   c ⇒ an account receivable for office supplies sold to the City of New York

   g ⇒ 100 ounces of gold

   h ⇒ a portfolio of Treasury bills

   The following assets are likely to be bad collateral:

   b ⇒ 1,000 cases of Beaujolais Nouveau, because it might depreciate quickly and be difficult to value.

   d ⇒ an inventory of 15,000 used books, because these are difficult to value.

   e ⇒ a boxcar full of bananas, because it will depreciate quickly.

   f ⇒ an inventory of electric typewriters, because they are obsolete.

   i ⇒ a half-completed luxury yacht, because it has little value unless completed.

16. Internet exercise; answers will vary.

17. Internet exercise; answers will vary.

Challenge Questions

18. Axle Chemical's expected requirement for short-term financing is:

$$(0.5 \times \$1,000,000) + (0.2 \times \$0) + (0.3 \times \$2,000,000) = \$1,100,000$$

If Axle Chemical takes out a 90-day unsecured loan for $2 million, then the interest paid at the end of the 90 days is:

$$\$2,000,000 \times [(1.01^3) - 1] = \$60,602$$

Under this arrangement, the expected cash surplus is:

$$\$2,000,000 - \$1,100,000 = \$900,000$$

This surplus will earn interest for an average period of 1.5 months at a 9% annual rate, for total interest of:

$$\$900,000 \times [(1.0075^{1.5}) - 1] = \$10,144$$

Therefore, the expected net cost of borrowing is:

$$\$60,602 - \$10,144 = \$50,458$$

If Axle Chemical uses the credit line, then the future value of the $20,000 commitment fee is:

$$\$20,000 \times 1.01^3 = \$20,606$$

Assuming that the cash requirement accumulates steadily during the quarter, the average maturity of the loan is 1.5 months and the expected interest cost is:

$$\$1,100,000 \times [(1.01^{1.5}) - 1] = \$16,541$$

The total cost of the credit line is therefore: $20,606 + $16,541 = $37,147. The credit line has the lower expected cost.

19. The main points to be considered are:

- The commercial paper is cheaper than the bank loan (9% compared to 10%). Large firms with good credit ratings can usually reduce the cost of credit by not borrowing from a bank.

- On the other hand, the firm will need to roll over the commercial paper ten times. That is acceptable as long as the firm's credit rating remains good, but commercial paper can be very expensive for companies with poor credit ratings, and may even dry up entirely. Also, liquidity in the commercial paper market varies over time. For example, during the Russian crisis in 1998, commercial paper became very expensive. The advantage of the bank loan is that the company is sure of the availability of the money for five years and is also certain regarding the margin above the prime rate. It is also important to note that the commercial paper will need to be backed by a line of credit, which will increase its cost.

- The floating rate loan from the bank appears to be cheaper than the 11% fixed rate loan from the insurance company, but it is important to remember that the difference between fixed and floating rates may indicate an expectation of a rate rise.

- The choice between the fixed-rate and the floating-rate loans may also depend on whether one or the other better hedges the firm's exposure to interest rates. For example, if the firm's income is positively related to interest rate levels, it might make sense to borrow at a floating rate; that is, when the firm's income is low, its cost of debt service is also low.

CHAPTER 32

Mergers

Answers to Practice Questions

7. Answers here will vary, depending on student choice.

8. Answers here will vary, depending on student choice.

9. a. This is a version of the diversification argument. The high interest rates reflect the risk inherent in the volatile industry. However, if the merger allows increased borrowing and provides increased value from tax shields, there will be a net gain.

    b. The P/E ratio does not determine earnings. The efficient markets hypothesis suggests that investors will be able to see beyond the ratio to the economics of the merger.

    c. There will still be a wealth transfer from the acquiring shareholders to the target shareholders.

10. Suppose the market value of the acquiring firm is $150 million and the value of the firm with a merger is $200 million. If the probability of a merger is 70%, then the market value of the firm pre-merger could be:

    ($150 × 0.3) + ($200 × 0.7) = $185 million

    If the acquiring managers used this value, they would underestimate the value of the acquisition.

11. This is an interesting question that centers on the source of the information. If you obtain the information from someone at Backwoods Chemical whom you know has access to this valuable information, then you are guilty of insider trading if you act upon it. However, if you come across the information as a result of analysis you have done or research you have performed (which anyone could have done, but did not do), then you are free to act upon the information.

12. a. Use the perpetual growth model of stock valuation to find the appropriate discount rate (r) for the common stock of Plastitoys (Company B):

    $$\frac{0.80}{r - 0.06} = 20 \Rightarrow r = 0.10 = 10.0\%$$

    Under new management, the value of the combination (AB) would be the value of Leisure Products (Company A) before the merger (because Company A's value is unchanged by the merger) plus the value of Plastitoys after the merger, or:

$$PV_{AB} = (1,000,000 \times \$90) + 600,000 \times \left(\frac{\$0.80}{0.10 - 0.08} \right) = \$114,000,000$$

We now calculate the gain from the acquisition:

$$Gain = PV_{AB} - (PV_A + PV_B)$$

$$Gain = \$114,000,000 - (\$90,000,000 + \$12,000,000) = \$12,000,000$$

b. Because this is a cash acquisition:

Cost = Cash Paid − PV_B = ($25 × 600,000) − $12,000,000 = $3,000,000

c. Because this acquisition is financed with stock, we have to take into consideration the effect of the merger on the stock price of Leisure Products. After the merger, there will be 1,200,000 shares outstanding. Hence, the share price will be:

$114,000,000/1,200,000 = $95.00

Therefore:

Cost = ($95 × 200,000) − ($20 × 600,000) = $7,000,000

d. If the acquisition is for cash, the cost is the same as in Part (b), above: Cost = $3,000,000

If the acquisition is for stock, the cost is different from that calculated in Part (c). This is because the new growth rate affects the value of the merged company. This, in turn, affects the stock price of the merged company and, hence, the cost of the merger. It follows that:

PV_{AB} = ($90 × 1,000,000) + ($20 × 600,000) = $102,000,000

The new share price will be:

$102,000,000/1,200,000 = $85.00

Therefore:

Cost = ($85 × 200,000) − ($20 × 600,000) = $5,000,000

13. a. We complete the table, beginning with:

Total market value = $4,000,000 + $5,000,000 = $9,000,000

Total earnings = $200,000 + $500,000 = $700,000

Earnings per share equal to $2.67 implies that the number of shares outstanding is: ($700,000/$2.67) = 262,172. The price per share is:

($9,000,000/262,172) = $34.33

The price-earnings ratio is: ($34.33/$2.67) = 12.9

b.   World Enterprises issued (262,172 – 100,000) = 162,272 new shares in order to take over Wheelrim and Axle, which had 200,000 shares outstanding. Thus, (162,172/200,00) = 0.81 shares of World Enterprises were exchanged for each share of Wheelrim and Axle.

c.   World Enterprises paid a total of (162,172 × $34.33) = $5,567,365 for a firm worth $5,000,000. Thus, the cost is:

$5,567,365 – $5,000,000 = $567,365

d.   The change in market value will be a decrease of $567,365.

14.   In a tax-free acquisition, the selling shareholders are viewed as exchanging their shares for shares in the new company. In a taxable acquisition, the selling shareholders are viewed as selling their shares. Whether the acquisition is tax-free or taxable also affects the resulting firm's tax position. If the acquisition is tax-free, the firms are taxed as though they had always been together. If the acquisition is taxable, the assets of the selling firm are revalued, which may produce a taxable gain or loss and which affects future depreciation, and, hence, depreciation tax shields.

It follows that buyers and sellers will only agree to a taxable merger when the tax benefits to one group outweigh the tax losses to the other and some middle ground is agreed upon.

15.   Table 32.3 becomes:

NWC	21	30	D
FA	92	88	E
Goodwill	5		
	118	118	

If the acquisition is tax-free, then the value of AB Corporation does not change. If the acquisition is taxable, the revaluation of fixed assets increases the allowable depreciation, but the write-up in asset value is a taxable gain. This reduces the value of AB.

Challenge Questions

16.   Answers here will vary, depending on student choice.

17.   Answers here will vary, depending on one's views of the proper role of government, as well as one's views of the role of financial markets.

CHAPTER 33

Corporate Restructuring

Answers to Practice Questions

10.   a.   True. Carve-out or spin-off of a division improves incentives for the division's managers. If the businesses are independent, it is easier to measure the performance of the division's managers.

b.   False. The limited life of a private-equity partnership reassures the limited partners that the cash flow will not be reinvested in a wasteful manner. It also tends to ensure that partnerships focus on opportunities to reorganize poorly performing businesses and to provide them with new management before selling them off.

c.   True. The remuneration package for the general partners typically includes a 20% carried interest. This is equivalent to a call option on the partnership's value and, as is the case for all options, this option is more valuable when the value of the assets is highly variable.

11.   In general, firms with narrow margins in highly competitive environments are not good candidates for an LBO or an MBO. These firms are often highly efficient and do not have excess assets or unnecessary capital expenditures. Further, the thinness of the margins limits the amount of debt capacity.

12.   RJR issued a lot of debt and repurchased shares to reduce the equity base. Sealed Air issued a lot of debt and paid a special dividend to all shareholders to reduce the equity base. RJR was seen as a company that needed to streamline operations and reexamine its capital expenditures and asset holdings. The firm was in a highly competitive environment, but had the advantage of brand name recognition for its products. Sealed Air needed to streamline its operations because it had grown inefficient due to the patent protection it had for its products. Sealed Air remained public in order to increase the pressure to perform by remaining exposed to buying and selling pressure in the market.

13.   Answers will vary depending upon the examples chosen.

14.   The story told in *Barbarians at the Gate* is a very complicated one. Those who favor mergers can find much evidence in this story to support their position, as can those who oppose mergers. In a similar fashion, those who espouse one particular theory or another as to why companies merge can find evidence here to support their position (and evidence to refute the positions of others). Thus, the answer will vary, depending on one's views.

15.   Private equity partnerships are usually run by professional equity managers representing larger institutional investors. The institutional investors act as the

limited partners while the professional managers act as general partners in the limited partnership. The general partners are companies that focus on funding and managing equity investments in closely-held firms. The incentive for general partners is a management fee plus a share in the company profits that they can increase if they successfully "fix" the firm. The limited partners get paid first but are not entitled to all the profits. Further, the limited life of the partnership precludes wasteful reinvestment. These partnerships are designed to make investments in various types of firms from venture capital start-ups to mature firms that need to re-invigorate management.

16. In a private-equity partnership, the carried interest represents the general partners' call option. The exercise price of this call option is the dollar amount of the limited partners' investment in the partnership. In order for the general partners' call option to be in the money, the general partners must earn back more than the limited partners' investment. Therefore, the general partners clearly have an incentive to earn a profit on the limited partners' investment. On the other hand, the general partners also have an incentive to take on risk; increased volatility increases the value of the call option, so the general partners might choose a risky investment over a less risky investment with a greater expected NPV.

17. Although agency costs can be significant for public companies, anyone who has dealt with a governmental institution (or, for that matter, a non-profit organization) has undoubtedly experienced the far greater problem of agency costs in organizations outside the private sector. Privatization can substantially reduce these costs, resulting in much greater efficiency. Competition in the private sector imposes a greater discipline within the enterprise, while also eliminating the impact of political influence. Management and other employees are often offered stronger incentives in a private enterprise than would be possible in a governmental organization.

18. Many of the problems with Chapter 11 bankruptcy could be mitigated by negotiating a prepackaged bankruptcy. Many problems arise from the fact that the two goals of Chapter 11 bankruptcy are often in conflict with each other: (1) to satisfy creditors and (2) to allow the firm to resolve its problems and continue to function as an ongoing business. Furthermore, there are conflicts within the different classes of securities holders. Senior creditors tend to favor a liquidation of the company so that their claims will be satisfied immediately, while junior creditors favor a reorganization of the business in the hope that they will receive some portion of their claims. There is also a conflict between secured creditors, who receive interest while the company is in Chapter 11 bankruptcy, and unsecured creditors who do not receive interest. These numerous conflicts increase the likelihood that extensive litigation will drain resources from the company while these issues are resolved. A prepackaged bankruptcy resolves these issues with a negotiated settlement.

CHAPTER 34

Governance and Corporate Control Around the World

Answers to Practice Questions

10.   a.   While it is true that managers have a fiduciary duty to shareholders, it is human nature for managers to put their own interests ahead of those of the stockholders when there is a conflict in objectives. It is impossible for stockholders to monitor the actions of all managers at all times, so agency problems are inevitable.

        b.   The types of mechanisms used to keep agency problems under control generally involve monitoring of management, contracts that relate management compensation to firm performance, and market mechanisms such as takeover threats and competition in the market for managerial employees.

11.   Other financial intermediaries include insurance companies, mutual funds and pension funds. In Japan, banks provide relatively more financing than do other financial intermediaries, while in the U.K., other financial intermediaries provide substantially more financing. In the U.S., banks are less important sources of financing compared to financial intermediaries, and in Europe, financing provided by banks and financing provided by other financial intermediaries are approximately equal.

12.   Transparency is essential in a market-based system, but is not necessarily a requirement for a bank-based system. In a bank-based system, banks have long-standing working relationships with the companies seeking financing, and banks have on-going access to information about the firm. In a market-based system, creditors and equity-holders require that financial information about companies seeking financing be available, sufficiently detailed and accurate if they are to participate in the market. This information, including audited financial statements, allows participants in the market to make judgments about a firm's profitability and prospects for the future. Without this information, investors are not willing to participate in the financial markets.

13.   A company with dual-class equity has two classes of common stock with different voting rights. One of the best known examples of a company with dual-class equity is Ford Motor Company; the Ford family owns a class of common stock with extra voting rights, which allows the family to control the company.

14.   New industries seem to develop in market-based financial systems such as the U.S., while bank-based systems, such as Japan and Germany, seem to be successful in sustaining established industries. The automobile industry, for example, grew and developed in the U.S., but Japan and Germany have sustained a competitive advantage in recent decades. As new industries or

products develop, there often appear to be several potential avenues for development; each requiring significant amounts of financing before the eventual industry leaders emerge. A bank-based system is not likely to provide this early-stage financing because of the uncertainty involved, but a market-based system provides financing from numerous investors with different views regarding prospects for development. Market-based systems also seem to be more effective in eliminating declining firms and industries.

15. Pyramids allow a wealthy family, for example, to control a group of companies with a relatively small investment. This allows the family to diversify their holdings while maintaining control of the group. In the U.S., investors can diversify their holdings in the financial markets, so a pyramid or a conglomerate is not necessarily a desirable alternative. In developing countries, however, the substandard financial markets do not provide a desirable mechanism for diversification and expansion.

16. A Japanese keiretsu is a network of companies with cross-holdings and numerous interrelationships. These include long-standing relationships among the companies in the keiretsu, and between the companies and the bank that is often associated with the keiretsu. The advantages of this form of organization include the ability to obtain debt financing from the keiretsu's bank or from other affiliated financial institutions. Financing can also be obtained from other companies in the keiretsu, avoiding the need for external financing. Keiretsus tend to have relatively stable cash flows and are often able to resolve issues related to the financial distress of a company in the keiretsu. A disadvantage of this form of organization is the fact that outside shareholders have little, if any, influence on the companies in the keiretsu. As a result, dividends are relatively low and takeovers are extremely rare.